THE CIVIL WAR AND
THE CONSTITUTION

KENNIKAT PRESS SCHOLARLY REPRINTS

Dr. Ralph Adams Brown, Senior Editor

Series in
AMERICAN HISTORY AND CULTURE
IN THE NINETEENTH CENTURY
Under the General Editorial Supervision of
Dr. Martin L. Fausold
Professor of History, State University of New York

THE CIVIL WAR AND
THE CONSTITUTION

1859-1865

BY

JOHN W. BURGESS, Ph.D., LL.D.

PROFESSOR OF POLITICAL SCIENCE AND CONSTITUTIONAL LAW, AND DEAN OF
THE FACULTY OF POLITICAL SCIENCE, IN COLUMBIA UNIVERSITY

VOLUME I

KENNIKAT PRESS
Port Washington, N. Y./London

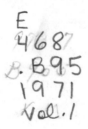

E
4687
B. B95
1971
Vol. 1

THE CIVIL WAR AND THE CONSTITUTION

First published in 1901
Reissued in 1971 by Kennikat Press
Library of Congress Catalog Card No: 77-137905
ISBN 0-8046-1473-3

Manufactured by Taylor Publishing Company   Dallas, Texas

KENNIKAT SERIES ON AMERICAN HISTORY AND
CULTURE IN THE NINETEENTH CENTURY

To the memory

of

SAMUEL B. RUGGLES, LL.D.,

for many years one of the most prominent of the

Trustees of Columbia College,

to whose efforts,

more than to those of any other single man,

the Faculty and School of Political Science

in Columbia University owe their foundation,

these two volumes

are reverently and affectionately inscribed

by the Author

PREFACE

The preface to "The Middle Period" was intended to serve for all the volumes of this series proceeding from my pen. I do not feel inclined to interfere with that arrangement now, and I shall not do so. Perhaps, however, it is due to my readers that I should make some explanation in regard to the delay in the appearance of these volumes after the publication of "The Middle Period." I can do this in a single sentence. I found the task of going carefully through the immense mass of Congressional debates, Executive orders, diplomatic correspondence and military reports so prolonged that, in the midst of the exactions of my University labors, I was unable to complete them earlier.

I desire, further, to express in these introductory lines my continued obligation to my friend and former pupil, and now, I rejoice to say, my colleague, Dr. Harry A. Cushing, for his invaluable aid in the preparation of these volumes.

John W. Burgess.

Columbia University,
June 12, 1901.

CONTENTS OF VOLUME I

LIST OF MAPS

THE CIVIL WAR

CHAPTER I

DAVIS, LINCOLN AND DOUGLAS

The Need of New Leaders—Davis, Lincoln and Douglas—Resemblances of the Three Men in Character—Differences
between the Three Men—In Personal Appearance—Circumstances of Birth and Education—And Mind and Character—
The Political Differences between Davis, Douglas and Lincoln in 1860.

THE Kansas-Nebraska Act, the Dred Scott decision,
and the anti-Lecompton triumph had brought the politics of the country into a nebulous condition. The need of
New centres of cohesion must be developed new Leaders.
around which the vapors should become solidified and
clarified, in order that the conflicting forces might appear distinct in principle and purpose. It was a situation which required the advent of strong personalities,
and their advance to the front, personalities who should
rear their heads above the dead level of democracy, and
around whom the people must gather for the great
struggle.

Between the years 1857 and 1860 these appeared.
They were Jefferson Davis, Abraham Lincoln, and
Stephen Arnold Douglas. The first and last Davis, Lin-
were then, by no means, new names to the coln and
country, and the bearer of the second had Douglas.
already before 1857 won an enviable local reputation.

1

Davis was the oldest and Douglas the youngest of the three, while Lincoln, who stood between the two in the chronology of birth, was strangely, not to say fatefully, connected with both in the events of his career.

Davis and Lincoln were born upon the soil of the same Commonwealth, Kentucky, the one in June of 1808, and the other in February of 1809. It has been said that they met for the first time at Dixon, in Illinois, in the year 1831, and that then and there, Davis, at that time a Lieutenant in the regular army, administered to Lincoln the oath of allegiance to the United States, as Captain of a company of Illinois volunteers mustered into the service of the United States for the Black-Hawk War. They met again in Congress between 1846–48, both members of the House of Representatives, when Davis upheld the cause of his country against Mexico, and then proved his patriotic devotion by resigning his seat and going to the front, as Colonel of the first Mississippi regiment, where he distinguished himself as a brave and successful soldier and commander on the fields of Monterey and Buena Vista; while Lincoln joined with the Northern Whigs in denouncing the war, and thereby ruined his political prospects in Illinois for several years afterward. They never met again personally, but as commanders-in-chief of the great hosts, who struggled through the bloodiest war of modern times, they became the commanding figures of our history in the first half of the seventh decade of the century.

Likewise Lincoln and Douglas, though born as far apart in place as Kentucky and Vermont, and in time as 1809 and 1813, met early upon the prairies, and became rivals in courtship, rivals in law practice, and rivals in politics, until at last their rivalry culminated in the great presidential contest of 1860, in which Lincoln triumphed, and Douglas pledged him allegiance in upholding the

Union in the conflict of arms which Davis was inaugurating against it.

In two things these three great characters resembled one another, viz., in personal bravery and in loyal tenacity to conviction. Nobody has disputed the former quality to either of them, but in regard to the latter there is, and has always *Resemblances of the three men in character.* been, difference of opinion. At this time it may be said that it is more universally attributed to Lincoln than to either of the others, and less so to Douglas. There was undoubtedly a difference in degree between them in this respect, but that is probably to be ascribed to the fact that Lincoln saw farther than Davis, and both farther and more clearly than Douglas. It would be difficult, if not impossible, to find any act in Davis's life which proves any lack of devotion to the truth, as he saw it, or any lack of readiness to sacrifice himself for it. And certainly the unbending attitude which Douglas preserved in the two great crises of his political career, the Lecompton struggle and the presidential nomination of 1860, and his ready and unreserved declaration of loyalty to his great rival at the outset of the struggle for the preservation of the Union, can be explained on no other satisfactory theory than that of self-sacrificing adherence to principle. If it was not always so with Mr. Douglas, it came to be so in the latter years of his great life. While as to Lincoln, so many of his old foes have come to recognize the correctness of the opinion of his friends, that absolute truthfulness was the fundamental principle of his character, that there is no need of adducing instances of his conduct in proof of it.

In most other respects, however, the three men were very different. In personal appearance, the contrast was very striking. Davis was tall, well-formed, erect, handsome, dignified, and graceful. He bore all the marks of a well-born, well-bred, cultured gentleman. Lincoln was very tall, lank, ungainly, homely, and awkward, but dignified and grave even to melancholy. No one could doubt, after a little contact with him, that he was on the inside a true gentleman, although the outward polish failed him almost completely. Douglas was rather short and thick-set, with a massive head, well-developed forehead, and deeply planted brilliant blue eyes, which in moments of excitement seemed to emit electric sparks. He was, withal, good-looking and very genial and courteous.

Differences between the three men. Personal appearance.

The circumstances of their birth and education differed also very widely. Davis was descended from Welsh ancestors on his father's side and Scotch-Irish on his mother's. His father was a country gentleman of considerable property, who resided first in Georgia, then in Kentucky, afterward moved to Louisiana, and finally settled in Mississippi. His mother was said to have been a lady of rare beauty and intelligence. He received his preparatory education in the ordinary schools about his home, was then sent to Transylvania University, at Lexington, Kentucky, and when near graduation from that institution, had a West Point cadetship conferred upon him. He graduated from the Military Academy in July of 1828, and immediately entered the regular army, as a second lieutenant, and was assigned to service on the western frontier. After seven years of arduous and well-performed duty, he resigned from the army, married the daughter of Colonel Zachary Taylor, afterward President of the United States, and settled down at Briarfield, in Mississippi, as a planter. The sudden death of his young wife, a few months after their marriage, broke his health and deranged his affairs. A severe illness, and a long **tour**

Circumstances of birth and education.

of travel necessitated by it, occupied the better part of the next two years of his life. From 1837 to 1845, he directed the cultivation of his plantation, won wealth, and read widely in political philosophy, political economy, and public law. In February of 1845, he married the accomplished daughter of W. B. Howell, of Natchez, and with her founded one of those typical Southern homes so justly noted for refinement and hospitality. In 1844, he was elected a presidential elector on the Polk ticket, and in 1845, he was elected Representative to Congress from the district in which he resided. From this time forward he was almost continuously in public life until the downfall of the Southern Confederacy in 1865.

No greater contrast to this brilliant preparation and education for political leadership can be imagined than the lowly and humble course through which Mr. Lincoln worked his way. His father was a dull, ignorant, lazy, shiftless, poor white, of Kentucky backwoods life, the son of a man of the same sort, who immigrated into Kentucky from Virginia, about the year 1790; and his mother was the daughter of one Lucy Hanks, whose family belonged likewise to the class of " poor white trash."

Lincoln's childhood, boyhood, and young manhood, were spent in the most abject poverty, and amid surroundings of the most humble, demoraliz- Lincoln's ing, and common character. About the time early history. he reached his seventh year, his worthless father had taken care of his family as long as he could in a country which had become somewhat civilized, and moved onward into a newer region. The more fertile maiden lands of Indiana seemed to offer richer winnings to the stupid, thriftless Kentuckian. Thither he took his family, and in a miserable cabin in the wilderness he housed them. For ten years now Abraham Lincoln worked for his father under greater severity than the av-

erage slave of the South worked for his master. During
this time he received altogether not more than one year
of schooling.   He had no books, except the Bible and a
copy of Æsop's Fables, and could get none.   He was
thoughtful, meditative, thirstful for knowledge, and
ambitious, and the uncongeniality and hopelessness of
his surroundings induced in him a dejection of spirit
and a settled melancholy, which immediately impressed
everyone who came into contact with him as one of his
chief peculiarities.   He had, indeed, already revealed his
rich vein of humor, which was not exactly the humor of
pessimism, but very much like the humor of despair.   His
tree-felling, rail-splitting, digging, ploughing and lifting,
had made him a full-grown, powerful man at seventeen.

At nineteen he took his first journey into the great
world as a "hand" on a flat-boat, destined for New
Orleans.   Upon this journey, and a subsequent one to
the same place, made some three years later, he saw
slavery under some of its most forbidding aspects, and
conceived thus early in his life a deep hatred for the
institution.   In the spring of 1830, just as he had attained his majority, and his legal freedom from his
father's control, the family moved again in search of
Removal to Illinois. richer lands.   They settled this time upon a
bluff overlooking Sangamon River, in Macon
County, Illinois.   Lincoln now went to work at all
kinds of jobs for himself.   He was a great rail-splitter,
and was occupied chiefly with such employment until he
fell in with one Denton Offut, a bluff, sanguine, enterprising fellow, without much capacity for making a
success of anything, but with indefatigable genius for
planning, who hired him to go upon his second journey
to New Orleans, and, on his return, gave him employment in a store at New Salem.   Offut's almost immediate failure in the mercantile business set Lincoln

afloat again, not, however, until the slovenly clerk had
made many acquaintances among Offut's customers, and
some reputation as a good story-teller and a promising
politician among the loafers who congregated every
evening in the back-room of Offut's store.

Lincoln now tried military life in the Black-Hawk
War, to which reference has already been made, and
owing to the popularity which he had acquired, and to
his great physical powers, he was elected Captain of his
company. At the close of this service, which lasted only
a few months, he returned to New Salem, and in 1832
tried to secure an election to the Legislature. Defeated
in this first political effort, he turned again to store-
keeping, bought the stock of the Herndon Brothers, and
set himself up, with one William Berry for partner, as a
merchant. In less than a year, this venture proved a
failure. Lincoln was now involved in debt, and scarcely
knew which way to turn. He worked around at odd
jobs, earning a bare pittance, and reading borrowed law
books at every spare moment. At this juncture the
Surveyor of the county, one John Calhoun, made him
Deputy Surveyor. He now studied his mathematics
with great assiduity, and soon became proficient in the
work of his office. At the same time he secured the place
of Postmaster of New Salem. The two positions gave
him the means of livelihood, and from this time forward
he was able to exist without being compelled to employ
any considerable portion of his time in manual labor.

He allied himself politically with the Whig party, and
developed his political opinions under the influence of
its national creed. In 1834, he was elected,
as a Whig, to the Illinois Legislature, and **Lincoln's
first political
experiences.**
again in 1836. In 1837, he migrated from
New Salem to Springfield, to which latter place the
capitol of the Commonwealth had just been removed,

in some degree through his influence and efforts. He was still so poor that he could not pay the sum of seventeen dollars for the necessary furnishings of a room in which to sleep, and was literally compelled to accept the hospitality of Joshua F. Speed, who offered to share room and bed with him. He was now twenty-eight years of age, and certainly this was a bad showing from the point of view of worldly success. He now began the practice of law, as the partner of John T. Stuart, but broke away from this career almost immediately for another term in the Legislature.

It was one of Lincoln's traits that he liked the society of men better than that of women. Nevertheless he was not blind to feminine attractions, and was not unsuccessful in his suits. In 1835, he entered into an engagement of marriage with a charming young girl of New Salem, Annie Rutledge, by name, who died before the consummation of vows. This sad event deepened greatly the habitual melancholy of his life. In 1840, he sought successfully the hand of Miss Mary Todd, a bright, vivacious, pretty, and, in comparison with himself, highly born and highly bred Kentucky girl. The strange conduct of Lincoln in not appearing on the evening appointed for the wedding, when the bride and guests were awaiting anxiously his coming, and the still stranger conduct of Miss Todd in marrying him nearly two years afterward, despite the mortification and chagrin which he had caused her, are scarcely subjects to be treated in a constitutional history of the United States, and yet these things had their influence in shaping the course of that history. They had their part in creating that domestic incompatibility between Mr. Lincoln and his wife, which drove him so constantly from the seclusion of his own fireside into the haunts of men, thus widening his acquaintance

Lincoln's marriage.

among men and increasing his influence with them, and which helped to cultivate in him that sense of aloneness, the twin of self-reliance, and that silent patience, which were such marked ingredients of his great personality.

Lincoln's nearest friend, Herndon, says that Lincoln finally married Miss Todd simply because he felt that he was bound in honor to do so; and that Miss Todd so far condoned the offence which he had given her by absconding upon the date originally set for the wedding as to marry him nearly two years later, because she had discerned his coming greatness, and because she desired the satisfaction of an ultimate triumph over the man who had so shamefully left her in the lurch upon the evening of January 1st, 1841.   It was certainly a very bad beginning, and it resulted most disastrously to the peace and comfort of Mr. Lincoln's domestic life, but it is altogether probable that such discipline as his constant unhappiness at home imposed upon him chastened his character, developed his self-reliance, his patience and his conciliatory spirit, and thus fitted him all the better for the great work which lay before him in the hidden future.   The year following his marriage to Miss Todd, Lincoln associated with himself, in the practice of law, William H. Herndon.   This arrangement proved most advantageous to both parties.   Herndon was faithful to Lincoln's political fortunes to the end, and their business union was dissolved only by the shot of the assassin Booth.

Mr. Lincoln began his political career upon the broader stage of national politics at the same time and in the same manner with Mr. Davis.   That is, he was a candidate for presidential elec- Lincoln in national politics. tor in the campaign of 1844.   He canvassed the Commonwealth of Illinois for Mr. Clay and won

considerable reputation by his speeches. He also entered Congress at very nearly the same time as Mr.
Davis, and they were both members of the House of
Representatives at the period of the Mexican war.
Lincoln's attitude toward the war was almost the very
opposite of that taken by Davis. While Davis supported the war policy, and shed his blood upon the battle-
field in its execution, Lincoln denounced it, and discouraged its execution as far as he could without actually
voting to withhold the necessary supplies. The splendid triumph of the American arms damaged greatly the
political prospects of many of the men who opposed
the war, and among them those of Mr. Lincoln. At the
expiration of his term he returned to private life, and
for the next five years devoted himself to the practice of
his profession. The agitation over the Kansas-Nebraska
Bill, and the repeal of the restriction upon slavery in the
Louisiana territory above the line of thirty-six degrees
and thirty minutes, called him again into the political
arena. From this time onward to 1860 he was developing in his thought and utterances that "body of Republican doctrine" which led to the final triumph of his
party and to his own election to the presidency. He
was chosen again to the Legislature in 1854, but almost
immediately resigned his seat, in order to improve his
chances, as he thought, for the United States senatorship,
which was to be filled at that session. In this plan he
was disappointed by the sharp practice of the five Free-
soil Democrats of the Legislature, who persisted in voting for Trumbull until it became manifest to Lincoln and
his supporters that they must go for Trumbull or see a
"Nebraska Democrat" elected, when Lincoln himself
gave the word to elect Trumbull. It was probably understood at the time that the friends of Trumbull, the
Free-soil Democrats, would assist to put Lincoln in the

seat then occupied by Mr. Douglas, at the close of the latter's term in 1858. Whether or not it was so planned, it so happened, and the summer and autumn of that year witnessed the ever-memorable debate between the two "Giants," in which the doctrines of the Douglas democracy and the Lincoln republicanism were quite distinctly formulated. Mr. Lincoln was again defeated for the senatorship, but his nobly fought campaign made him the nominee of his party for the presidency in 1860, and destroyed the chances of Douglas for uniting the Democratic party of the South with that of the North in the great struggle of that year.

Mr. Douglas, finally, was a descendant of very different stock from the ancestry of Mr. Lincoln. He was as highly born as Mr. Davis. To be exact upon that point it must be said that he was even more highly born than Mr. Davis. On his father's side he came from the Douglases of Scotch fame, and on his mother's from that William Arnold, of Rhode Island, who was the associate of Roger Williams in the founding of that Province, and whose son was appointed by King Charles II. its first governor under the royal charter. Mr. Douglas's father was a respectable, not to say distinguished, physician of Brandon, Vermont. *Douglas.*

Dr. Douglas died on the 1st day of July, 1813, when the subject of this sketch was about two months old. He was poor at the time of his death, and his wife and two children were provided for during the next fifteen years by Mrs. Douglas's brother, a well-to-do farmer of Vermont, by the name of Fisk. The inability of Mr. Fisk to defray the expenses of an academic education for young Stephen caused him to begin life for himself. He was only fifteen years of age, but went forth bravely to meet the hardships of the struggle for existence. He walked from Brandon to Middlebury with all of his possessions in a little pack upon his back, and apprenticed himself to a cabinet maker. For two years he worked industriously at his trade until his health failed. He then attended Brandon Academy for a year, devoting himself with great enthusiasm to classical study. Meanwhile his mother had married Mr. Gehazi Granger, of Canandaigua, New York, and had removed her residence to that place. Thither young Douglas now went by the invitation of his step-father, and became a student in the once famous Canandaigua Academy. For three years he pursued the courses of instruction in that institution with great avidity and success, and, during a portion of the time, also read law in the office of the Hubbells. He here began to develop his talent for extemporaneous debate and political management.

In June of 1833 he started westward, locating first in Cleveland, Ohio, as a clerk in the law office of the Hon. S. J. Andrews. His health soon suffered here from the malaria of the country, and by the advice of his physician he left Cleveland, but instead of returning to the East he went farther westward. He tried Cincinnati, Louisville, and St. Louis, with no success. He then pushed on to Jacksonville in Illinois, arriving there in the last days of November (1833), with only thirty-seven cents in his pocket. He found nothing here to do, and was obliged to sell some of his books for bread. In a few days he was again compelled to face hunger. To attempt to practise law, at such a moment, was out of the question. He would starve before he could find a client. He heard of a chance to organize a school at a place called Winchester, a few miles distant from Jacksonville, and one November morning he walked over to the little town and set himself up as a teacher of a three months' school. He now had bread and shelter, and could devote a little spare time to continuing his law reading.

On the 4th of March, 1834, when not yet quite twenty-one years of age, he received his license to practise before the Supreme Court of the Commonwealth. He was a successful practitioner from the first. The same month in which he obtained admission to the bar was signalized by his entrance into political life. He made a strong political speech at Jacksonville in support of President Jackson's Antibank policy. It was considered by those who heard it and many of his subsequent efforts as among his best. It was upon this occasion that he was hailed for the first time as the "Little Giant." The result of this immediate success at the bar and on the hustings was his election, in February of 1835, as prosecuting attorney for the first judicial district of the Commonwealth over the highly accomplished and much respected John J. Hardin. He was an able, fearless and successful prosecutor, and his services in this capacity contributed greatly to the establishment of law and order in the then comparatively new community.

In the winter of 1835–36, he began the work of organizing the Democratic party in Illinois. Down to that time it had been customary in Illinois for candidates for public place to present themselves, or be presented by a small *Douglas as a party organizer.* number of political friends, and to conduct their own canvasses, either alone or with the aid of a few such friends. Douglas now conceived the plan of winning Morgan County, the county of his residence, from the Whigs by a strict organization of the Democratic party in county convention, which should nominate candidates, and plan and control the campaign for their election. He would thus be able to oppose a regular ticket, with only a single candidate for each place, to the loose methods of the Whigs. He succeeded in his purpose, and although the Whigs were driven by this movement also to unite upon a single ticket, yet they were beaten by the Douglas organization, and the county passed under the control of the Democratic party for a long period. This was the beginning of the "Douglas Machine" in Illinois. In this election Mr. Douglas himself was chosen to the Legislature, and on the first Monday of December, 1836, when only a little over twenty-three years of age, he began his career as a legislator. In four months from this date his fame had reached Washington, and he received from the new President, Mr. Van Buren, the appointment to the office of Land Register at Springfield, in Illinois. Mr. Douglas held this office for a little longer than one year, and during this time, he was working upon the problem of organizing the Democratic party in the Congressional districts and in the Commonwealth, after the model of the Morgan County organization.

In November of 1837, he was nominated by the Democratic district convention of the northern district in the Commonwealth as candidate for the House of Representatives of the National Congress. His opponent was the Hon. John T. Stuart, Lincoln's former partner, and one of the ablest and most popular citizens of Illinois. Mr. Douglas was defeated by only five votes, and it was a question whether this was not attributable to an error in the making up of the ticket.

For the next two years he devoted himself to the practice of his profession, but in the presidential contest of 1840, he again mounted the hustings, and, pitted against Cyrus Walker and Mr. Lincoln, opened the campaign in Illinois. This was the beginning of his political rivalry with Mr. Lincoln which was to culminate in the great struggle of 1860. Probably it was owing to his efforts more than to those of any other one man that the Commonwealth of Illinois chose Democratic electors.   In January of 1841, he was appointed Secretary of State of Illinois, and, in a little over one month afterward, he was elected by the Legislature a judge of the Supreme Court of the Commonwealth.   He was not yet twenty-eight years of age, but he made an able, fearless and just magistrate.   In December of 1842 he was put forward by his friends as a candidate for United States Senator, although he had not completed his thirtieth year.   He came within five votes of an election in a total of one hundred and eleven votes cast by the Legislature in joint session.

In the spring of 1843, he was again nominated as a candidate for a seat in the National House of Representatives.   His competitor this time was Douglas in the Hon. O. H. Browning, a man of great Congress. ability and popularity.   He immediately resigned his judicial office, and in a most hotly waged contest won the election.   From this time forward to the end of his life, he was a member of the National Congress.   He served in the House until 1847 and after that in the Senate.   He was early appointed chairman of the House committee on Territories, and, upon his transfer to the Senate, was soon elected chairman of the Senate committee on the same subject.   In these positions he developed those peculiar doctrines about Territorial government and relations entitled " Popular Sovereignty," or " Squatter Sovereignty," which led to the unsettling of the customary views upon these subjects, and to the rupture of the old agreements and understandings in regard to the question of slavery in the Territories which have been recounted and described in the preceding volume of this work.

Such was the origin and such the education of the

three great personalities around whom and whose doctrines the history of the country chiefly turned in those
momentous years from 1857 to 1861, and around two of
whom it continued to turn for four years more as the
chiefs of the mighty hosts of war, who decided at last
by the issue of arms what could not be settled by peaceful adjustment.

These differences of origin, surroundings, and education account, in large degree, for the differences in mind
and character obtaining between them.
The Celtic blood, military education, and
slave-holding experiences of Mr. Davis will
easily explain the chief points in his intellectual and moral constitution. He saw very clearly,
but not deeply. He was logical rather than intuitive,
and possessed little real imagination. From given premises he reasoned with great exactness, but had neither
the inductive power nor the power of insight necessary
to the discovery of the principles or axioms upon which
he based his syllogisms. The letter of the Constitution,
as the fathers made it and understood it, was his political bible, and he manifested nowhere the slightest appreciation of the consideration that the fathers might have
failed to give exact expression, in the instrument, to the
political and social conditions of the country, or of
the consideration that those conditions might have so
changed through the natural course of human development as to require either a revision of the instrument,
or the employment of methods of liberal interpretation,
such as would enable the political forces and ideas, existing at any given moment, to find some expression through
it. He ridiculed the idea of the "higher law," which is
only an unfortunate name for a profound truth, the truth
that jurisprudence has its basis in ethics, and must develop with the unfolding of the common consciousness

Differences in mind and character between Davis, Lincoln, and Douglas.

of right and wrong. Mr. Davis's rhetoric corresponded in character closely with his logic. It was pure, perspicuous, and rather terse. It must have been a great relief to the Senate, after listening to the ornate sentences, mixed metaphors, and far-fetched similes of most of the Southern members, to have Mr. Davis tell them briefly, plainly, and distinctly, just what it was all about. As discussion and debate approach the point of action such personalities are indispensably necessary to formulate the creeds for which men fight and die. His bearing and conduct were likewise in accord with the character of his thought and speech. He was dignified, grave, almost severe, and decided even to imperiousness. He was rather impatient, and rather inclined to suspect those who differed with him in opinion of being influenced by wrong motives. But withal he was noble, kind, generous in his feelings, if not in his intellect, brave, self-sacrificing, and grandly devoted to duty as he understood it. It was not accident that such a mind and character stood as the representative, Davis's representative character. in 1860, of that narrow but distinct view of the Constitution, which claimed that the " States " were copartners in the Territories, and that the emigrant from any " State " into a Territory carried with him the law of the " State " from which he emigrated with reference to property, and the representative of that imperious demand which claimed the protection of the rights based upon such law by the Government of the United States for so long as the Territorial status should continue. Mr. Davis had advanced this theory as far back as 1848 in his famous 12th of July speech upon the question of the organization of Oregon Territory. Mr. Calhoun had given utterance to it before Mr. Davis, and so had Mr. Rhett ; but Mr. Calhoun died ten years before the

matter was ripe for the trial by battle, and his mantle
fell upon Mr. Davis; while Mr. Rhett was too extravagant
in his notions and expressions, too utterly lacking in
the elements of commandership, to rival Mr. Davis as the
chief representative of the Southern view and purpose.

The Celtic component in Mr. Douglas's blood also was
clearly manifested in his intellectual constitution. He
was more superficial than Mr. Davis in his
mental action, and also less clear. On the
other hand, his volubility was extraordinary.
In fact, his tongue frequently ran away with his brain.
He was always the readiest man in debate, whether he
had studied the subject under discussion or not, although it cannot be said that he did not study carefully
his subject. He was vacillating concerning the details
of his opinions, but he clung to the general principles
involved in them with great tenacity, though not with
the fanaticism of Mr. Davis. He differed greatly from
Mr. Davis in feelings and disposition. He was always
brim full of good cheer, hail fellow well met with everybody, and perfectly adored by the young men who surrounded him. He was a thorough believer in the wisdom and capacity of the people, especially of the
people of the great West, and in their innate fitness for
self-government. He was a real thorough-going, boast-
ful, vainglorious Democrat, while Mr. Davis, though professing democracy and believing himself to be a Democrat, was a high-toned, reserved, aristocratic gentleman
of the old school. Mr. Douglas was impulsive, but not
quick to anger, generous with his assistance to everybody
who sought it, honest and upright in all private deal-
ings, but decidedly inclined to the Celtic view that all
things are fair in politics. He was constantly on the
lookout for some new thing, and made a great point of
never being left behind. It was not at all accidental

Personal traits of Douglas.

that the doctrine that the people resident within a Territory should be entrusted with about the same degree of self-government as those residing within a Commonwealth found its chief exponent in him. He was just the man to believe that the Western adventurers, hunters, and cowboys were as fully equipped for statesmanship as the transcendentalists of Boston or the gold bugs of New York, and needed no period of pupilage or guardianship under the Washington Government to prepare them for civilization and the customs of settled life. He was also just the man to fall into helpless confusion when it came to the work of distinctly fixing and formulating the practical details of this doctrine, and to bury the real question at issue under a mountain of verbiage.

He was never able to give a clear and satisfactory answer to Mr. Lincoln's noted question, in the famous joint debates in Illinois in the year 1858, *The debate between Lincoln and Douglas in 1858.* whether there was any way, under the doctrine of " Popular Sovereignty," for the people in a Territory to prohibit the existence of slavery during the Territorial period. He had declared his adherence to the Dred Scott decision, and that decision was considered by him and his party to hold that Congress had no power to prohibit slavery in the Territories. Of course, if Congress had no power to do it, neither the Territorial legislature nor the people resident within a Territory could do it, since a Territory is a purely Congressional creation, and can have no powers except such as are conferred upon it by Congress, and Congress is not authorized to confer upon a Territory any powers which Congress itself cannot exercise, or empower the President of the United States to exercise.

Lincoln's famous question, as he finally formulated it, was : " Can the people of a United States Territory, under the Dred Scott decision, in any lawful way, against the wish of any citizen of the United States, exclude slavery from its limits, prior to the formation of a State constitution ? " Douglas's intellectual insight was not clear enough and penetrating enough to discover the inconsistency between the *dictum* of the Dred Scott opinion and his doctrine of "Popular Sovereignty," or really to appreciate it after it had been pointed out to him. This is very evident from the fact that there was a way out of the difficulty, simply to hold, as the best lawyers do now and did then, that the point decided in the Dred Scott case was only that a negro descended from a slave mother was not, and could not be, a citizen of the United States, and that the declaration in the opinion about the inability of Congress to prohibit slavery from the Territories was mere *dictum obiter*. Under this view of the case there was no necessary inconsistency involved in professing allegiance both to the decision and to the doctrine of "Popular Sovereignty." But Douglas did not take this way out. There is no evidence in anything he said that he saw this way out. His very superficial answer was that the people within a Territory might, despite the Dred Scott decision, under his doctrine of "Popular Sovereignty," exclude slavery from the Territory, prior to the forming of a "State" constitution, by failing to enact the police regulations for the protection of slave property therein, and by Territorial legislation unfriendly to the maintenance of such property. It did not take Lincoln five minutes to show that slavery could exist without any police regulations in its favor, that it did so exist in the earliest period of its history in the country, that Dred Scott himself was held in slavery in Minnesota Territory without any such regulations, that under the Dred Scott decision, as Judge Douglas and the Democrats understood it, the enactment by any Territorial legislature of regulations unfriendly to slave property would be in violation of the Constitution of the United States itself, and that the failure of a Territorial legislature to enact regulations for the protection of slave property would be the transgression of a duty laid upon it by the Constitution of the United States.

After this, Douglas did get down deep enough in thought to obtain some faint glimmerings of the inconsistency in which he was involved. He subsequently stated his answer in different language. He said that the Constitution of the United States, as interpreted by the Dred Scott decision, "did not carry slavery into the Territories beyond the power of the people of the Territories to control it as other property." It did not take Mr. Lincoln five minutes more to show that, since the Constitution of the United States contained the provision that no one should be deprived of his property without due process of law, and since the Dred Scott decision held, according to Mr. Douglas's understanding, that slave property was recognized by the Constitution, the Territorial control of slave property, as other property, could never mean a power in the people of a Territory to destroy slave property, but must mean only a power to protect it for the benefit of the owner. Mr. Douglas was never able to comprehend fully the self-contradiction under which he labored, nor to extricate himself from the political embarrassments resulting therefrom. His answer, probably, saved him from defeat in the Senatorial contest of 1858, but it lost him the nomination of the Democratic party, as a whole, for the presidency in 1860, and, of course, it thereby destroyed his chances of election to the presidency.

Douglas's idea of the Dred Scott decision.

Superficial as he always was when compared with Lincoln, yet he had a most effective way, to the ordinary mind, of stating, pressing, and refuting things. He would His method take a point advanced by an opponent, deof argument. velop it into a general proposition, which carried falsehood on its very face, and would then attack it savagely and demolish it triumphantly. It was in this manner that he dealt with Lincoln's famous *dictum* that the Union could not permanently exist half slave and half free, but must ultimately become all slave or all free. Douglas developed this into the proposition that there must be uniformity of law and custom in all respects in the several Commonwealths in order to the perpetuity of the Union, and then proceeded to show how this idea would bring about the establishment of a centralized empire upon the ruins of the federal republic. Mr. Douglas really believed that he had completely answered Mr. Lincoln's proposition, and he made a vast number of his hearers believe likewise. Many of the critics of Mr. Douglas incline to the view that this habit was a bit of conscious sophistry on his part, but it is far more probable that it was the natural result of his superficial mental processes, of the rough and ready character of his thinking.

In very decided contrast with the intellectual power and methods of Mr. Davis and Mr. Douglas, stood those of Mr. Lincoln. Mr. Lincoln was slow in his mental movements, and phlegmatic and melancholy in his temperament, but his thinking was unceasing and progressive, and it went down, down, down into depths of which neither Davis nor Douglas had ever dreamed. Lincoln's intellectual power and methods. He was conservative and law-abiding in his instincts and conduct, fully as much so as either of the others, but law with him must be based on ethical right in order to be perpetual, and in order to command permanent

obedience.   One of his maxims was that "he who
moulds public opinion goes deeper than he who makes
statutes or pronounces decisions; he makes the execution of statutes and decisions possible."   The care, patience, and thoroughness with which he worked out his
political science and his constitutional law are the highest evidence of the power and incessant persistence of
his thought.   With him it was quite possible that a decision of the Supreme Court might be erroneous, yea,
that a constitutional provision itself might be erroneous ;
and while he would yield obedience to such a decision
or provision as being subject to the jurisdiction of the
Government, he saw no treason in endeavoring to expose
the error in it to the people, or in urging the people to
rectify it in the legally appointed way.   He not only saw
no treason in such conduct, but he saw positive political duty in it.   The legalism of Davis and of Douglas
would, according to Lincoln's view, have prevented all
reform in the law itself.   While Davis and Douglas took
the Constitution as interpreted by the Supreme Court
to be the sole and original basis of all there was of the
United States, and saw only anarchy back of the Constitution, Lincoln was able to see the Nation behind the
Constitution, with its ideals of law and justice, and its
plastic power to mould law and justice into the forms of
these ideals.

Notwithstanding the depth of his philosophy, he did
not lose himself in transcendental politics.   He had
thought out his constitutional law as carefully and as thoroughly as he had his political ethics.   He was the master both of Davis
and of Douglas upon the ground of positive law and
constitutional history, as well as upon the ground of
public morality.   When Douglas in loud triumphant
accents proclaimed that Lincoln had taken the posi-

*Lincoln as a
constitutional
lawyer.*

tion that the Union could not permanently exist half slave and half free, as the fathers made it, Lincoln quietly reminded him that the fathers never *made* the Union half slave and half free, but found it so, or rather, found it almost entirely slave, and by authorizing Congress to prohibit the African slave-trade after 1808 to any part of the United States, and by prohibiting slavery from going into the North-west Territory, gave unmistakable evidence that they regarded slavery as a temporary status, and intended to put it on the course of ultimate extinction, and thought they had done so. In a few of his terse, logical sentences, he showed that Mr. Douglas's "Popular Sovereignty" doctrine was the innovation, the departure from the ideas and purposes of the fathers of the Constitution, while the Republican doctrine of preventing the extension of slavery by Congressional statute was in strict accord therewith. Nothing ever exceeded the vigor and the clearness with which he exposed the sham of "Popular Sovereignty" in the Territories when taken with the Dred Scott decision, as the Democrats understood the decision. He summed the whole miserable sophism up in a single sentence, and called it the doctrine which taught "that a thing may be lawfully driven away from where it has a lawful right to be."

The soundness of Mr. Lincoln's distinctions between the social sphere, the political sphere, and the sphere of civil liberty, are to-day unquestioned by any true jurist and political scientist. But when he made them, they were to most minds very much like discoveries. Mr. Douglas never seemed able to comprehend them. As Lincoln humorously remarked, Douglas seemed to think that a man must have a negro woman for his wife, if he did not want her for his slave.

The most surprising thing about Mr. Lincoln's mental

constitution was his real conservatism. His low birth, his common, even vulgar rearing, and his poverty, are conditions which have for their results, in most cases, radical, reckless hatred of vested interests and readiness to embrace revolutionary methods. But Mr. Lincoln never once recommended anything except that wise reform which is necessary in this imperfect, changing world to preserve what is sound in existing conditions ; and he never once recommended revolutionary methods to attain such reform. Extraordinary patience, forbearance and conciliatoriness were chief elements in his thinking and his conduct. Mr. Douglas exerted himself to the utmost to show that Lincoln's famous utterance at Springfield on June 17th, 1858, in the presence of the convention which nominated him as the candidate of the Republican party of Illinois for United States Senator, was revolutionary. Lincoln said : " A house divided against itself cannot stand. I believe this Government cannot endure half slave and half free. I do not expect the Union to be dissolved ; I do not expect the house to fall, but I do expect it will cease to be divided. It will become all one thing or all the other. Either the opponents of slavery will arrest the further spread of it, and place it where the public mind shall rest in the belief that it is in the course of ultimate extinction, or its advocates will push it forward, till it shall become alike lawful in all the States, old as well as new, North as well as South."

Mr. Douglas at once made this proposition his chief point of attack, and declared that it meant the extinction of slavery in the "States" where it existed by revolutionary means. But Mr. Lincoln first reminded him that it was rather of the nature of a prophecy than of a party platform, and that it did not even express a preference for a free republic over a slave empire. He said, however, that he was willing to give Judge Douglas the advantage, if such it might be, of the assumption that he preferred the extinction to the extension of slavery ; but he contended that this was the spirit of the Constitution itself, and that the trend of our history had been toward this consummation, at least down to 1850. He showed plainly that constitutional means might be employed for this purpose, among them the prohibition of slavery in the Territories, and the prevention of foreign importation of slaves, means that had been employed down to 1850. And he solemnly averred that he intended the employment of no other means than those which were lawful. It is true that the proposition was a little in advance of what the Republicans in Middle and Southern Illinois were prepared for, but it had no necessary element of revolution in it. In fact it was a conservative proposition in the truest sense of the word. Had it been accepted by the slave-holders, and supported by them, it would probably have preserved slavery in the Commonwealths where it then existed for many years beyond the actual date of emancipation. The absence of prejudice and the love of truth can alone explain this quality of Mr. Lincoln's mental constitution. Though one of the "plain people," he had not the slightest tinge of the demagogue in him. He was ambitious; but his ambition was rather of the altruistic sort. To attain a power and an influence which might be effective in producing some great good for humanity, was his own interpretation of his ambition, and it can scarcely be questioned that he read himself correctly.

It was not adventitious that three such characters as those just described were the exponents of the doctrines which met in the famous contest of 1860, and it was no

more adventitious that each stood for what he did—
Davis, lucid but superficial, insisting that the letter of
the law as interpreted by courts should be lived up to,
as both right and politic, and demanding that
since the Constitution carried slavery into the
Territories, under the latest judicial interpretation, as he understood it, Congress and
the President must protect it there, as other
property; Douglas, less lucid and more superficial,
endeavoring to hold to the same literal legalism with
one hand, and to his Democratic panacea, his " Popular
Sovereignty " doctrine, with the other, and perishing at
last from their inconsistency ; and Lincoln, equally lucid
in thought and language with either, but far more profound, truthful, and self-forgetful, holding that Congress was empowered by the Constitution to exclude
slavery from the Territories, and contending that the
ethics of the nineteenth century required that Congress
should so use the power as to purify every foot of them
from the great curse.   While founding powers upon
law, he thus founded policy upon morality.   In this he
differed, *toto cœlo,* from the others, both of whom made
interests the basis of policy.

When the political contest became acute the Douglas
doctrine was virtually swept from the field, and the op-
posing forces were ranged under the principle of Congressional prohibition of slavery from the Territories,
on the one hand, or Congressional protection of slavery
in all the Territories, on the other.   This was clear,
exact, and comprehensive, and the triumph of the first
at the polls in 1860 was the earnest of its triumph on
the battle-field in 1865.

The political differences between Davis, Douglas and Lincoln in 1860 summed up.

CHAPTER II

ANTI-SLAVERY SENTIMENT IN THE SOUTH BETWEEN 1857 AND 1860

Statistics of Slave-ownership, in 1860—Reasons for the Lack of Inquiry into the Sentiments of the non-Slaveholders in the South in Regard to Slavery—Hostility to Slavery and to the Slave-owners at the South, in 1860, Chiefly Social—Social Hostility Was Leading, however, to Political Differences—The Leadership of the Southern Whigs After the Death of Henry Clay—Hinton Rowan Helper, and His Book—Anti-Slavery Sentiment at the South, in 1858, Estimated—The Common Fear of Slave Insurrection—The Harper's Ferry Catastrophe, and Its Results—The Leaders of the South and Slave Insurrection—The Harper's Ferry Outrage and the Solid South—End and Means in Civilization.

THE most generous estimate that can be made will show that not over two millions of the eight millions of whites inhabiting the slaveholding Common-
Statistics of Slave-owner-ship, in 1860. wealths, in the sixth decade of the century, were directly interested in slave property. The usual statement, as derived from the Census of 1850, is that there were about three hundred and twenty-five thousand slave owners in the South at that date. Counting each one of these as the head of a family of five or six white persons, we obtain about the number above stated as directly interested in such property. Some six millions of whites then had no such interest, and the inquiry as to what their sentiments were in regard to slavery is one of the most neglected parts of our history.

There are reasons for this, of course. The first of these is the great difficulty of discerning any such sentiments, since the press of the South was either in the hands of, or under the pay of, the slaveholders. That is, the anti-slavery sentiments in the South left no such literary results as would enable succeeding generations to gain any satisfactory knowledge of their character or their extent. The second reason is that the development of these sentiments received a rude shock, in 1859, by the Harper's Ferry massacre, before they had gained sufficient strength and clearness to make a manifestation, before, really, the mass of those who entertained them knew that they were anti-slavery sentiments. But that such sentiments did exist and were becoming formidable, no one who had any accurate personal acquaintance with the South during that period will dispute.

Reasons for the lack of inquiry into the sentiments of the non-slaveholders in the South in regard to slavery.

The hostility to slavery, or rather to the slave-owners at the South in 1860, was chiefly social, but in some degree also political. In some portions of the South a certain town civilization had been developed, which had become conscious, to say the least, of its lack of full sympathy with the plantation order of life. Large cities were indeed few in number, but throughout the whole of Kentucky and Tennessee, and in the major part of all of the other Southern Commonwealths, a very large number of handsome and fairly enterprising and prosperous county towns had grown up where there resided lawyers, merchants, bankers, teachers, and some mechanics, men who had little property interest in the perpetuation of slavery, who felt their own intellectual superiority to the country squires and their fox-hunting, horse-racing, quarrelsome sons, and who consequently

Hostility to slavery or to the slave owners at the South in 1860 chiefly social.

asserted social independence of them and social equality
with them. There were constant social feuds between
the young men of the towns and the young squires of
the country in athletic contests, and sometimes in intellectual jousts, but chiefly over the fair ones of the towns,
who, in spite of their urban residence, rather inclined to
look with more favor upon the dashing knights of the
country. So high did this hostility run at times, and
so constant had it become in the years between 1845
and 1860, that a tolerably fair picture of the condition
of the Middle Ages was obtainable from the state of society which prevailed in these parts of the South. It
needed only a clear consciousness on the part of this
young bourgeoisie that the power of their country rivals
lay in the institution of slavery to have turned their en-
mity against that institution. In fact, the merchants
in these towns had already begun to see that their pecu-
niary interests were suffering from the system of plantation slavery. The masters of these great plantations
had developed the practice of purchasing their supplies
immediately from the wholesale dealers in Northern
cities, and the smaller slaveholders had begun, by
threats of doing likewise, to secure from these Southern
town merchants special low rates of charges for their
supplies. These merchants had thus been made to see
that a large population of small farmers and towns-
people would be far more advantageous to their interests than the oligarchy of plantation lords with their
retinues of slaves.

While, as above indicated, this hostility between the
bourgeoisie and the planters was mainly social, still it
had influence in determining political preferences. Those
who would express their hostility politically to the slaveholding planters went with the Whig party, and then the
so-called Know-nothing party, and lastly the American

Union party. The great leader of the Whig party in the South, especially in the Southwest, to the time of his death, was, of course, Henry Clay. He was opposed to the extension of slavery into the Territories, and in favor of gradual emancipation in the slaveholding Common- Social hostility was leading however, to political differences. wealths. Had he lived in 1860, there is little question that he would have been a Republican in principle. The Whig party in the Southwest was not, and could not be, a pro-slavery party in the same sense as was the Democratic party in that section. It looked upon slavery as a temporary necessity, and entertained the hope and the purpose of its ultimate extinction. Its strength was in the towns, and its members were chiefly, though not exclusively, from among the developing bourgeoisie already described. The large slaveholders who belonged to it were generally men of superior intelligence and tender hearts, who ruled their slaves in mercy and kindness, felt compassion for their condition, and were not averse to considering plans for their improvement, and for their ultimate emancipation.

The death of Clay left the party momentarily without a chief. The rivalry for the leadership was, however, soon narrowed down to John J. Crittenden, The leadership of the Southern Whigs after the death of Henry Clay. of Kentucky, and John Bell, of Tennessee. At the time of Clay's death, Crittenden was Attorney-General in President Fillmore's Cabinet, and Bell was a Senator in Congress from Tennessee. Bell's noble stand against the repeal of the Missouri Compromise, in 1854, made him the Whig leader in the South, especially in the Southwest, as was clearly manifested by his nomination for the presidency in 1860 ; but the fact that almost all of the Whig members from the South, in the Congress of 1853–54, voted in favor of the repeal, while all of the Whig members

from the North voted against it, caused the absorption
of the Whig party in the North by the Republican party,
and threw it into great confusion in the South. Had
Bell possessed the power and influence of Clay, he might
have reorganized the Whig strength in the South, and
have held it true to its quasi-anti-slavery principle. He
did succeed to a considerable degree in so doing, and
except for the untoward events of 1859 in Northern Virginia, his success would have been much larger, if not
complete. The signs were certainly quite favorable in
1858.

At that juncture there appeared a most significant
expression of the feelings of the bourgeoisie of this section from a native of North Carolina, one
Hinton Rowan Helper. It is true that the
Senators in Congress from North Carolina,
Mr. Biggs and his successor, Mr. Clingman, repudiated
the North Carolina citizenship of Mr. Helper, and undertook to brand him as a disreputable character. On
the 5th of April, 1858, Mr. Biggs, who had been irritated
by a reference made by Senator Wilson, of Massachusetts,
to Mr. Helper's book, as a true representation of Southern
conditions, gave the Senate an account of Mr. Helper,
which, while it was an extravagant exaggeration of
Helper's youthful faults, manifested the intense hostility of the slaveholders to the publication of the differences in political opinion in reference to slavery obtaining at the South.

It is quite evident from all that came out that Helper
was an exceedingly intelligent, brave, and resolute fellow for his years. He had certainly discovered, before
he was thirty years of age, what most of the statesmen
of the South gave no evidence of understanding until
driven thereto by four years of disastrous war, namely, the immense superiority of the resources of the

North over those of the South.   Helper described himself as a native of the South, born and bred in North
Carolina, of slaveholding parents, although he himself
had engaged in mercantile pursuits in the town of Salis-
bury, a Southerner in instinct, thought, and habit, and
having the desire and purpose to live and die in the
South.   He was in the North somewhere at the time his
book appeared.   In the preface of this book, entitled
the "Impending Crisis of the South," which gave such
mortal offence to the slaveholders of the South, Mr.
Helper addressed himself with great earnestness to his
Southern brethren, besought them to read his book without prejudice, and declared that an irrepressible desire
"to do something to elevate the South to an honorable
and powerful position among the enlightened quarters
of the globe" had been the principle which had actuated
him in the preparation of the work.

The language of the book is generally too violent;
some of the conclusions reached were exaggerations; and
threats were indulged in with a frequency   The impend-
and to a degree that gave the composition   ing crisis.
an incendiary flavor; but the statistics were reliable, and
proved satisfactorily the vast superiority of the wealth,
resources, and civilization of the North over those of the
South; the history was correct, and demonstrated the
apostacy of the slaveholders from the principles of their
ancestors in the establishment of the Republic; the conclusion as to the moral sense of the modern civilized
world upon the question of slavery was truthful; and
the expressions of opinion by the world's great thinkers
and actors, upon which the conclusion was based, were
numerous, well chosen, and convincing; while the hostile
class-spirit manifested throughout the book against the
"Oligarchs," "Slaveocrats," "Lords of the Lash,"
"Terror Engenderers of the South," was in large degree

participated in by the classes to which the name bourgeoisie has been above given. It is, in fact, probably
quite true that Helper's denunciations of the great slaveholders were an approximately fair expression of a quite
general feeling among them, or, at least, a large part of
them. Left entirely to themselves, this hostility to the
class of large slave-owners would probably have developed
into an attack upon slavery itself, as it did in Mr. Helper's
mind. Any pressure from without, however, for the
hastening of such a development would, on the other
hand, call forth a spirit of resentment, the Southerner's
besetting sin, that would allay internal strife and con-
fuse the mind in the work of getting at the secret of the
feeling which was slowly creating this anti-slavery class
in the Middle South.

Mr. Helper's plan for the abolition of slavery was
the natural outcome of the class hostility just described. He recommended the political organization of
the non-slaveholders, with the slaveholders in favor of
abolition, for the purpose of capturing the Commonwealth governments, the social boycott of the slaveholders by this class, and the levy of such heavy taxes upon
slave property by the regenerated governments as would
make it entirely worthless. Mr. Helper's scheme also
contemplated the removal of the negroes from the South,
and a great immigration of whites from the Northern
section of the Union and from Europe. In all of this
he was giving expression to impulses and feelings existing throughout the Middle South that had almost
risen to the stage of mental consciousness. And, on the
whole, it may be said that, in 1858, slavery had little
Anti-slavery strength in Delaware and Maryland, and no
sentiment at great strength in Kentucky, Tennessee, Mis-
the South, in
1858,estimated. souri, Western Virginia, North Carolina,
Northern Georgia, Northern Alabama, and Northern

Texas, and that its strength in these parts was on the decline. These facts were not then appreciated at the North. The North then judged the sentiments of the South only, or almost only, by the speeches and votes of the Southern Senators and Representatives in Congress, and by its slavery-subservient press. The great slaveholders were, however, cognizant of them, and were anxious to bring matters to a crisis before the hostile development close around them should proceed further.

There was one feeling, however, which the white population in the South of all classes shared in common, and that was the fear of slave insurrection. It was a curious trait in the character of the slaves that what hostility they manifested against the whites was directed chiefly against the non-slaveholders and the poorer slaveholders. It was, however, fully as significant as curious, since it is entirely intelligible. The richer slaveholders lived in greater state, of course, wore finer raiment, rode in more splendid equipages, had more courtly manners. Such a master had only to exercise a little friendly condescension in order to win the respect, reverence, and good-will of the slave. Moreover, the patrol duty was imposed chiefly upon the commoner whites. Thus, while the master granted the pass to the slave, it was the poor white who held him up, examined it, and, if it was not satisfactory, imposed the stripes. Hence the non-slaveholders and the smaller slaveholders knew well that a servile insurrection would be to them and to their families an even more terrible danger than to the great masters. If, therefore, the fear of "negro rising," as they were accustomed to call it, could be excited and sustained in their breasts, the developing social conflict between them and the great slaveholders would be repressed, and, instead of it, they would become conscious of a solidarity of interest with the slave-

The common fear of slave insurrection.

holders against the negroes, which would grow more intense as the fear which produced it increased, and subordinated all other sentiments to itself. The great slaveholders understood this, and were not so very greatly disturbed by the existence of any such excitement, as they would otherwise have been. It was a capital string for them to play upon, especially if the original impulse to hostile plans and movements among the slaves could be imputed to the wickedness of the inhabitants of the non-slaveholding Commonwealths.

Seen from the point of view of the influence of such fears upon the growth of the still half-conscious anti-slavery spirit existing throughout large sections of the South, nothing could have been more untoward, wickedly harmful, and positively diabolical than the John Brown raid on Harper's Ferry on the night of the 16th of October, 1859. If the whole thing, both as to time, methods, and results, had been planned by His Satanic Majesty himself, it could not have succeeded better in setting the sound conservative movements of the age at naught, and in creating a state of feeling which offered the most capital opportunities for the triumph of political insincerity, radicalism, and rascality over their opposites. No man who is acquainted with the change of feeling which occurred in the South between the 16th of October, 1859, and the 16th of November of the same year can regard the Harper's Ferry villainy as anything other than one of the chiefest crimes of our history. It established and re-established the control of the great radical slaveholders over the non-slaveholders, the little slaveholders, and the more liberal of the larger slaveholders, which had already begun to be loosened. It created anew a solidarity of interest between them all, which was felt by all with an intensity which overcame every other sentiment.

The Harper's Ferry catastrophe and its results.

It gave thus to the great radical slaveholders the willing physical material for the construction of armies and navies, and for the prosecution of war.

There was, indeed, little in the exact facts of the event which strictly necessitated these results. The long and thorough examination made by the Senate committee did not reveal the conscious complicity of anybody in the atrocity outside of the twenty-one villains who followed Brown. This committee was composed of Senators Mason of Virginia, Davis of Mississippi, Fitch of Indiana, Collamer of Vermont, and Doolittle of Wisconsin. It is no reproach to the memories of the two gentlemen first named to say that they sought diligently to find some connection between Brown and influential men at the North in the commission of this great crime. The facts of the case as drawn from the two reports of this committee, the majority report signed by Senators Mason, Davis, and Fitch, and the minority report signed by Senators Collamer and Doolittle, were, briefly told, that Brown, after having been cut short in his nefarious career in Kansas by the triumph of the "Free State" party, which repudiated him, had organized a little force of his Kansas desperadoes at Springdale in Iowa ; had instructed them in military tactics ; had taken them to Chatham in Canada, in the spring of 1858, where he claimed to have organized a provisional government, as a first step toward an attack upon some Commonwealth of the Union in which slavery was lawful ; had then gone with his party into Ohio, where he permitted them to separate subject to his call ; had sent one of them, John E. Cook by name, to Harper's Ferry with instructions to remain there, find out everything, and report to him ; had appeared himself, under the assumed name of Smith, with two sons

The Congressional investigation of it.

and a son-in-law, in the neighborhood of the place about July of 1859, and taken a farm some five miles from the town on the Maryland side of the Potomac ; and had here secretly gathered his followers, his arms, and his ammunitions. From this point he, with seventeen of his gang, sneaked into Harper's Ferry on the night of the 16th of October, between the hours of eleven and twelve, when the little village was wrapped in peaceful slumber. They seized upon the railroad bridge across the river, the engine house, the watch house, the arsenal and the rifle works; held up a train on the Baltimore and Ohio Railroad which was attempting to cross the bridge ; and shot to death a free negro named Hayward, a porter on the train, whose only offence was that he fled in terror when ordered to halt and stand. They employed the remainder of the night in going to the homes of prominent Virginia gentlemen, such as Colonel Lewis Washington, Mr. Allstadt, and Mr. Byrne, making prisoners of them, assuming to free such of their men-slaves as they could find, and forcing the newly emancipated into their ranks. As day broke, they seized all the white men who appeared in the streets, and confined them in the watch house and the engine house. News of the outrage having by this time reached Charleston and Martinsburg, the citizens of these towns armed themselves, proceeded to the scene of action, attacked the watch house in which most of the prisoners were confined, and succeeded in liberating them. By this time a company of marines, commanded by Colonel Robert E. Lee, arrived, stormed the engine house, liberated the rest of the prisoners, and captured Brown and the survivors of his band, with the exception of a single man. The Virginia negroes, who had been pressed into the service, threw down their arms and deserted their liberator at the first opportunity.

The whole attempt was a complete fiasco, and was to any calm and judicious mind satisfactory proof both of the impotence of secret insurrectionary movements prepared in the North, and of the lack of any insurrectionary spirit among the slaves themselves. But there were some suspicious things connected with the affair which even calm and judicious people required to have explained. Where, for example, did Brown get the money to support his band of twenty-two men for so long a period, and to procure arms for fifteen hundred men, as he had done, and have them transported to his Maryland farm-house. He was a notorious dead beat himself, had never succeeded in any legitimate business, had never earned any money, had had two wives and some twenty children, and had left them to shift for themselves in penury and misery, while he was careering around reforming things. Somebody had assisted him, that was certain ; and it was probable that a good many persons had helped him. It was possible, of course, that they did so with full knowledge of his purpose, but this was by no means a necessary conclusion.

Evidences of complicity in the Harper's Ferry incident.

The evidence taken by the Senate committee showed that a large number of men and some women were in the habit of going about through the North, giving abolition lectures and sending the net proceeds from the sale of tickets or the voluntary contributions to Brown. No statement of plans or account of expenditures was required of him. He always resisted any approach toward anything of the kind. Brown had gotten into his first paying business, and he was determined not to have it ruined by publicity. And it certainly did seem that some of the people with whom he had gotten in were so anxious to keep out of sight that they were quite contented not to know what he was doing. The evidence before the committee also showed that such men as Gerritt Smith, Dr. Samuel G. Howe, and Mr. George L. Stearns had given Brown large sums of money without requiring from him any information in regard to the use of it.　Mr. Stearns went so far in his testimony before the committee as to say that, while he would have disapproved of the Harper's Ferry plan had he known of it before it was undertaken, he had come to view it as one of the greatest events in our history, that he thought it would free America.　Finally, the evidence before the committee showed that the most important and expensive weapons which Brown had, the two hundred Sharp's rifled carbines, were the property of the "Massachusetts State Kansas Committee," and that the two hundred pistols had been bought and paid for by Mr. Stearns.　It appeared that the "Massachusetts State Kansas Committee" had, some time before, transferred the carbines to the "National Kansas Aid Committee," and that this latter committee had sent them to Chicago ; that Brown had asked the National Committee for them, but that this Committee had required of him some information in regard to his purposes, and that, having received no satisfactory reply, had refused his request, and had voted to return the arms to the Massachusetts Committee ; and that Mr. Stearns, then chairman of the Massachusetts Committee, had delivered them to Brown at Tabor, in Iowa, for safe keeping.　It also appeared that one Forbes, whom Brown had employed to teach military tactics to his band at Springdale, but who subsequently quarrelled with Brown, had revealed to Senator Henry Wilson and Dr. Howe something of the dangerous character of Brown's plans, and that these gentlemen had communicated with Mr. Stearns about them, and had expressed their uneasiness that Brown should have been entrusted with the arms belonging to the Massachusetts Committee, and that Mr. Stearns did nothing for their reclamation.

It was certainly a most reckless and reprehensible thing, to call it by the mildest name, in Mr. Stearns and the Massachusetts Committee to entrust those arms to a man of Brown's antecedents. They had been procured to furnish the " Free State " settlers in Kansas with the means of defence against attack upon their persons and their homes.   Disorder in Kansas had been quelled by the triumph of the " Free State " party, and the arms were not needed there or anywhere else for any lawful purpose.   They should certainly have been returned to the immediate custody of the Committee, and given into the charge of some person whose character was a guarantee that they would not be put to any unlawful use.   There is no question that these revelations were a little disquieting even to cool and impartial minds.   They seemed to show that there were many respectable people at the North who were willing to put the means of doing mischief into the hands of desperate men, and then designedly keep themselves in ignorance of how these means were being employed.   They were immensely disquieting to Southern minds that were not cool and impartial, and it must be conceded that a majority of Southern minds of that day belonged to this class, and, as for that, a majority of minds everywhere.

Disquieting character of the revelations.

Long, however, before the reports of this Senate committee were published to the world, even before the motion for its appointment had been made, much more disquieting things in connection with the outrage had occurred than the revelations of the report would have been had they been made in November of 1859, instead of in June, 1860. These were the demonstrations indulged in

Demonstrations of sympathy with Brown at the North.

throughout many parts of the North on the day of the execution of Brown. Brown and his band had murdered five men and wounded some eight or ten more in their criminal movement at Harper's Ferry. If they had done nothing more than kill the free negro Hayward, they had made themselves common murderers, and were deserving of nothing but the punishment for murder and the execration of all decent men. Add to this the consideration that Brown certainly intended the wholesale massacre of the whites by the blacks in case that should be found necessary to effect his purposes, and it was certainly natural that the tolling of the church bells, the holding of prayer-meetings for the soul of John Brown, the draping of houses, the half-masting of flags, etc., in many parts of the North, should appear to the people of the South to be evidences of a wickedness which knew no bounds, and which was bent upon the destruction of the South by any means necessary to accomplish the result. It was reported throughout the South that the Senate of Massachusetts came within three votes of passing a resolution for adjourning on the day of the execution.

It was of course possible for people far removed from any peril to make a distinction between approval of Brown's act and commiseration for his fate, and to attribute all of these demonstrations to the latter feeling; but it was simply impossible for those surrounded by all the dangers which Brown's movements threatened to call up to appreciate any such distinctions. To them they appeared the veriest cant and hypocrisy. Especially did terror and bitterness take possession of the hearts of the women of the South, who saw in slave insurrection not only destruction and death, but that which to feminine virtue is a thousand times worse than the most terrible death. For those who would excite such a movement or sympathize with anybody who would excite such a

movement, the women of the South felt a hatred as un-
dying as virtue itself.   Men might still hesitate, and
consider, and argue, but the women were united and
resolute, and their unanimous exhortation was : " Men
of the South, defend the honor of your mothers, your
wives, your sisters, and your daughters.   It is your
highest and most sacred duty ! "

It has been often said that the leaders among the
slaveholders knew that there was no such danger of
slave insurrection as the masses believed there   The leaders
was, and also knew that the sympathy at the   of the South
                                                and slave in-
North for any such movement, or for any-   surrection.
body who would take part in any such movement, was
not one thousandth part as great as the masses believed it
to be, but designedly kept this knowledge to themselves,
and either remained silent when they might have quiet-
ed fears, or by wicked misrepresentations increased these
fears and intensified the hatred born thereof.   This was
probably true in many cases, but not to the extent and
degree generally supposed at the North.   The leading
slaveholders had no such clear knowledge of the character and impulses of their slaves, or of the intentions of
the North, as subsequent opinion has attributed to them.
They themselves were not wholly free from the fear which
possessed the masses, and they could not have created
this terror among the masses except for the actual attempt to excite slave insurrection, and the apparently
widespread sympathy for the same in many parts of the
North.   From the Harper's Ferry outrage onward the
conviction grew among all classes that the   The Har-
white men of the South must stand together,   per's Ferry
                                                outrage and
and must harmonize all internal differences   the solid
in the presence of the mortal peril, with   South.
which, as a race, they believed themselves threatened.
Sound development in thought and feeling was arrested.
The follies and the hatreds born of fear and resentment

now assumed the places of common sense and common kindliness. And war and bloodshed became a necessity for the relief of burning hearts.

A sound philosophy will undoubtedly hold that there is a plan of world civilization, and that man cannot thwart its ultimate realization; but it will also hold that man can and does, in large degree, at least, determine the nature of the means employed in the attainment of the predestined results. Whether they shall be destructive or constructive, or more or less destructive, whether they shall be vicious or virtuous, honorable or degrading, these are things which are within the power and control of man. Here lies his responsibility. Here is his realm of duty. It is from this point of view that the event at Harper's Ferry must be judged. And from this point of view it was crime, and nothing but crime, common crime and public crime, crime that made violent and destructive means possible and actual, and seemingly necessary for the attainment in the United States of that principle of the world's civilization which has decreed the personal freedom of all men. Unless we are fatalists or Jesuits in philosophy, we are bound to condemn this crime to the end of time, and execrate the committers of it, even though we should ascribe to it the emancipation of the bondmen. It is an affront to Divinity itself to assert that the world's civilization cannot be realized except through violence and destruction, blood, crime, and sin. It is the cardinal fallacy of orientalism to hold that what has happened must have been inevitable, not only as to the end secured, but also as to the means by which the end was secured. It is the passionate haste of sinful man which dares to hurry the plans of Providence by the employment of means which rob the plans of their glory and their divinity.

End and means in civilization.

CHAPTER III

THE PRESIDENTIAL ELECTION OF 1860

The Cincinnati Platform of 1856 and the Dred Scott Doctrine of
1857—Buchanan and Douglas After the Dred Scott Decision—
Threatened Breach in the Democratic Party—The Davis Reso-
lutions of February 2, 1860—The Revised Draft of Mr. Davis's
Resolutions—The Purpose of These Resolutions, and of Others
Like them—Criticism and Debate upon Mr. Davis's Resolutions
—Assembly of the National Convention of the Democratic
Party—The Platform as Proposed by the Majority of the Com-
mittee—The Platform as Proposed by the Minority of the Com-
mittee—The Resistance of the Northern Democrats to the
Platform of the Majority of the Committee—Secessions from
the Convention—The Failure to Make a Nomination, and the
Adjournment of the Convention—The Seceders' Convention—
Advance in the Slaveholders' Demands—The Events of the In-
terim between the Adjournment and Reassembly of the Democratic Conventions—Adoption of the Davis Resolutions—The
Republican National Convention—The Republican Platform
—The Doctrine of the Platform Concerning Slavery in the Territories—The Tariff Plank—Its Connection with the Question
of Free Territories—The Nomination of the Candidates by the
Republican Convention—The Constitutional Union Party, and
Its Convention—The Nomination of John Bell for the Presidency by It—The Danger to the Slaveholders in the South
from This Party—Reassembly of the Convention of the Southern Democracy—Reassembly of the Convention of the Northern Democracy—Work of the Two Conventions—The Political
Campaign of 1860—The September and October Elections—
The Election of November, 1860.

THE fundamental doctrine of the Cincinnati platform of 1856, the doctrine of "Popular Sovereignty"

The Cincin-
nati platform
of 1856 and the
Dred Scott
doctrine of
1857.

in the Territories, had, as we have seen, been
contradicted by the Dred Scott opinion of
1857. Notwithstanding this fact, however,
the Northern Democrats led by Mr. Douglas
continued to hold, as we have also seen, that in some
way or other, either by unfriendly police regulation,
or by refusing friendly police regulation, the people of
a Territory might make the existence of slavery in it
impossible, if they so willed, during the Territorial
period, and prior to the formation of a Commonwealth
government. Except for this claim Mr. Douglas could
not have secured the election of a majority of Democrats as members of the Illinois Legislature in 1858,
and his own election by that Legislature as United
States Senator, against the combined efforts of the Republicans and the Buchanan Democrats.

President Buchanan had, after the Dred Scott decision,
given up the doctrine of "Popular Sovereignty" in

Buchanan
and Douglas
after the Dred
Scott decision.

the Territories entirely, and for this reason,
together with the defeat of his Lecompton
plan for Kansas, effected chiefly by the opposition of Mr. Douglas, he and the wing of the Democratic party which he represented had developed a bitter
hostility to Mr. Douglas, which was manifested first in
the senatorial contest in Illinois in 1858, and then upon
the larger field of the presidential contest in 1860. Mr.
Lincoln had foreseen the latter result during the senatorial contest, and had said that Mr. Douglas could not
so answer the famous Freeport question as to secure
both the senatorship in 1858 and the presidency in 1860.
He did so answer it as to secure the senatorship. tI
now remained to be tested whether the answer would
prevent his attainment of the presidency.

During the year 1859, the contradiction between the "Popular Sovereignty" doctrine and the Dred Scott opinion became more and more clear and more and more generally appreciated, until by the opening of the spring of the year 1860 it was evident that the Democratic party would, in the coming campaign, probably split upon this issue, the Northern Democrats holding to the former doctrine, and the Southern Democrats to the latter.   If this should actually come to pass the Democratic party, as a national party, would be disrupted, and the last bond of party unity between the two sections would be severed. The outlook was most portentous.   Not many men recognized the greatness or the imminence of the danger, and the mass of men went forward to meet it with a lightness of heart which can be attributed only to ignorance. Meanwhile the agitation of the slavery question in Congress was kept up with ever-increasing excitement in the Senate over the question of investigating the Harper's Ferry outrage, and in the House over the resolution introduced by Mr. J. B. Clark, of Missouri, in condemnation of Mr. Helper's book and of those members of Congress who had approved of it and recommended its perusal to the people.

Threatened breach in the Democratic party.

Such was the state of feeling and opinion in Congress and throughout the country, when, on the 2d day of February, 1860, Mr. Jefferson Davis introduced into the Senate of the United States the noted resolutions which indicated the doctrines upon which the Democrats of the South would stand in the coming contest.   These resolutions were six in number.   The first affirmed the sovereignty of the "States," and the subordinate character of the United States Government, and denounced the intermeddling of one "State," or a combination of the citi-

The Davis resolutions of February 2, 1860.

zens of one "State" with the domestic institutions of another. The second proclaimed negro slavery to be an important domestic institution in fifteen "States" of the Union, recognized and protected by the Constitution of the United States, and declared any attack upon it by any "State" of the Union, or by the citizens of any "State" of the Union, to be a manifest breach of faith, and a violation of the most solemn obligations. The sixth asserted the constitutionality of the existing Fugitive Slave law and denounced the attempts of "State" Legislatures to defeat its purpose by the passage of the so-called "personal liberty bills," or in any other manner. The third, fourth, and fifth of the series contain, however, the real gist of the questions at issue, and must, therefore, be quoted *verbatim*. They ran as follows:

"Resolved, that the unity of these States rests on the equality of rights and privileges among its members, and that it is especially the duty of the Senate, which represents the States in their sovereign capacity, to resist all attempts to discriminate either in relation to person or property, so as, in the Territories—which are the common possession of the United States—to give advantages to the citizens of one State which are not equally secured to those of every other State:"

"Resolved, that neither Congress nor a Territorial Legislature, whether by direct legislation or legislation of an indirect and unfriendly nature, possesses the power to annul or impair the constitutional right of any citizen of the United States to take his slave property into the common Territories; but it is the duty of the Federal Government there to afford for that, as for other species of property, the needful protection; and if experience should at any time prove that the judiciary does not possess power to insure adequate protection, *it will then become the duty of Congress to supply such deficiency:*"

"Resolved, that the inhabitants of an organized Territory of the United States when they rightfully form a constitution to be admitted as a State into the Union may then, for the first time, like the people of a State when forming a new constitution, decide for themselves whether slavery, as a domestic institution, shall be sustained or prohibited within their jurisdiction; and if Congress shall admit them as a State, they shall be received into the Union with or without slavery, as their constitution may prescribe at the time of their admission."

Mr. Davis asked that these resolutions should be printed and made a special order for the following Wednesday, which was agreed to. Their consideration was, however, postponed from time to time, until on the 1st of March Mr. Davis asked to be allowed to withdraw them and offer them anew in a somewhat modified form, since conference with friends had convinced him that a slight change in them was desirable.

An examination of the revised draft shows that the only change of any importance was in the fourth resolution, which in the revision was divided into two resolutions, the first of which read: "Resolved, that neither Congress nor a Territorial legislature, whether by direct legislation, or legislation of an indirect and unfriendly character, possesses power to annul or impair the constitutional right of any citizen of the United States to take his slave property into the common Territories and there hold and enjoy the same while the Territorial condition remains:" and the second of which reads: "Resolved, that if experience should at any time prove that the judiciary and executive authority do not possess means to insure adequate protection to constitutional rights in a Territory, and if the Territorial government shall

The revised draft of Mr. Davis's resolutions.

fail or refuse to provide the necessary remedies for the purpose, it will be the duty of Congress to supply the deficiency." No objection was made to the substitution of this revision of the resolutions for the original draft, and they were so substituted.

The purpose of these resolutions was the construction of a creed for the Democratic party in the rapidly approaching presidential election, and the defeat of Mr. Douglas's candidacy. Some five other sets of resolutions, having the like purpose, had been already offered when Mr. Davis presented these. Among them, those brought forward by Mr. Davis's colleague in the Senate, Mr. Brown, were most noted for their radical character. They provided for positive and immediate action by Congress for the protection of property in slaves in every Territory already organized, or to be organized in the future.

The purpose of these resolutions, and of others like them.

Mr. Brown criticised Mr. Davis's resolutions as being weak and worthless. Evidently there were already people in Mississippi more advanced than Mr. Davis himself on the subject of the claimed constitutional duty of the United States Government to protect slave property in the Territories. The debate upon Mr. Davis's resolutions began on April 2d, and from that time forward the other sets of propositions having the same purpose, in whole or part, dropped out of consideration. Mr. Davis was anxious to get a vote so soon as possible upon his declaration of principles, and, for this reason, discouraged extended debate upon them ; but the Senators kept up the battle of words, and the Democratic National Convention met before a single one of the resolutions had been put to vote.

Criticism and debate upon Mr. Davis's resolutions.

This convention assembled at Charleston, South Carolina, on the 23d day of April. Delegates were present from every Commonwealth in the Union, then thirty-three in number, Minnesota having been admitted in May of 1858, and Oregon in February of 1859. Counting by heads, it was well known that Mr. Douglas and his now fatally modified " Popular Sovereignty " doctrine preponderated ; but the convention appointed its committees by Commonwealths, and as the Democrats of California and Oregon adhered to the Southern party, the majority in the committees fell to Mr. Douglas's opponents. The committee on the platform being so constituted naturally reported a party creed upon which Mr. Douglas could never stand without the grossest stultification, and upon which, in so far as it referred to slavery in the Territories, he had declared he would not stand even for the presidency. Moreover, the presiding officer of the convention, the Hon. Caleb Cushing, was a Dred Scott decision Democrat, and a warm personal friend of Senator Jefferson Davis. The influence of the chair was thus against Mr. Douglas.

Assembly of the National Convention of the Democratic party.

The platform, as finally perfected by the majority of the committee, and presented by its chairman, Mr. Avery, of North Carolina, to the convention, declared, " that the government of a Territory organized by an act of Congress is provisional and temporary, and during its existence all citizens of the United States have an equal right to settle with their property in the Territory without their rights either of person or property being destroyed or impaired by Congressional or Territorial legislation ; that is, it is the duty of the Federal Government, in all its departments, to protect, when necessary, the rights of person and property in the Territories, and wherever else its constitutional authority extends ; that when the settlers in a Territory having an

The platform as proposed by the majority of the committee.

adequate population form a State constitution, the right of sovereignty commences, and, being consummated by admission into the Union, they stand on an equal footing with the people of the other States, and the State thus organized ought to be admitted into the Federal Union, whether its constitution prohibits or recognizes the institution of slavery." It also contained provisions favoring the annexation of Cuba, the construction of a railway to the Pacific, and the protection of the rights of naturalized citizens, and denouncing the acts of the Commonwealth Legislatures of the North passed for the purpose of defeating the execution of the Fugitive Slave law.

The minority of the committee also presented, through the Hon. Henry B. Payne, of Ohio, the draft of a platform to the convention. It differed from the report of the majority only in the article upon the subject of slavery in the Territories. The proposition of this report in reference to that all-absorbing matter was as follows : " Inasmuch as differences of opinion exist in the Democratic party as to the nature and extent of the powers of a Territorial Legislature, and as to the powers and duties of Congress, under the Constitution of the United States, over the institution of slavery within the Territories: Resolved, that the Democratic party will abide by the decisions of the Supreme Court of the United States on the questions of constitutional law."

The platform as proposed by a minority of the committee.

Mr. Avery stated, in presenting the report of the majority of the committee, that " Popular Sovereignty" in the Territories was as dangerous to Southern interests as the Wilmot proviso itself, be- cause experience had shown that the South could not compete successfully with the North in the settlement of the Territories, since it was

Mr. Avery's statement in connection with the majority report.

costing the emigrant aid societies of the North only about two hundred dollars to place a voter in the Territories, while it cost a Southern man about fifteen hundred dollars to place himself in a like position. Of course, he meant a Southern man encumbered with a retinue of slaves. Mr. Avery went on to attack the proposition of the minority to hold to the Cincinnati platform as modified and interpreted by the proposed pledge to "abide by the decisions of the United States Supreme Court on the questions of constitutional law," and also the proposition of Mr. Benjamin F. Butler to reaffirm the Cincinnati platform without any explanations or modifications. He declared that the Cincinnati platform was susceptible of two meanings, and told his Northern brethren plainly that the South was no longer to be befooled and befogged with ambiguous statements, but was now determined to have something which would mean the same thing everywhere. It was in vain that the Northern Democrats pleaded that they should not be weighted down with a platform which meant certain defeat of the party in the North, and, therefore, in the whole country. The great slaveholders preferred the chances of defeat to any further uncertainties about their rights in the Territories, or about the disposition of the North concerning them. They knew that a solidarity of feeling between them and the lesser slaveholders and the non-slaveholders had been, at last, attained, which had not before existed, and which might be lost again. They felt instinctively that now was the time to take the firm stand, and bring their Northern friends squarely up to the mark.

To their surprise the Northern Democrats developed an independence and a resoluteness which they had never before manifested. Under the leadership of Mr. Henry B. Payne and Mr. George E. Pugh, they triumphantly carried the report of the minority of the committee on the platform in the convention by a vote of one hundred and sixty-five to one hundred and thirty-eight. All the Northern Democrats, except the delegates from California and Oregon, and part of the delegates from Massachusetts, New Jersey, and Pennsylvania, voted for the report. Twelve delegates from the border Commonwealths of the South also voted for it.

The resistance of the Northern Democrats to the platform of the majority of the committee.

So soon as the result was made known the Southerners began to secede from the convention. The Alabama men led off. The chairman of the delegation, Mr. L. P. Walker, informed the convention that the "State" of Alabama in convention assembled had instructed her delegates not to submit to a "squatter sovereignty" platform, but to withdraw from the general convention, if such a one should be adopted. The Mississippians immediately followed. Then the delegations from South Carolina, Florida, and Texas went out. Finally, all but two of the Louisiana delegates, all but one of the Arkansas delegates, and twenty-six of the thirty-four Georgians, withdrew.

Secessions from the convention.

There still remained, however, in the convention, a substantial majority of the whole number of delegates chosen from all of the Commonwealths. They proceeded to ballot for candidates for President and Vice-President upon the two-thirds rule adopted by the convention. Mr. Douglas received a good majority, but could not reach a majority of two-thirds of all of the votes cast. After fifty-seven unsuccessful ballots, the convention adjourned, May 3d, to reassemble in Baltimore on the 18th of the following June. Before adjourning, it passed a resolution recommending the party organizations, in the several Commonwealths, whose delegates

The failure to make a nomination, and the adjournment of the convention.

had withdrawn from the convention, to elect and send
forward new members to occupy the seats of the seceders.

The seceding delegates had assembled in separate
convention under the presidency of Senator James A.
Bayard of Delaware. They adopted the
resolutions reported by the majority of the
committee of the general convention on the
platform, the Avery principles, talked for four days,
and then adjourned to meet on the second Monday of
the following June at Richmond, Virginia. The division
of the Democratic party on sectional lines was now an
accomplished fact. It remained to be seen whether it
was final, or whether six weeks of reflection would bring
wisdom and conciliation.

The seced-
ers' conven-
tion.

To the historian there is no question that the slaveholders had demanded an advance upon the Cincinnati
doctrine of 1856, which was then universally
accepted as a finality. That doctrine was,
as we know, non-intervention by Congress,
either in the Commonwealths or the Territories, upon
the subject of slavery. The slaveholders now said that
by non-intervention in the Territories upon that subject
they understood, both in 1860 and 1856, the same sort
of neutrality which Congress observed toward slavery
in the District of Columbia, which was that Congress,
having found slavery an existing institution in the District, could, as a neutral body toward it, legislate only
for its protection. If Congress should fail to do this,
they now said, Congress would be acting against it,
and would thus violate neutrality with regard to it.

Advance in
the slavehold-
ers' demands.

In a very concise and able speech upon Mr. Davis's
resolutions, made in the Senate Chamber on April 2d
preceding, Senator Wigfall of Texas had developed this
idea in a most subtile juristic manner. He took the
ground that no legislature merely in the political sys-

tem of the United States, whether it were Congress or the Legislature of a Commonwealth of the Union, could

Mr. Wigfall's reasoning upon the meaning of Congressional neutrality in regard to slavery in the Territories.

determine in what property should consist; that that could be done only by the sovereign in the system; and that the only powers which government had, or could have, in a republican system, in reference to property, were powers to protect that which the sovereign had defined to be property. Hence the conclusion, that if government failed to protect property it was attempting to thwart the will of the sovereign power, was disobedient, and thus really intervening against the organic law. This reasoning was sound, in respect to the question of slavery in the Territories, provided the sovereign in the Territories was sovereign over the Government of the United States, and had established property in slaves in the Territories.

Now, this doctrine was not held by the Democratic party in 1856. It appeared first in the Dred Scott opinion in 1857, *and what the slaveholders proposed at Charleston was to make the Dred Scott opinion the platform of the party*. Whatever may be said about the rightfulness or wrongfulness, the wisdom or unwisdom of this, it was certainly a new thing, and it certainly marked an advance by the slaveholders beyond their position in 1856. It was an encroachment upon the North. The slaveholders said, and with some show of reason, that they asked only what the Supreme Court had declared to be their constitutional right, a right which was, therefore, as old as the Constitution, and of which they had been deprived by Congressional legislation. But it was at least questionable whether the Supreme Court had *decided* the point contended for by the slaveholders. Justice Curtis asserted that it had not, as we have seen, and the consensus of opinion

among the best constitutional lawyers of this day is that
he was correct. Admitting, however, for the sake of
argument that the Court had decided the point, the
whole duty of Congress would have been discharged by
furnishing the courts and the executive with the general
power to execute judicial decisions. The nullification
of an act of Congress by a judicial decision does not
obligate Congress to pass any other act. The proposition of the minority of the committee on the platform
met the case entirely in pledging the Democratic party
to abide by the decisions of the Supreme Court in questions of constitutional law. The demand of the slaveholders that the opinion of the court should be incorporated in the platform was, under the most generous
aspect in which it can be viewed, a demand that the
duty of obedience to judicial decision in a specific case
should be so magnified and exaggerated as to make the
decision a binding rule of political action—an irrefutable
principle of political opinion. This was certainly a new
demand. It was a demand to which the Democrats of
the North could not accede, unless they were willing to
make the Supreme Court the determiner of policy and
opinion as well as of law, unless they were willing to
acknowledge sovereignty itself as belonging to the Supreme Court, unless they were willing to accept an
oligarchic state as the form of the American system.

Between the date of the adjournment of
the two Democratic conventions in early
May and their reassembling in the middle
of June, events which were to exercise an
influence upon their final action crowded
in thick and fast.

*The events
of the interim
between the
adjournment
and reassem-
bly of the
Democratic
conventions.*

In the first place, the discussion in the Senate upon
the Davis resolutions continued and grew more earnest
and excited. On the 7th of May Mr. Davis himself

made a powerful effort to crush Mr. Douglas and his
" Popular Sovereignty " doctrine to earth. On the 15th
Mr. Douglas undertook to answer and controvert the
main points of Mr. Davis's resolutions and speech. To
the historian it appears that he did do so conclusively,
but to the Democratic Senators it manifestly appeared
that he did not. The vote was taken upon the resolutions separately beginning on the 24th and
ending on the 25th. Mr. Douglas aside of
course, every Democratic Senator, except Mr.
Pugh, voted for all of the resolutions, and they were all
adopted by a majority of almost two to one, and without
any modification in principle. So far as the Democratic
members of the Senate of the United States could make
it so, the confederatization of the political system of the
United States was complete. They had also thrown
themselves upon the side of the Southern Democracy,
which signified their encouragement to the seceders from
the Charleston convention to persevere in the division
of the party and dissolve the last bond of political party
unity between the North and the South.

Adoption of
the Davis res-
olutions.

The second great event of the interim was the assembly of the Republican National convention at Chicago,
on the 16th day of May. It was called a
national convention, although, in fact, it was
geographically sectional, no delegates from
the slaveholding Commonwealths being present, except
from what were then called the " border States." The
organization of the convention was quickly accomplished,
and the platform was promptly drafted and unanimously
adopted. It was evident that there was no disposition
to allow differences of opinion upon points of minor
importance, or even points of considerable importance,
to interfere with success at the polls. The enthusiasm
of a new party, composed chiefly of comparatively young

The Repub-
lican National
Convention.

men, determined upon the arrest of a great evil, gave forceful unity to feeling, thought, and action, and promised victory from the outset.

The platform was something of a pronunciamento both in length and style of composition. It reaffirmed the Declaration of Independence. It denounced disunion. It anathematized Buchanan's ad- The Republican platform for its Kansas policy, its financial extravagance and corruption, and its inhuman conception of the relation of slave and master. It pronounced for a homestead law, for a railroad to the Pacific, for river and harbor improvements, for the full and efficient protection of the rights of naturalized citizens, etc.

But the two subjects of transcendent importance with which it dealt were slavery in the Territories and a protective tariff. In regard to these it will be best to quote *verbatim* the resolutions. They ran as follows : " Resolved, that the new dogma that the Constitution, of its own force, carries slavery into any or all of the Territories of the United States is a dangerous political heresy, at variance with the explicit provisions of that instrument itself, with contemporaneous exposition, and with legislative and judicial precedent ; is revolutionary in its tendency and subversive of the peace and harmony of the country ; that the normal condition of all the territory of the United States is that of freedom ; that, as our Republican fathers, when they had abolished slavery in all our national territory, ordained that 'no person should be deprived of life, liberty or property without due process of law,' it becomes our duty by legislation, whenever such legislation is necessary, to maintain this provision of the Constitution against all attempts to violate it ; and we deny the authority of Congress, of a Territorial legislature, or of any individuals, to give legal existence to slavery in any Territory of the United States :

"Resolved, that, while providing revenue for the support of the general government by duties upon imports, sound policy requires such an adjustment of these imposts as to encourage the industrial interests of the whole country ; and we commend that policy of national exchanges which secures to the workingmen liberal wages, to agriculture remunerative prices, to mechanics and manufacturers an adequate reward for their skill, labor and enterprise, and to the nation commercial prosperity and independence."

There was no doubt about the meaning of this platform in respect to the question of slavery in the Territories, no ambiguity in the statement of the principle. The Republicans agreed with the Southern Democrats that property is a fundamental conception, that the definition of property, the determination of what it shall embrace, is, therefore, a subject of constitutional law. They differed from the Southern Democrats, on the other hand, differed as widely as direct contradiction can, in regard to the status of the individual in the Territories, as fixed by constitutional law. The Republicans held that the Constitution not only did not carry slavery into the Territories, but that it made the freedom of every human being the nominal status in the Territories, *by not expressly legalizing slavery, and by providing that "no person shall be deprived of life, liberty or property without due process of law."*

The doctrine of the platform concerning slavery in the Territories.

The Southern Democrats held, as we have seen, that property in slaves existed everywhere in the country at the time of the formation of the Constitution of the United States, that it was recognized as lawful everywhere by that instrument, and that its abolition or prohibition anywhere rested in every case upon some positive enactment to that effect. The Southern Democrats were nearer right in their constitutional history than the Republicans, and both were wrong in their constitutional law. The Republicans were wrong in holding that Congress could not legalize property in slaves in the Territories; and the Democrats were wrong in holding that Congress could not abolish or prohibit property in slaves in the Territories. Where a constitution creates a government of general powers, as distinguished from one of enumerated powers, that government can, so far as constitutional power is concerned, do anything which the sovereign can do, unless forbidden by the sovereign in some provision of the Constitution. Such a government can determine in what property shall consist, unless restrained from so doing by an express provision of the Constitution. The Government of the United States was a government of general powers in the Territories, and the Constitution of the United States did not then prohibit it from defining property therein, either generally or specifically. The Republican interpretation of the clause in the Constitution relied upon by the Republicans for disabling Congress from legalizing property in slaves in the Territories, viz., that "no person shall be deprived of life, liberty or property without due process of law," was as far-fetched as the doctrine of the Southern Democrats, that the United States had no sovereignty at all, and, therefore, could not define property, was false. No definition which the Supreme Court had to that time given or indicated of the phrase "due process of law," would have deprived Congress of the power of legalizing slavery in the Territories ; while the Democratic doctrine that the United States had no sovereignty, and, therefore, could not determine in what

The antithesis between the Republican and Democratic platforms.

property should consist anywhere, and that the separate "States" *alone* had that power in our political system, and could themselves exercise it only as a *constituent power*, can stand the test neither of historic fact nor of the sound principles of political science. Every tyro in American constitutional history knows that property in slaves was legalized, and abolished, in many Commonwealths of the Union by mere legislative enactments, and that the Commonwealth Legislatures have from the first been defining and redefining the rights to property within the general limitations of constitutional law. And even Mr. Jefferson Davis himself said, in his 7th of May speech, "I admit that the United States may acquire eminent domain. I admit that the United States may have sovereignty over territory ; otherwise the sovereign jurisdiction which we obtained by conquest or treaty would not pass to us. I deny that their agent, the Federal government, under the existing Constitution can have eminent domain. I deny that it can have sovereignty." Here is certainly a distinction between the United States as sovereign and the United States as government, and the attribution of that power to the United States which could define property. Had Mr. Davis been called upon to explain what he meant by the phrase "United States as sovereign," he would probably have said that he meant the separate "sovereign States" in partnership. It does not matter, however, how he might have explained it, here was an admission from the chief of the Southern Democracy that there was another kind of sovereignty in our system than that of the separate "States," which he, for this once, called the sovereignty of the United States. It was sufficient to show that the theory upon which the Southern Democrats rested to prove that Congress could not prohibit slavery in the Territories would not hold in all the cases which occurred to the minds of those same Democrats themselves.

While thus it is easily seen that the doctrines of both of these platforms respecting the power of Congress over the subject of slavery in the Territories were erroneous, yet they contained the advantage of a direct issue. The one distinctly and flatly contradicted what the other asserted, and *vice versa*.

The other very important provision of the Republican platform, the advocacy of a protective tariff, was expressed in a crude, half-hesitating, though politic, manner. The country had been since 1857 passing through a period of financial panic and business stagnation, chiefly in consequence, as it was thought, of the lowering of the duties by the Act of 1857. The tariff law of 1846 had brought a surplus of revenue into the Treasury, which the Congress of 1857 thought to curtail by reducing the duties. The immediate effect of the reduction was, however, largely increased importation, and a steady drain upon the specie of the country. The panic followed with its inevitable attendant, long business depression. From the autumn of 1857, the protection feeling was growing, especially throughout the North, and when the Republican convention met a great number of the leading men of the country were of the opinion that a revival of prosperity could be effected only by an increase of the duties up to the protective point. The Whig element in the Republican party was naturally easily won for it, but the Freesoil Democrats of the party were attached to the principle of free trade, and had to be led up gently to a protective policy. Hence the moderation and almost ambiguity of the tariff provision in the platform.

The doctrine advanced was very cleverly connected

with the question of freedom in the Territories. It indicated that the two things which stood in the way of better pay for free labor in the North, were the unpaid labor of the slave at the South, and the low wages of labor in Europe. In its endeavor to neutralize or minimize the influence of both of these forces, the Republican party now represented itself as the true friend of the laboring man of the North. Some of the shrewdest of the Republican leaders, among them Mr. James G. Blaine, have affirmed that the Republican party could not have carried the election of 1860 without this provision of the platform. Pennsylvania, they think, would not have gone Republican on the slavery question alone. If their view is correct, it demonstrates most decidedly the political cleverness of the leaders in the convention at Chicago.

Its connection with the question of free Territories.

The unanimity of the convention, expressed in the enthusiastic vote upon the platform, manifested itself again in the choice of the candidates. Down to within a few months before the meeting of the convention, Mr. Seward, on account of his activity in the organization of the party, and his leadership of it in Congress, and in the great Commonwealth of New York, as well as on account of his great ability as a statesman and a politician, had been generally regarded as the man for the first place on the ticket. But the wiser heads had, by the opening of the year 1860, begun to see that Mr. Seward was not the surely available candidate necessary to success. It was thought that his opinions upon all points, secondary as well as cardinal, were too well known, and that, consequently, too many differed with him upon one subject or another. It was also thought that he was too radical, and his " higher law " doctrine was interpreted to mean

The nomination of the candidates by the Republican convention.

that he would disregard the Constitution in his hostility to slavery. And it was thought, finally, that he lacked in conciliatoriness of spirit toward the South, and that he was especially hated by the slaveholders. Still more weighty, however, were the considerations that Mr. Greeley had turned against him, and was doing everything in his power to defeat his candidacy, and that the leaders in Pennsylvania and Indiana were asserting that he could not carry these Commonwealths. The East had, however, no other candidate of great strength, and it was not, under the circumstances, unnatural that the West should claim the prize, and, with the advantage of western surroundings about the convention, win it.

Lincoln has sometimes been represented as a sort of "dark horse," but this claim manifests very little appreciation of his qualities, or of the great shrewdness with which his candidacy was managed. His speeches from 1858 to 1860 contain the best, most concisely stated, conservative body of Republican doctrine to be found in all our political literature, and his candidacy for the nomination had been an established fact for at least a year before the meeting of the convention. His managers, chief among whom were the Hon. David Davis, the Hon. O. H. Browning, and Governor Richard B. Oglesby, three of the most astute politicians that the country has ever produced, presented him, not as the rival of Seward, but as a substitute for Seward, in case Seward should be found unavailable. They were greatly aided, and at no point embarrassed, by Lincoln himself, who was also an old and skilled hand in politics. They furthermore had the advantage of the *entourage*. About all Illinois had assembled in and around the locus of the convention, cheering and shouting and singing just at the right moment to advance Lincoln's cause. There was also shrewd trading in his behalf.

The Pennsylvanians were asked the price of their support, and a place in the cabinet was pledged for it to Mr. Cameron. Lincoln knew nothing of this, at the moment, of course. He was at his home in Springfield, and was telegraphing David Davis to make no contracts that would bind him. Davis, however, paid no attention, of course, to Lincoln's directions.

On the first ballot Seward led, but fell sixty votes short of the nomination. On the second Lincoln came up even with him, within three and a half votes. On the third Lincoln was nominated. It was something of a surprise to the country, and the abolitionists were not happy over it. Wendell Phillips inquired : " Who is this huckster in politics, who is this county court advocate ? " But the nomination was no mistake. The convention had builded better than it knew itself. Lincoln was not only more available than Seward, but he had sounder morals and better judgment than Seward, or any of the others. He was far better equipped than any of them to meet the great emergency.

After the nomination of the candidate for the presidency, a very important question confronted the convention. It was the long-settled custom of the Republic that the two names upon the ticket should come from the two sections, North and South. The national character of the parties was thus indicated. The question now was whether the Republican party would follow this precedent or would manifest its sectional nature by abandoning it. There were delegates present in the convention from Delaware, Maryland, Virginia, Kentucky, and Missouri ; and there were able men from some of these Commonwealths who were sound anti-slavery men, good Republicans in principle, and already affiliated with the party. Among them were Edward Bates and the Blairs

The question of the second place on the ticket.

of Missouri, Cassius M. Clay, of Kentucky, and the brilliant Henry Winter Davis, of Maryland. It does seem as if it would have been judicious as well as conciliatory to have nominated one of these men for the second place on the ticket. It would have enabled the Republicans to represent themselves as a national party. There is little doubt that the nomination of Hannibal Hamlin for the vice-presidency, from the extreme northeastern Commonwealth of the Union, gave far more offence to the South than the nomination of Lincoln for the presidency. It certainly appeared to stamp the Republican party as a sectional party. It seems to have been thought that it was necessary in order to make sure of the East. It is certainly true that under no combination of candidates which could have been made would the Republicans have carried any slaveholding Commonwealth, and, if the East was in any danger of disaffection, it was good policy, from the point of view of success in the election, to strengthen the line in that quarter. Of course it can never be known whether the nomination of Mr. Hamlin saved any Northern Commonwealth at the polls or not. One cannot, however, help feeling that the purposes of the Republican party would have been better understood at the South had a man of known intelligence and probity from the South been selected for the second place on the ticket.

Of even greater importance than the movements of the Republican party in determining the course which the Democratic leaders would take upon re- The Constiassembling in nominating convention was tutional Union party and its the attitude now assumed by the remnant of convention. the old Whig party, which had, after its disruption in 1855, taken the name of " the American Party," and now manifested its obsoleteness by calling itself " the

Constitutional Union Party." All the parties, except perhaps the abolitionists, were as yet Constitutional Union parties. They all proposed to stand on that general ground. The question had progressed, however, far beyond that general statement of principles. The question now at issue was as to the meaning of the Constitutional Union in reference to a given point, viz., slavery in the Territories. Upon this specific question the "Constitutional Union Party" was silent. Its platform was expressed in a single line. It was: "The Constitution of the country, the Union of the States and the enforcement of the laws." Undoubtedly the party conceived, in May of 1860, that it had a timely object in view. Undoubtedly it meant to say that under no circumstances whatever would it yield to disunion sentiments; that the Union, with or without slavery, but always the Union, was its cardinal principle. But, as we shall see further on, it did not stand by its colors when the fire grew hot and near.

The convention of the party met in Baltimore, on the 19th day of May, and nominated John Bell, of Tennessee, and Edward Everett, of Massachusetts, as its candidates for the presidency and the vice-presidency. Both of these statesmen were "old-line Whigs," and gentlemen of the "old school," courteous, kind, conciliatory, patriotic, and high minded. They had both served the country long and nobly, and everybody knew that their characters were guarantees of peace, union, mutual regard of rights, deference in matters of opinion, temperance in speech, and gentleness in manners. But the age was passed for all these virtues. In their place vulgar radicalness in thought, belligerency in feeling, coarseness in language, and brutality in conduct were to be found on all sides.

The nomination of John Bell for the presidency by it.

There was not from the first the slightest chance of their election. They were formidable from but a single point of view—from the point of view of the necessity to the slaveholders of the unity of the South under the rule of the Southern Democracy. The South must be made solid and kept solid. The slaveholders must not risk the loss of a single Southern Commonwealth for the chance of winning a Northern one. They must beat Mr. Bell in all the Commonwealths of the South, and they knew they could not do this with any Northern man for their candidate.

The danger to the rule of the slaveholders in the South from this party.

Such was their conviction when their leaders reassembled, on the 11th of June, at Richmond. They manifested no disposition whatever to compromise with their Northern brethren on the question of the platform, and now was added the danger of losing control of some of their own communities by the success of Mr. Bell at the polls. They remained some days in Richmond revolving plans, and then adjourned to meet on the 28th in Baltimore.

Reassembly of the convention of the Southern Democracy.

The regular convention of the Democratic party met, pursuant to adjournment, at Baltimore, on the 18th of June. In place of any approach of the two bodies, however, toward each other, the delegates to the regular convention from Delaware, Maryland, Virginia, North Carolina, Tennessee, and Missouri withdrew, in whole or part, and went over to the other side. The Hon. Caleb Cushing, of Massachusetts, resigned the presidency of the regular convention, and was made the presiding officer of the seceders' body, when its members reassembled on the 28th.

Reassembly of the convention of the Northern Democracy.

The regular convention then nominated Mr. Douglas

for the presidency and Mr. Fitzpatrick, of Alabama, for
the vice-presidency, and upon the refusal of Mr. Fitzpatrick to accept the nomination, substituted the Hon. Herschel V. Johnson, of
Georgia, in his place.

Work of the two conventions.

The seceders organized their convention on the 28th,
consisting of delegates from twenty-one Commonwealths,
under the presidency of the Hon. Caleb Cushing, adopted by a unanimous vote the platform proposed by Mr.
Avery at Charleston, and nominated John C. Breckenridge, of Kentucky, and Joseph Lane, of Oregon, as
candidates for the presidency and vice-presidency. Mr.
Yancey pronounced the valedictory in a style which can
be described by no more appropriate title than "fire-
eating," and they went forth to their mad work, which
resulted in their own destruction.

The campaign was earnest and serious. It was a battle of principles as well as of candidates. Mr. Douglas
led his own hosts, speaking both in the North
and in the South, and endeavoring to inspire
his followers, his hearers, and the readers of
his speeches, with some of his own enthusiasm. The
greatest debaters of the country went on to the hustings,
and everywhere the issues were discussed with great
force. The machinery for rousing the feelings of the
masses, not given to decision by judgment, was also put
in motion. Music, parades, torchlight processions, fire-
works, etc., were seen and heard on all sides.

The political campaign of 1860.

As the campaign advanced two things, at least, became manifest. The first was the fact that Lincoln was
gaining in the North at the expense of Douglas. The
obstinacy of the Southern Democrats at Charleston and
Baltimore had greatly angered many of the Northern
Democrats and was operating to drive them into the
Republican ranks. The second was the increasingly

threatening attitude which the slaveholders were assuming toward the Union in case of the election of Lincoln. It came to be generally believed before October that they would not submit to a Republican administration. The Republicans, however, refused to be intimidated by the situation and were determined to test the question whether a constitutionally elected President would be refused recognition by any part of the country. In several of the Northern Commonwealths, the other parties betrayed much more agitation. In New York, New Jersey, and Rhode Island, they arranged a fusion ticket, dividing the number of electors assigned to each of these Commonwealths between them in the proportion of their relative voting strength in each, thus uniting their strength against Lincoln. In the Southern Commonwealths, the adherents of Breckenridge were as tenacious as the Republicans in the North. They would not fuse with the Douglas Democrats, even to rescue the "border States" from the "Constitutional Unionists." Their purpose to rule or ruin became more and more manifest from day to day.

As the October elections in Pennsylvania and Indiana approached, the tension became almost unbearable. Everybody knew that these elections would indicate the result of the presidential election in the next month. Maine and Vermont had, in September, gone Republican by large majorities. Still uncertainty, as to the two pivotal Commonwealths, was not wholly dispelled. It was well known that the Republicans could not carry Pennsylvania upon the question alone of slavery prohibition in the Territories. The managers in Pennsylvania, therefore, shrewdly brought the question of protection to the front and made it a principal, if not the principal, issue of the campaign. Mr. Curtin himself, the Republican candi-

date for Governor, made protection the chief subject of
his addresses, and the shrewdest among the Republican
politicians have attributed his success in the campaign
to that fact.   Both Pennsylvania and Indiana were won
by safe majorities, and it was now reasonably certain
that Mr. Lincoln would receive the electoral vote of all
the Northern Commonwealths, except perhaps New
Jersey and Rhode Island, and would be elected President.

When the news of the results of the elections in Pennsylvania and Indiana reached the South, it was received
by a few with sinister delight, but despondency and terror mastered the minds and
wills of most.   It was said, and by the masses
believed, that such men as John Brown and
Hinton Rowan Helper would be appointed to the
United States offices in the South, and that every official bureau would become a rendezvous for conspirators
against the peace and security of the South, and a hatch-
ing-place of negro insurrections.   If such was really the
intention of the administration, which now seemed on
the eve of being chosen to power, it was said, and largely
believed, that there was no way of escape from murder,
rape and pillage, except by withdrawal from the Union.

The terror-
izing of the
masses at the
South by their
leaders.

Never did a nation go to the ballot-box with a more
serious spirit than did the people of these United States
on that noted November day of 1860.   The
Tuesday following the first Monday fell that
year on the sixth, and on the morning of the
seventh it was known that the Republicans had won a
complete victory in every Northern Commonwealth, except New Jersey, and had elected four of the seven electors in New Jersey.   Lincoln and Hamlin would have
one hundred and eighty of the three hundred and three
electoral votes.   The two Northern candidates, for

The elec-
tion of No-
vember, 1860.

whom no tickets had been put in the field in any of the Southern Commonwealths, except those along the Northern border, had been chosen. The Northern section of the Union had, at last, got the Government, and the question became now the query whether it could administer it throughout the whole Union.

An analysis of the popular vote will show that the Republican Electors had received only about two-fifths of the popular vote, 1,857,610 out of 4,645,390. It will also show that the Southern Democracy had not carried the South, counting by the popular vote. The Bell electors had received in the South 515,973 votes, the Douglas electors 163,525 votes, and the Breckenridge electors 571,871 votes. That is, the Union candidates, as we may call them, had received together 679,498 votes against 571,871 for the candidate whose following contained the disunion elements. Such figures indicated that the Republican party was not strong enough to undertake a radical programme, and that the slaveholders were not powerful enough to refuse recognition to the Republican Administration. The prospect of an understanding and an arrangement seemed fair, and good and wise men resolved to lend their influence and their energies to the accomplishment of the same. A little patience, calmness, good judgment and patriotism seemed all that was necessary to preserve the country in its accustomed course of action.

CHAPTER IV

SECESSION

THE theory upon which the claimed right of secession was based was that the United States were a confederation of sovereignties, connected with each other by an agreement, from which each might recede at its own pleasure, without any legal power on the *The seces-* part of the others to prevent it. It was *sion theory.* held by most of those who espoused this doctrine that secession was both a sovereign and a legal right. In support of the view that it was a sovereign right, they argued that a sovereign is not subject to law, and that there can be, therefore, no limitation upon a sovereign's rights. In support of the view that it was a legal right, they cited that clause of the Constitution, the tenth amendment, which provides that powers not delegated to the United States by the Constitution, nor prohibited by it to the " States," are reserved to the "States" respectively or to the people, and argued from it that, no power having been delegated to the United States to forbid secession, and no prohibition having been placed by the Constitution on the right of the " States " to secede, the right was reserved to the "States" or to the people by the Constitution itself.

It would be strange indeed if the fathers of the Union did intentionally legalize disunion and anarchy, and it was unfortunate that they used words which *Criticism* could be tortured into such a meaning. It *of it.* is altogether incredible that they attached any such signification to the language of the tenth amendment, and there is not the slightest grammatical necessity for the invention of any such by their successors. For, in the first place, that provision of the Constitution which declares that the " Constitution of the United States, and the laws of the United States which shall be made in pursuance thereof, and all treaties made, or which shall be made, under the authority of the United States, shall be the supreme law of the land," undoubtedly con-

tains the prohibition of the power of any Commonwealth of the Union to withdraw itself from the jurisdiction of that "supreme law of the land." And, in
the second place, the reservation of powers not delegated to the general government nor prohibited to the
"States," is not to the "States" alone, but "to the
States respectively *or to the people.*" Unless the last four
words of the provision mean the same as the first three,
that is, unless they are tautologic, why may not the
clause be interpreted to mean that if any power to determine the question of disunion is reserved to anybody
by the Constitution, that reservation is to the people
of the whole United States? This is certainly the
more natural interpretation. It is, however, entirely
evident to any impartial mind that the Congress
which proposed this amendment never intended to
reserve by it the power of disunion or secession to
anybody. They were evidently thinking only of the
powers of local government in the Commonwealths,
and the civil rights of the citizens, when they drafted
this article.

The argument of the secessionists from the constitutional provision was, from every point of view, a mere
jugglery with words. Some of the better thinkers
among them made no use of it at all, but fell back upon
the doctrine that secession was a sovereign right alone.
They sought to distinguish between a sovereign right
and a right of revolution. There is a certain distinction. The right of revolution is the right of a body
claiming sovereignty, of a body which is, at the given
moment, in the process of organizing, establishing,
and vindicating its sovereignty by successful violent
resistance to existing legal power. It is what the Ger-
mans would call the right of a sovereignty *im Werden
begriffen,* and which Mr. Emerson would have trans-

lated, the right of a sovereignty in the making. The secessionists denied that secession was this kind of a sovereign right. They held it to be the right of an already established and recognized sovereign. Here is certainly a very important distinction. It would deliver secession entirely from the stage of rebellious experiment, the stage of hazarded right between the outbreak of resistance to existing legal power and the triumph of that resistance, provided the seceding body were acknowledged to be already a sovereign body, as the secessionists claimed the "States" of the Union were. If revolution should be committed in such a case, it would not be by the seceding sovereign, but by the body defeating the attempted secession, and thereby subjecting the old sovereignty to a new sovereignty developed in and through the struggle.

It is from this point of view that the secessionists still contend that secession was right in principle, a "lost cause," although the attempt to realize it was overcome by superior power; a result which, in sound political science, stamps violent resistance to existing order as rebellion. The secessionists can be shown to have been in the wrong, *legally*, only by demonstrating that the "States" of the Union were not, at the time they attempted secession, sovereign bodies, which, indeed, can be easily done. But, *ethically*, the triumph of the principle of the sovereignty of the nation over the doctrine of "State sovereignty," in the appeal to arms, establishes the presumption of the righteousness of the former and the unrighteousness of the latter, no matter whether the sovereignty of the nation was the already recognized legal order, or only became such through the course and result of the struggle.

We have become generally conscious of these distinc-

tions, however, chiefly through our experiences since
1860. At that date a large majority of the people
of the country confounded sovereignty with the powers of residuary government, and recognized what
they conceived to be a certain kind of sovereignty
as belonging to the "States." Many of the secessionists honestly befooled themselves, as well as befooled
others, by their sophistries based upon these confused
premises. The majority of the secession leaders were
undoubtedly sincere in the belief that they were right
in principle.

Naturally the Commonwealth in which the doctrine
of "State sovereignty" had been elaborated into a system of positive science, so to speak, and had
South Caro-
lina and seces- been so generally embraced as to have be-
sion.
come the political creed of its inhabitants,
assumed the rôle of leader in the secession movement.
Chance seemed also to favor South Carolina with the opportunity. It was the only Commonwealth in which
the presidential electors were still chosen by the Legislature. This occasioned the meeting of the Legislature
on November 5th, several weeks earlier than it would
otherwise have assembled, and several weeks before the
meeting of the Legislature of any other Commonwealth except that of Georgia. The South Carolina
Legislature remained in session to learn the result
of the election, and in the height of the first excitement throughout the South over the choice of Mr.
Lincoln, issued the call for the convention of the
people of the "State," the sovereign body, according to the South Carolina doctrine, in our political
system.

The chief secessionists of the Commonwealth had
reached an understanding upon the subject some ten
days previous to the assembly of the Legislature. The

Governor, Mr. Gist, United States Senators Hammond and Chesnut, the members of the delegation to the national House of Representatives, and several others of the leaders were present at the conference held at Senator Hammond's house, and all joined in the opinion that, in the event of Mr. Lincoln's election, the convention should be called, and should pass a secession ordinance ; or, as they expressed it, should resume the exercise of the powers delegated by South Carolina to the United States.

There were many members of the Legislature who desired to avoid precipitation, and to consult with the political leaders in the other Commonwealths of the South, and await co-operation, but the secessionist chiefs paid no attention to their remonstrances, which were indeed feeble and hesitating. Senator Chesnut and the United States judicial officers in South Carolina resigned their positions before the Legislature had even voted to call the convention, and Senator Hammond did the same thing immediately after the vote, anticipating, thus, and prejudicing, the work of the convention.

The Legislature passed the act calling the convention on the 12th day of November. It appointed the 6th day of the following December for the election of the delegates to it, and the 17th for their assembly in convention. On the next day, the 13th, the Legislature elected Francis W. Pickens Governor, who immediately proceeded to form a cabinet or ministry, after the manner of the executives of sovereign nations.

Meanwhile the Legislature of Georgia had assembled and was debating the question of calling a convention. On the 14th day of the month (November), Mr. Alexander H. Stephens made his noted speech against the proposition of Mr. Robert Toombs to refer the question of secession immediately to the voters by submitting to them for ratification a resolution of the Legislature not to submit to the rule of the Abolitionists. Mr. Stephens carried the day, and the convention was called to meet on the 17th of the following January.

Georgia and secession.

President Buchanan was naturally greatly disturbed by these movements in South Carolina and Georgia, and on the 17th of the month (November), he addressed an inquiry to his legal adviser, Attorney-General Black, concerning the President's power in case a "State" should undertake secession, or resistance to the laws of the United States.

Mr. Black's opinion concerning the powers of the President to prevent secession.

The opinion sent by Mr. Black to the President, under date of November 20th, is one of the most unfortunate state papers of our history. It was the foundation of the President's even more unfortunate message of December 3d. Mr. Black instructed the President that the President had the power to take such measures as he might deem necessary to protect the public property of the United States, and to recapture it when unlawfully seized by anybody; and that he had the power to use the army and the navy and the militia to assist the civil officers of the United States in the execution of the laws "whenever the laws of the United States shall be opposed or the execution thereof obstructed in any State by combinations too powerful to be suppressed by the ordinary course of judicial proceedings, or by the power vested in the marshals"; but that in case there were no civil officers of the United States within the supposed "State" to execute the laws of the United States, the President could not use the military to uphold the powers of the United States Government in such

"State" at all. "If," said Mr. Black, "troops may
be sent to aid courts and marshals, there must be courts
and marshals to be aided.   The existing laws put and
keep the Federal Government strictly on the defensive.
You can use force only to repel an assault on the public
property, and aid the courts in the performance of their
duty."   Mr. Black did not, however, content himself
with reducing the President to impotence in case the
United States civil officers in any "State" should
resign, and no persons could be found to succeed them,
which would be the situation produced by secession ; but
he argued that if Congress should undertake to authorize
the President to send the military into such a "State"
to enforce the laws of the United States, Congress would
thereby simply declare war upon that "State," a thing
which Congress had no power, under the Constitution,
to do, and that the attempt to do it would amount to
the expulsion of such a "State" from the Union, making it a foreign enemy, between whom and the United
States all future relations would be regulated by the
principles and customs of international law. He declared
that "there was undoubtedly a strong and universal
conviction among the men who framed and ratified the
Constitution, that military force would not only be useless, but pernicious, as a means of holding the States
together."

Had Mr. Black been a secessionist himself, he could
not have stated the case more strongly against the
Government of the United States. He was,   Mr. Black's
on the other hand, a stanch Union man, a reputation
                                          and influence
great jurist, a man of letters, a pure patriot, as a man and
                                          a lawyer.
and a man of high moral and religious character.   He was, however, a Pennsylvania Democrat of
the "States-rights" school, and he believed that the
Abolitionists and the Republicans were the enemies of

the Union.   He was evidently not averse to pointing out, with great emphasis, the danger which the country had, as he thought, unrighteously incurred by allowing the triumph of the Republican party.

President Buchanan had the very highest respect and regard for Mr. Black's learning, judgment, and integrity. They were also close personal friends, and shared each other's feelings concerning the critical situation into which the country had been brought.   It was natural, then, that the President's message to Congress should, in dealing with the secession movement, contain the same destructive doctrines, and that the weaker intellect of the President should have accentuated them in higher degree.

President Buchanan's message of December 3, 1860, in regard to secession.

The President began the message with a declaration that the threatened danger to the Union was caused by "the long-continued and intemperate interference of the Northern people with the question of slavery in the Southern States." He said that the immediate peril arose neither from the claims that Congress or the Territorial Legislatures might control the question of slavery in the Territories, nor from opposition to the execution of the Fugitive Slave Act, but "from the fact that the incessant and violent agitation of the slavery question throughout the North for the last quarter of a century had at last produced its malign influence upon the slaves and inspired them with vague notions of freedom."   In short the President asserted that the sense of domestic security at the South had been attacked by the intemperate and incessant agitation of the question of slavery at the North, and that union between the North and the South could not continue, if the people of the South should come generally to feel that the security of their homes and firesides could not be preserved under it.

He said that if the people of the North would only let
the people of the Southern " States " alone in regard to
their domestic institutions, and would obey the Constitution and laws of the United States in respect to slavery, the existing peril would pass away. He declared
that no " State " had any constitutional right to withdraw from the Union, but he conceded that the people
of any " State " or section have the revolutionary right
to resist intolerable oppression, and relieve themselves
of it if they can. He insisted, however, that the election of a sectional President, if accomplished in accordance with the Constitution and the laws, was not oppression, and did not necessarily lead to oppression.
He stated that the duty of the President was " to take
care that the laws be faithfully executed," but he contended that the laws could be executed only by civil
officers, and, if there were no civil officers in a " State,"
that the President could not undertake to have the
laws of the United States executed by the military forces,
since according to the laws enacted by Congress the
military power could be used only in aid of the United
States marshals, and then only after the inability of the
posse comitatus of the marshal had been demonstrated.
He concluded, however, that he might hold the property of the United States by force, if attacked. He
simply stood upon the ground, in respect to his powers,
furnished him in Mr. Black's opinion.

It would have been better had he stopped with the
confession of his own impotence to cope with secession,
bad as that was. It could have been re-   Criticism of
garded as an appeal to Congress for larger the message,
and statement
means and a freer hand in the discharge of of its most
his duty to see to the faithful execution of destructive
propositions.
the laws ; but, like Mr. Black, he went on to declare
the impotence of Congress also in the face of secession.

He repeated with emphasis Mr. Black's proposition that the coercion of a " State" attempting secession was the making of war upon that "State," a power not confided by the Constitution, according to his view, to Congress or to any department of the Government. He evidently intended to convey the view that an act of Congress vesting the President with the power to use the military for the enforcement of the laws in any "State" in which there were no United States civil officials was tantamount to a declaration of war by Congress upon such "State." He deprecated the exercise of any such power, even if the Government possessed it, as destructive of the Union, which, he declared, rested upon public opinion, and could never be cemented by the blood of its citizens shed in civil war.

He concluded his message upon this subject by recommending the settlement of the differences between the North and the South by a constitutional amendment, which should include "an express recognition of property in slaves in the States where it now exists or may hereafter exist," an express declaration of "the duty of protecting this right in all the common Territories throughout their Territorial existence, and until they should be admitted as States into the Union, with or without slavery, as their constitutions may prescribe," and "a like recognition of the right of the master to have his slave, who has escaped from one State to another, restored and delivered up to him, and of the validity of the Fugitive Slave law enacted for this purpose, together with a declaration that all State laws impairing or defeating this right are violations of the Constitution, and are consequently null and void."

The President's solution of the question of slavery.

President Buchanan was a man of fair judgment, of pure patriotism, and of fine feeling. He was well-read in history and political science, and was a good lawyer. How he could have written such a message is to the men of the present almost past comprehension. It was the greatest encouragement to secession which could have possibly been given. It meant, whether the President so intended it or not—and he certainly did not intend it —that the secessionists should have until the 4th of the following March to withdraw their "States" from the Union, and organize a new government of their own without any serious impediment from the Administration at Washington. The President undoubtedly hoped to appease the secessionist leaders, and induce them to refrain from destroying the Union, but he had wofully misread the real character of the men whose courtly manners had enlisted his sympathies. The message was the most convincing demonstration of the inherent error and viciousness of the "States-rights" theory of the Union, which had to that moment appeared. It was to be surpassed only by secession itself.

It has been said in justification of the President that he had the letter of the old law with him, and that his sense of duty as well as his conservative nature led him therefore in the direction which he pursued. But what was there in the letter of the old law that prevented the President from sending true Union men from the loyal Commonwealths into a Commonwealth attempting secession to occupy the civil offices of the United States within the latter, and then sustaining their authority by the aid of the military forces of the Union ? And what was there in the letter of the old Constitution that prevented Congress from authorizing the President to use the military officers for the immediate execution of the laws of the United States ? Clearly the President was befooled by his "States-rights" theories, his timid nature, and his personal regard for the Southern leaders.

These leaders were overjoyed by the tone of the message, not that they thought it might lead to compromise and conciliation, but because it pronounced the impotence of the United States Government to prevent them from destroying the Union. Some of them had been consulted by the President in regard to its contents, and he certainly had accepted their representation of the state of feeling at the South.

Acceptability of the message to the Southern leaders.

Of all men the President stood in the position to defeat secession by simply filling the civil offices of the United States with loyal men, and then sustaining these officers by his military power, but he would have regarded the sending of citizens of one Commonwealth into another to occupy the United States offices in the latter, as such a departure from long-established usage as to amount almost to a violation of the Constitution. Moreover, he was old and timid, and was surrounded by disloyal advisers, who not only misled him, but who, in some way or other, roused the fear of assassination in his mind if he crossed too far their purposes. There was undoubtedly one other consideration which moved the President, and that was the feeling that those who had brought the danger upon the country, the Abolitionists and Republicans, as he thought, should shoulder the responsibility of meeting it. He thought it was fair to leave the problem for his successor to wrestle with. When, then, his trusted friend and legal counsellor, Mr. Black, whom he knew to be able and loyal, took the same view of the impotence of the Government in the event of secession that his secessionist advisers did, it is hardly to be marvelled at that he struck the suicidal blow. He did not go quite as far as they wanted him to go. They asked that he would acknowledge secession to be a constitutional right of each

Probable influences that led the President to send such a message.

"State," and some of them even suggested that he ought to justify its exercise in the existing contingencies. But he went far enough to encourage them in high degree, and to fill the souls of loyal men with gloomy forebodings.

Between the communication of Mr. Black's opinion and the presentation of the President's message to the Houses of Congress, the Legislatures of Mississippi and Florida had met, and passed acts calling conventions to consider the question of secession. The spirit manifested in both of them was hostile to the Union, and it was evident that dangerous movements threatened. When, therefore, Congress came to the consideration of the President's message, its members were entirely aware of the serious nature of the work before them. Motions were immediately made in both Houses to refer that part of the message treating of the perilous state of the country to a special committee in each. In the House of Representatives the motion was quickly adopted, with but little debate. In the Senate, on the other hand, the debate upon it lasted for nearly two weeks, during which it became entirely evident that the members from the "planting States" had made up their minds for secession. Six of the Southern Legislatures, those of South Carolina, Georgia, Mississippi, Florida, Alabama, and Louisiana, had now called conventions; and the members of the Senate of the United States from these Commonwealths simply informed the Senate that the question of the "federal relations" of their "States" was now to be decided in these conventions, and no longer by any branch of the United States Government. One of the Senators from Georgia, Mr. Iverson, said that all the Southern "States" would decide this question in the sovereign conventions of their people, and that nothing could prevent the following of this course. Referring to the refusal of Governor Houston of Texas to permit the call of a convention in that "State," he said : "Some Texan Brutus will arise to rid his country of the hoary-headed incubus that stands between the people and their sovereign will." Senator Wigfall, of Texas, immediately repudiated this imputation of barbarism to his community, and said that Texas would find means of seceding from the Union, without having recourse to assassination. Mr. Jefferson Davis said that the difficulty was deeper than any acts of Congress could reach, that it was the fact that a Union of hostile sections had taken the place of a Union of friendly "States." He declared that a change of view and feeling among the Northern people was the only remedy for the case. It was, thus, manifest that nothing which Congress could do would be satisfactory to the secessionists. It was equally manifest that the Northern Democrats, and a large number of the Republicans, would go almost any length to conciliate them.

The passage of the ordinance of secession by unanimous vote in the South Carolina convention, on the 20th of the month (December), brought
The Secession of South Carolina. matters to the direct issue, and caused great alarm in Congress and throughout the country, much as some of the Northern journals jeered at it. The thing which had been threatened for thirty years, threatened so often indeed as to have lost some of its terrors, had now come at last, when men had almost ceased to expect it. It is true that the causes alleged for it by the South Carolinians were false and puerile, and that the manner of its realization was a travesty of dignity and a mockery of statesmanship, but there it was, and must be dealt with as a stern fact.

First of all, what would the President do about it ? He was bound to execute the laws in South Carolina, as else-where in the Union. He had no power to The President in the face of the emergency. recognize the independence of South Caro-lina. He must proceed as though no ordi-nance of secession had been passed. It is true that he had no judges and marshals in South Carolina, as we have seen, but he could appoint them, and he had col-lectors of the revenue, and was in possession of the forts. He had delayed strengthening the garrisons so as not to excite the secessionists ; and General Cass, his Secretary of State had, on the 12th of the month (December), re-signed his position on account of difference of opinion with the President on this subject. This action on the part of the venerable statesman was so popular through-out the North as to make the President feel that he had committed a grave error. The new Secretary of State, Mr. Black, also felt the force of the popular approval of General Cass, and realized that he himself had made a serious mistake, both as regarded his views of the con-stitutional powers of the President, and of the temper of the people of the North, and also of the temper of the people of the South. In addition to this, the suc-cessor of Mr. Black in the office of Attorney-General, Mr. Edwin M. Stanton, proved to be a powerful sup-port to the stronger view of the President's powers. He, Mr. Black and Mr. Holt, the Postmaster-General, who though a Southerner, was a stanch Union man, now displaced the Southerners in the confidence of the President, and roused the Administration to the dis-play of more courage and firmness. It was well that this happened when it did. If these changes had been deferred a few days, it is probable that Mr. Buchanan would have committed himself irretrievably to the seces-sionists.

On the 26th (December), the three commissioners, Messrs. Adams, Barnwell, and Orr, appointed by the South Carolina convention to treat with the Government of the United States for the delivery of the forts, lighthouses, magazines, and other United States property in South Carolina, to the authorities of the now self-declared independent nation of South Carolina, and for other purposes, appeared in Washington. On the 28th, they sent to the President the following extraordinary communication :

The South Carolina Commissioners and the President.

" To the President of the United States : Sir : We have the honor to transmit to you a copy of the full powers from the convention of the People of South Carolina under which we are authorized and empowered to treat with the Government of the United States, etc. . . . In the execution of this trust, it is our duty to furnish you, as we now do, with an official copy of the ordinance of secession, by which the State of South Carolina has resumed the powers she delegated to the Government of the United States, and has declared her perfect sovereignty and independence. It would also have been our duty to have informed you that we were ready to negotiate with you upon all such questions as are necessarily raised by the adoption of this ordinance, and that we were prepared to enter upon this negotiation with the earnest desire to avoid all unnecessary and hostile collision, and so to inaugurate our new relations as to secure mutual respect, general advantage, and a future good-will and harmony beneficial to all parties concerned. But the events of the last twenty-four hours render such an assurance impossible. We came here the representatives of an authority which could, at any time within the past sixty days, have taken possession of the forts in Charles-

Their communication to the President.

ton harbor, but which, upon pledges given in a manner that we could not doubt, determined to trust to your honor rather than to its own power. Since our arrival here an officer of the United States, acting, as we are assured, not only without but against your orders, has dismantled one of the forts and occupied another, thus altering, to a most important extent, the condition of affairs under which we came. Until these circumstances are explained in a manner which relieves us of all doubt as to the spirit in which these negotiations shall be conducted, we are forced to suspend all decision as to any arrangements by which our mutual interests might be amicably adjusted. And, in conclusion, we would urge upon you the immediate withdrawal of the troops from the harbor of Charleston. Under present circumstances they are a menace which renders negotiation impossible, and, as our recent experience shows, threatens speedily to bring to a bloody issue questions which ought to be settled with temperance and judgment."

The insolence of this communication is apparent enough on its face. The representatives of a petty power, as yet unrecognized, and destined never to be recognized, announcing to one of the most powerful governments in the world that they would not treat with it was a ridiculous spectacle. But when we come to consider what this power was which these men professed to represent, and to inquire into the reasons for this bantam audacity, we must conclude that they were not far removed from stark madness.

It seems that on the 8th day of the month (December) the members of the House of Representatives in Congress from South Carolina had gone to the Presi- The expla-
dent and undertaken to give him some nation of it.
assurances about the matter of the forts in the harbor at Charleston. The President asked them to put what

they had to say in writing. They did so, and presented the same to him on the 10th. This document read as follows : " To his Excellency James Buchanan, President of the United States : In compliance with our statement to you yesterday, we now express to you our strong conviction that neither the constituted authorities, nor any body of the people of the State of South Carolina, will either attack or molest the United States forts in the harbor of Charleston, previously to the action of the convention, and, we hope and believe, not until an offer has been made, through an accredited representative, to negotiate for an amicable arrangement of all matters between the State and the Federal government, provided that no re-enforcements shall be sent into those forts, and their relative military status shall remain as at present."

When this document was read to the President by these gentlemen he objected to the use of the word " provided," lest it should be held to imply an agreement on his part, and said that he would not enter into any agreement with them upon the subject. They replied to him that they did not understand it as implying any agreement whatever on his part. The next day Mr. John B. Floyd, the Secretary of War, issued an order to Major Anderson, in command of the forts in Charleston Harbor, of the following tenor : " You are carefully to avoid every act which would needlessly tend to provoke aggression ; and, for that reason, you are not, without evident and immediate necessity, to take up any position which could be construed into the assumption of a hostile attitude ; but you are to hold possession of the forts in the harbor, and, if attacked, you are to defend yourself to the last extremity. The smallness of your force will not permit you, perhaps, to occupy more than one of the three forts ; but an attack on, or an attempt to take possession of, either

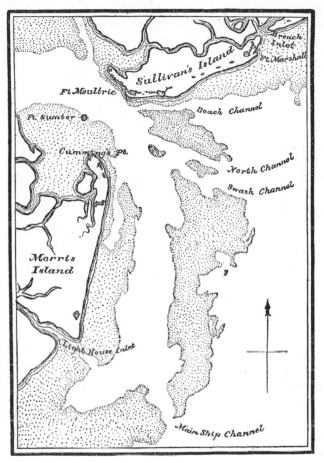

Charleston Harbor.

of them, will be regarded as an act of hostility, and you may then put your command in either of them which you may deem most proper, in order to increase its power of resistance. You are also authorized to take similar defensive steps whenever you have tangible evidence of a design to proceed to a hostile act." This order from Mr. Floyd was not brought to the notice of the President until the 21st day of the month (December). He saw no reason to disapprove it, and did not do so. Major Anderson was at the moment in Fort Moultrie with a very small force of men. He became convinced that he was in a dangerous position, and believed that an attack upon him by the South Carolinians was imminent. On the night of the 26th he, therefore, left Fort Moultrie and occupied Fort Sumter, which he considered a stronger position.

These acts by Major Anderson were the events referred to by Messrs. Adams, Barnwell, and Orr as precluding any discussion in regard to the amicable adjustment of the mutual interests of South Carolina and the United States, since they held the same to be a violation of the faith of the United States Government with South Carolina, as pledged by the President.

The President would have been entirely justified in consigning this communication from these gentlemen to his waste-basket, but he took counsel of his fine sense of courtesy instead of a proper sense of the dignity and prerogatives of his office, and sent them an answer. Thanks, however, to the influence of Black, Stanton, and Holt, the answer, though most polite and kindly in its language, was a firm declination to withdraw the United States troops from Charleston Harbor or to have anything to do with the commissioners except in the character of private gentlemen.

The President's answer.

The day after the transfer of the United States troops from Fort Moultrie to Fort Sumter, the South Carolinians seized Castle Pinckney and Fort Moultrie, and raised the flag of the State of South Carolina upon them. On the same day they raised their flag over the United States Custom House and Post Office in Charleston, and took possession of these properties. It was undoubtedly the condition of readiness to accomplish these things into which the South Carolinians had brought themselves that had caused Major Anderson to conclude that an attempt might be made at any time upon one or the other of the forts.

The South Carolina gentlemen answered the President's reply to them with a communication, which he, with all his conservatism, kindliness, courtesy,

Reply to the President's answer. conciliatoriness and timidity declined to receive. They wrote the President that they had no solicitude about the character in which he might recognize them. They accused him of misconceiving and misconstruing their first note to him. They declared that he had made pledges to South Carolina, impliedly if not expressly, and that he did not deny this when they called upon him to redeem them. They charged him with failing to redeem those pledges by not ordering Major Anderson back to Fort Moultrie ; and cited as proof, both of the giving of the pledges and their violation, the action of the Secretary of War, Mr. Floyd, who resigned his seat in the cabinet for the avowed reason that the action of Major Anderson had violated the plighted faith of the Government, and that the failure of the President to restore the status in Charleston Harbor had dishonored him. They accused him of seeking to escape from the obligations of his pledges by misrepresenting the contents of their first communication, and by exaggerating the import of what had been done by the South Carolinians on the day following the movement of Major Anderson.

The paper ended with the following pronunciamento : " By your course you have probably rendered civil war inevitable. Be it so. If you choose to force this issue upon us, the state of South Carolina will accept it, and, relying upon him who is the God of justice, as well as the God of hosts, will endeavor to perform the great duty which lies before her, hopefully, bravely and thoroughly."

The effect of this extraordinary communication upon the President was most beneficial. He saw now plainly that the Southern members of his Cabinet had used their positions to betray the Government, and to compromise him and his honor before the country ; and he saw that the South Carolinians were traitorously bent upon seizing the forts and property of the United States, which he had declared he should defend with all the means in his power. He began now to feel the bitterness against them which follows the discovery of misplaced and abused confidence ; while they, together with the Southern Senators who had had his ear, now turned upon him with the rage of men disappointed, at the last moment, in the accomplishment of their purposes. Even the self-contained and debonair Mr. Benjamin denounced Mr. Buchanan as "a senile executive under the influence of insane counsels."

The effect of the controversy with the Commission - ers upon the President.

The people of the North were made to understand by these attacks that the President had at last nerved himself to break with the secessionists, and do his duty for the Union. Hope and encouragement now began to displace the despondency and despair which had rested upon the mind and heart of the North since the fatal message of December 3d.

The North encouraged by the President's stand.

Meanwhile the Congressional committees of conciliation had been in session struggling with the great question of pacification, under the form of propositions amendatory of the Constitution. In
the Senate committee, composed of Messrs.
Davis, Douglas, Toombs, Hunter, Powell,
Bigler, Rice, Seward, Collamer, Doolittle, Wade,
Grimes, and Crittenden, seven Democrats, five Republicans, and one Independent, the Southern Democrats,
Davis, Toombs, and Hunter, took the ground that they
would accept nothing which the Republicans would not
support. They gave as their reason for this, their belief that any settlement effected without the concur-
rence of the Republicans would prove futile. We must
credit them with sincerity, although it was gravely suspected that they sought in this way to prevent any
agreement at all, and at the same time to throw the
blame for the failure upon the Republicans. The demands which these men made of the committee as the
price of their further allegiance, and that of the South,
to the United States were formulated by Mr. Toombs.
They were, in his own language, " that the people of
the United States shall have an equal right to emigrate
to and settle in the present, or any future acquired, Territories, with whatever property they may possess, in-
cluding slaves, and be securely protected in its peaceable
enjoyment until such Territory may be admitted as a
State into the Union, with or without slavery, as she
may determine, on an equality with all existing States ;
that property in slaves shall be entitled to the same protection from the Government of the United States, in
all of its departments, everywhere, which the Constitution confers the power upon it to extend to any other
property, provided nothing herein contained shall be
construed to limit or restrain the right now belonging

The Congressional committees of conciliation and their work.

to every State to prohibit, abolish, or establish and protect slavery within its limits ; that persons committing crimes against slave property in one State, and fleeing to another, shall be delivered up in the same manner as persons committing crimes against other property, and that the laws of the States from which such persons flee shall be the test of criminality ; that fugitive slaves shall be surrendered under the provisions of the Fugitive Slave Act of 1850, without being entitled either to a writ of Habeas Corpus, or trial by Jury, or other similar obstructions of legislation in the State to which they may flee ; and that Congress shall pass efficient laws for the punishment of all persons in any of the States who shall in any manner aid and abet invasion or insurrection in any other State, or commit any other act against the law of Nations, tending to disturb the tranquillity of the people or government of any other State."

Mr. Toombs and his Southern associates required that these propositions should be incorporated in the Constitution as irrepealable, unamendable amendments. In respect only to one of them were they willing to accept a modification. They agreed to compromise upon Mr. Crittenden's proposition for a division of the Territories between North and South on the line of thirty-six degrees and thirty minutes. It was upon this point chiefly that Mr. Crittenden's famous resolutions differed from the demands formulated by Mr. Toombs.

Upon other points the Crittenden resolutions were but little more than a restatement of the Toombs propositions. They proposed by irrepealable, unamendable amendments to the Constitution to disable Congress from touching slavery in the "States," or the Territories, or in the District of Columbia so long as the institution should exist in Maryland or Virginia, or in places subject to the exclusive jurisdic-

The Crittenden resolutions.

tion of the United States Government in slaveholding "States"; from interfering with commerce in slaves between slaveholding "States" and Territories; and from prohibiting members of Congress and United States officers from bringing slaves with them into the District of Columbia for domestic use.

The Crittenden resolutions also proposed by an irrepealable, unamendable amendment to the Constitution to secure payment by the Government to the slavemasters for the loss of their slaves, whenever the loss should be occasioned through interference with the officers charged with the capture and rendition of such slaves by the people of the community in which the apprehension was sought to be made, or in which the rescue was effected.

These resolutions proposed further to make the existing provisions of the Constitution in respect to the rendition of fugitive slaves, and in respect to the counting of the slaves in the apportionment of the representation in Congress and in the presidential electoral colleges, irrepealable and unamendable. And they finally pronounced the legality and sacred obligation of the Fugitive Slave Act of 1850, and recommended to the Northern Commonwealths the repeal of their personal liberty laws, which were held to contravene it. Naturally Davis, Toombs, and Hunter were willing to take this statement of their demands, although coupled with a division of the Territories by the line of the thirty-six degrees and thirty minutes to the Pacific, instead of recognizing the legality of slavery in all of them. Of course the other Democrats on the committee could ask no more than the triumvirate named.

But the Republicans were obliged to answer *non possumus*. The cardinal principle of the Republican creed was the arrest of the further extension of slavery. It was with them not simply a party platform, or a political policy, which might be sacrificed without the violation of any principle of justice or morality, but it was the fundamental ethical principle of their existence.   To agree to Mr. Toombs's demands, or to Mr. Crittenden's propositions, would have been for the Republicans political and moral suicide.

The position of the Republicans.

Mr. Seward said that he was ready to vote for an irrepealable, unamendable amendment to the Constitution securing slavery in the "States" where it already existed; that he was also ready to vote for proper laws for the punishment of citizens of one "State" invading another and stirring up insurrection, or for aiding and abetting in the same; and that he disapproved of all "State" legislation in contravention of the acts of Congress required by the Constitution for the execution of the provision for the rendition of fugitive slaves.   The other Republicans considered these propositions to be quite generous, but the Southerners regarded them so slightly as to affirm that the Republicans never indicated by word or sign any concession which they would be willing to make.

Mr. Seward's propositions.

The historians and publicists are bound to say that Mr. Seward's propositions were not only generous, but, upon one point, too generous.   An irrepealable, unamendable provision in a Constitution in regard to anything is a rotten spot, which threatens decay to the whole Constitution.   It is a standing menace to the peaceable development of any political system.   It is the most direct contradiction possible of one of the most fundamental principles of political science, the principle that the amending power in a constitution, the legally organized sovereign power in the political system of a country, must be able to deal with

Criticism of Mr. Seward's propositions.

any and every subject. If matters are excepted from its jurisdiction, then they can be dealt with only by revolution—that is, by the forcible intervention of superior physical power not recognized by existing law. In other words, the withdrawal of any subject from the amending power is the destruction of constitutional development as to that subject, and the destruction of constitutional development in general will work the inevitable overthrow of the Constitution and constitutional government. For, despite the sneers of Mr. Toombs, politics are progressive, and if they cannot progress through the regular forms of amendment, they will do so through the violent course of revolution. It was this consideration which moved the framers of the Constitution to construct the regular method of amendment as a constitutional provision, the most important provision of the Constitution; and now the proposition to withdraw from its operation the most serious and burning question of our political ethics was a proposition to set the clock of ages back a century and more, so far as concerned the advancement of liberty and of the science of government. It simply could not be accorded. It was an attempt to thwart the purposes of the unseen but almighty power which conducts the development of man toward his ultimate destiny.

Naturally with such demands as those made by Mr. Toombs, or with such propositions as those advanced by

Failure of the Senate committee to agree upon a proposition. Mr. Crittenden, and declared by the Southerners to be the ultimatum, no agreement could be arrived at by the Senate committee. The committee quickly recognized the situation, and on the last day of the month (December), reported to the Senate their inability to agree.

When the committee had been sitting only a single day, Senator Toombs telegraphed an address to the peo-

ple of Georgia through the Savannah *News,* in which he
declared to them that his demands had been received by
the Republican members of the committee Mr. Toombs's
address to the
people of
Georgia.
with derision ; that they had rejected the
Crittenden propositions, and had announced
that they themselves had no guarantees to offer ; that
they were, furthermore, fair representatives of the Republican majority of the House committee on the same
subject ; that, therefore, nothing was to be expected
from either of these committees or from Congress ; and
that he, therefore, advised the secession of Georgia before the 4th day of the coming March. Mr. Toombs
undoubtedly thought that the moral impossibility of
the Republicans yielding to his demands was an impossibility which was created by the execrable immorality
of their principles. However that may be, he recognized very quickly that impossibility, and hastened to
advise his friends and constituents that they must hang
no hopes upon Republican concessions.

The Republicans of the House committee were more
yielding than their party brethren of the Senate committee, and the prospect seemed for a time The proceedings in the
House com-
mittee.
fairly good that this committee might be able
to agree upon a *modus vivendi* between the
North and the South. It had been at work, however,
for nearly a month, without attaining a final result,
when the Senate committee reported inability to agree.
There was indeed some ground for believing that it too
would fail to accomplish anything, certainly in the
minds of those who were indifferent to its failure or success.

Five days more now passed after the Senate committee's report without the reaching of any conclusion by
the House committee. Already on the 13th of December, Mr. Reuben Davis, member of the committee from

the Mississippi delegation, had procured from some twenty of his Southern associates in Congress a man-
ifesto to their constituents and to the people of the South generally, in which it was de-clared that "all hope of relief in the Union, through the agencies of committees, congres-sional legislation, or constitutional amendments, is ex-tinguished, and we trust the South will not be deceived by appearances or the pretence of new guarantees. The Republicans are resolute in the purpose to grant noth-ing that will or ought to satisfy the South. We are sat-isfied that the honor, safety, and independence of the Southern people are to be found only in a Southern Confederacy, a result to be obtained only by separate State secession, and that the sole and primary aim of each slaveholding State ought to be its speedy and ab-solute separation from an unnatural and hostile Union."

The mani-festo of Mr. Reuben Davis and his asso-ciates to the South.

This was the tenor of almost all of the information furnished the Southern people from their representa-tives in Washington during that fateful month. Still the Southern people hesitated.

Hesitation of the Southern people.

Eight of the most reputable citizens of Geor-gia joined in a telegram to Senators Douglas and Crit-tenden, dated at Atlanta, December 26th, inquiring of these Senators, if the advices from Mr. Toombs that there were no hopes for Southern rights in the Union were correct, and declaring that they were for the Union if only their rights would be respected therein. These loyal Senators replied that Southern rights, as the rights of every "State" and section, could be protected in the Union, and exhorted them not to despair of the Republic.

The progress of secession was evidently halting, and it appeared still possible to arrest it peaceably, when the Senators from Georgia, Alabama, Mississippi, Florida, Louisiana, Arkansas, and Texas held that fateful caucus

of January 5, 1861, and sent out from it the advice to
the people of these Commonwealths to secede from the
Union. The Republican historians generally
ascribe the passage of secession ordinances by
these "States" to that advice. The secessionist historians, on the other hand, regard
this view as erroneous. These latter declare that secession was a great popular movement, and that the influence of the Southern members of Congress at Washington
was in restraint of it, rather than calculated or intended
to advance it. Mr. Davis, in his work upon the "Rise
and Fall of the Confederate Government," gives the text
of the resolutions adopted by this caucus and sent to the
constituents of its members. They read as follows :

The caucus of Southern Senators of January 5, 1861.

"Resolved, that in our opinion, each of the States
should, as soon as may be, secede from the Union ; that
provision should be made for a convention to organize
a confederacy of the seceding States, the convention to
meet not later than the fifteenth of February, at the city
of Montgomery, in the State of Alabama ; that in view
of the hostile legislation that is threatened against the seceding States, and which may be consummated before the
fourth of March, we ask instructions whether the delegations are to remain in Congress until that date, for
the purpose of defeating such legislation ; and that a
committee, consisting of Messrs. Davis, Slidell, and Mallory, be and are hereby appointed to carry out the object
of this meeting."

Mr. Davis said, " the significance of these resolutions
was the admission that we could no longer advise delay,
and even that was unimportant under the
circumstances, for three of the States concerned had taken final action on the subject
before the resolutions could have been communicated to them." Mr. Davis referred, of course, to

Mr. Davis's interpretation of the resolutions of the caucus.

the passage of the secession ordinances by the conventions in Mississippi, Florida, and Alabama, which took place on the 9th, 10th, and 11th of January, respectively. Mr. Davis does not, it is true, explain why resolutions adopted on the 5th of the month at Washington could not have been communicated to the secession conventions at Jackson, Tallahassee, and Montgomery before the 9th, 10th, and 11th of the month, with telegraphic lines and postal service in full operation between Washington and the principal cities in the South, nor does he assert that they were not. He simply claimed that they could not have been. In this he may have been mistaken, although it is hardly probable.

Mr. Davis said again and again that the great mass of the people of Mississippi considered him too slow, and

Mr. Davis too slow. that some suspected him of a stronger attachment to the Union than to the rights of the South. He certainly did take a more serious view of the situation than did most of his Southern colleagues. He expressed the opinion that war would follow, and that the South was not well prepared for that eventuality. He declared, however, that, as a firm believer in the doctrine of the sovereignty of his "State," he would obey her decision.

While, then, it is probably true that the Republican historians have somewhat exaggerated the importance of

True estimate of the event of January 5th. the event of January 5th in making it the cause of the passage of the secession ordinances by all of the "Cotton States," except South Carolina, yet we must still hold that it removed the last obstacle out of the way of that course of procedure. Had the advice of the caucus been the exact opposite to what it was, it is certainly very probable that not another "State" would have joined South Carolina in her mad project.

Whether the resolutions of this caucus became immediately known to the President, and whether, therefore,
they exerted any influence in provoking him The Presi-
to his special message of January 8th (1861), dent's special message of
we are not able with certainty to say. The January 8th, 1861.
suspicion, however, that such was the case
is very natural, and there is internal evidence of it in
the message itself. The President was now fully under
the influence of the Unionist members of the reorganized Cabinet, although General Dix did not come into
the Cabinet until the 11th. He evidently consulted only
the Unionist members in the preparation of this message. In it, he firmly declared that he must execute the
laws of the United States throughout the entire extent
of the country with all the means, both civil and military, placed in his hands, and that he purposed to do so.
He appealed to Congress to settle the differences by
compromise and mutual concession, but at the same
time he affirmed that the right and duty of the President "to use military force defensively against those
who resist the Federal officers in the execution of their
legal functions, and against those who assail the property of the Federal Government, are clear and unde-
niable."

He informed Congress that he had not, to that time,
sent any re-enforcements to Charleston Harbor, in order
not to arouse any excitement there, and he sent with
the message an extract from a communication from
Major Anderson, which contained information that,
contrary to assurances, the South Carolinians were preparing for a hostile movement, and also the statement
that the transfer of his command from Fort Moultrie to
Fort Sumter had been caused by the conviction that the
troops were in great danger of being captured in Fort
Moultrie. The President also transmitted with his

message the communications which had passed between him and the South Carolina commissioners.

At the date of this message all the forts and coast defences in South Carolina, Georgia, and Alabama, except
The seizure of the forts. Fort Sumter, had been seized by the respective "State" authorities, although Georgia and Alabama had not yet enacted their secession ordinances. It is now a well-settled fact that these seizures were made in Georgia and Alabama upon the advice of the men who still sat in the Congress of the United States, as Senators and Representatives from those Commonwealths.

It was evident from the tone of President Buchanan's message that he had nerved himself to do something for
The "Star of the West" affair. the vindication of the authority of the Government. On the very day that the message was read in Congress, it was revealed to the world what it was. He had most naturally resolved to strengthen Major Anderson's garrison in Fort Sumter sufficiently to enable it to hold the place against attack. He had sent re-enforcements and supplies to the Major from New York on the steamer "Star of the West." This vessel reached Charleston Harbor on the 9th (January), and attempted to approach Fort Sumter. It was fired upon, by the South Carolinians, from Fort Moultrie and Morris Island, and was struck. It then put back, and returned to New York, without having reached Fort Sumter at all. The South Carolinians had raised the hand of violence against the Government of the United States, and the whole military power of the United States ought to have been sent at once to the support of Fort Sumter, and for the recapture of the United States property in South Carolina. The firing upon the "Star of the West" was really the beginning of the war of the rebellion. The United

States Government had just as much right to send troops to Fort Sumter, as to keep troops in Fort Sumter. The constitutional right to do both was perfect, and firing upon United States soldiers going to Fort Sumter, under orders from the President, was just as much a hostile act as firing upon United States soldiers in Fort Sumter. The Administration simply chose not to so regard it. President Buchanan was resolved to avoid the issue of arms, if he possibly could do so. Congress was not prepared for it, and it is not certain that the people of the North would then have rallied to the President's support. And so, a distinction was made between resistance to the Government on its way to Fort Sumter and resistance to the Government already in Fort Sumter, in order to avoid accepting the gage of battle thrown down by the South Carolinians. It does seem, however, that a determined President, in command of ten thousand good soldiers might, at the moment, have nipped the rebellion in the bud. The legal right to act, and the legitimate occasion for acting, were both perfect. It was the physical means, and the disposition to use them, that were lacking.

As it was, the ignominious backdown of the Administration encouraged the secessionists and humiliated the North. The Secretary of the Interior, Mr. Thompson, of Mississippi, and the Secretary of the Treasury, Mr. Thomas, of Maryland, now resigned, declaring that in attempting to re-enforce Major Anderson the President had broken his pledges, and that they could therefore remain no longer in connection with him. The appointment of General John A. Dix of New York to the secretaryship of the Treasury, and the transfer of Mr. Holt to the War Department now, however, placed the Administration upon much firmer ground, so that, after all, the "Star of the

The effect of the failure to relieve Major Anderson.

West" affair was not wholly injurious. The Cabinet was, at last, purged of the secessionist element and became solidly and sincerely loyal to the Union.

Two days after the repulse of the "Star of the West" from Charleston Harbor, Governor Pickens demanded

The demand of Governor Pickens for the surrender of Fort Sumter. of Major Anderson the surrender of Fort Sumter. The Major refused, but suggested that, if the Governor would refer the matter to the President, he would send one of his own subordinates to bear the communication. The Governor immediately deputed his Attorney-General, I. W. Hayne, to go to Washington and demand the surrender of Fort Sumter. When Mr. Hayne arrived in Washington, the Senators from Georgia, Alabama, Mississippi, Louisiana, Florida, and Texas immediately met him, and persuaded him not to make this demand of the President until their "States" could form a confederation with each other and with South Carolina. They agreed with Mr. Hayne that, in consideration of his delay, they would themselves jointly request the President to give an assurance that the garrison in Fort Sumter would not be re-enforced. They made the request, and the President, through the Secretary of War, immediately declined to give any such assurance, but distinctly declared that, if Major Anderson's safety should require re-enforcements, every effort would be made to supply them. This happened on the 22d of January.

Meanwhile Congress had continued its efforts for pacification. The House Committee had reported on

The continuance of the efforts of Congress for pacification. the 13th. It, too, had been unable to come to any unanimous agreement. Two reports were therefore presented from the committee. The chairman of the committee, Mr. Corwin, presented the report of the majority. This report denounced the acts of Northern "State" Legislatures for obstructing the execution of the Fugitive Slave law, and the conduct of mobs and combinations of private persons for the same purpose, as contrary to the Constitution, inconsistent with comity and good neighborhood between the "States," and dangerous to the peace of the Union ; and recommended the repeal of all such legislative acts, and in their stead the passage of laws securing the rights of the citizens of each "State" in every other, and requiring the punishment of all persons guilty of attempting to set on foot the invasion of any "State" or Territory, or aiding or abetting therein. This report also declared the existence of slavery in fifteen "States" of the Union, and affirmed that no authority outside of the "State" concerned could deal with the institution in that "State"; but pronounced it to be "the duty of the Federal Government to enforce the Federal laws, protect the Federal property, and preserve the Union of the States," and denied that there was any sufficient cause, coming from any quarter, for the dissolution of the Union.

The practical propositions of the report were, first, an amendment to the Constitution, which should provide against the initiation of any future amendment in regard to slavery, except at the instance of a "State" in which slavery existed, and against the ratification of any such amendment when thus proposed, except by the vote of every "State" of the Union ; second, an amendment to the Congressional act for the rendition of fugitives from justice, so as to give the "State" from which the fugitive should escape full jurisdiction over the case and secure the rendition by means of the United States courts ; and, third, the immediate admission of New Mexico as a "State" into the Union with such territorial dimensions as to give almost all the domain of the Union south of the line of thirty-six degrees and thirty minutes to slavery.

Seven of the Southern members of the committee joined in a minority report, the propositions of which were substantially the Crittenden scheme presented to the Senate.

Finally, two of the Northern members, Mr. M. W. Tappan of New Hampshire and Mr. C. C. Washburn of Wisconsin, made another minority report, which concluded with a proposed resolution, reading as follows : " Resolved, that the provisions of the Constitution are ample for the preservation of the Union, and the protection of all the material interests of our country ; that it needs to be obeyed rather than amended ; and that our extrication from our present difficulties is to be looked for in efforts to preserve and protect the public property and enforce the laws, rather than in new guarantees for particular interests, or compromises, or concessions to unreasonable demands."

Before, however, these reports were debated at all in the House, a resolution was passed in the Senate which appeared to put an end to all attempts at any compromise in which it should be necessary for that body to participate. On the 3d day of January, Mr. Crittenden had again presented in the Senate his resolutions of December 18th, which, as we have seen, were offered by the Southerners in the committee of the Senate as the basis of a compromise. In the midst of the discussion upon them in the Senate, Mr. Clark, of New Hampshire, gave notice that he should move a substitute for them which read : " Resolved, that the provisions of the Constitution are ample for the preservation of the Union, and the protection of all the material interests of the country ; that it needs to be obeyed rather than amended ; and that an extrica-

Mr. Clark's resolution in the Senate.

tion from the present dangers is to be looked for in
strenuous efforts to preserve the peace, protect the public
property, and enforce the laws, rather than in new guarantees for particular interests, compromises for particular difficulties, or concessions to unreasonable demands ;
that all attempts to dissolve the present Union, or overthrow or abandon the present Constitution, with the
hope or expectation of constructing a new one, are dangerous, illusory and destructive ; that in the opinion of
the Senate of the United States, no such reconstruction
is practicable, and therefore to the maintenance of the
existing Union and Constitution should be directed the
energies of all the departments of the Government, and
the efforts of all good citizens."

On the 15th (January), Mr. Clark moved the adoption
of this substitute for Mr. Crittenden's propositions ; and
on the 16th the motion was actually voted, by   Passage of
a majority of twenty-five against twenty-   Mr. Clark's
three, through the abstention of six Southern   resolutions.
Senators, viz., Benjamin and Slidell of Louisiana, Hemp-
hill and Wigfall of Texas, Iverson of Georgia, and Johnson of Arkansas.   The Senators from the "States"
which had passed secession ordinances had ceased to act,
and Mr. Toombs of Georgia was not present.   Had he
been, he would no doubt have acted with the other six.
In fact, it is asserted on good authority that it was with
his knowledge and counsel that the six abstained from
voting, though in their seats, in order to be able to say to
the people of the South that the Senate had refused any
compromise whatsoever.   It is certainly true that Mr.
Benjamin telegraphed to the people of Louisiana, immediately after this vote, the fateful words : "We cannot
get any compromise."   Senator Andrew Johnson declared that he sat just behind Mr. Benjamin when the
vote was being taken, and that he asked Mr. Benjamin

why he would not vote, and that Mr. Benjamin replied that " he would control his own action without consulting me or anybody else." Mr. Johnson then and there divined his purpose and retorted, " vote and show yourself an honest man."

On the 18th, Mr. Cameron moved to reconsider the vote upon Mr. Clark's propositions, and the Senate passed the motion, so that the Crittenden measures were restored to the calendar of the Senate. But the vote of the 16th had done the work for the secessionists. The Georgia convention passed its secession ordinance on the 19th, and the Louisiana convention did likewise on the 25th, making thus the original six that formed the Southern Confederacy.

Reconsideration of Mr. Clark's resolutions.

The delegations from these " States " in the House of Representatives withdrew from that body as the passage of the secession ordinance in their respective " States " was officially announced to them. They took their leave generally through the form of cards, signed jointly by the members of each delegation, through which they informed the House of the secession of their " States " from the Union, and expressed the opinion that this act worked the revocation of their own representative functions. A few of them indulged in speeches, reproaching the North, the Government and the Republicans, and bidding them defiance.

Withdrawal of the Southern Senators and Representatives from Congress.

On the other hand, the Senators from Mississippi, Alabama, Florida, Georgia, and Louisiana made farewell addresses, each for himself. Mr. Toombs of Georgia and Mr. Brown of Mississippi were the only exceptions. They allowed themselves to be represented by their respective colleagues, Mr. Iverson and Mr. Davis. Between the 21st of January and the 4th of February, the Senators listened to the words of their departing colleagues.

One would naturally expect to find in these speeches an enumeration of the grievances imposed upon the "seceding States" by the Government, from whose jurisdiction they now declared themselves withdrawn, but nothing of the kind was offered.

The farewell addresses of the Southern Senators.

When reference was made to the tyranny of the Government at all, it was tyranny anticipated, not tyranny actually existing. To that moment all the departments of the Government had accorded everything which the slaveholders had demanded for the security of their peculiar institution. It was impossible for them to accuse it of tyranny in regard to any of its measures whatever. These Senators were, therefore, reduced to the necessity of proclaiming, as their only grievance against the Government, the prospect that after the 4th of the following March, the President and a majority of the House of Representatives in Congress would belong to a party which had declared that it would resist by all lawful means the further spread of slavery, because it thought that slavery was wrong.

In default of any actual grievances against the Government of the United States, these men were obliged to seek some elsewhere. They arraigned the Legislatures of the Northern Commonwealths for their personal liberty laws in defiance of the fugitive slave provision of the Constitution, and the Fugitive Slave Act of Congress, and at last they presented as their oppressor the anti-slavery spirit of the North. Against this some of them were exceedingly bitter.

There is no doubt that the personal liberty laws of some of the Northern Commonwealths, while intended only, in most cases, to protect their own colored citizens against kidnapping, did come into conflict with the Fugitive Slave Act of Congress; but the remedy for that in our system was a

"Personal liberty" laws in the North.

decision of the United States Courts against the validity
of such laws, and the execution of the Fugitive Slave
law by the United States Government.   In fact that
remedy had been applied, as we have seen, even to the
extent of employing the military power in the enforcement of that law, and nobody had spoken of this as the
coercion of a "sovereign State."   The Supreme Court
of the United States had decided eighteen years before,
as we have seen, that the sole responsibility for executing the fugitive slave clause in the Constitution
rested upon the United States Government, upon Congress to provide the means and measures, and upon the
President and the courts to enforce them.   Even though,
therefore, these personal liberty laws of some of the
Northern Commonwealths did come into conflict with
the Constitution and laws of the United States, they
could be regarded as violations of the " Compact " in
no other sense than any other Commonwealth law
which might be declared to be in this situation, and
they required no other remedy ; while as to the grievances against the anti-slavery spirit of the North, we
can only say, as Lincoln said two years before this remarkable episode took place in the Senate chamber, that
they meant that the secessionists would not be satisfied,
except upon the condition that the people of the North
should think and feel and express themselves upon the
subject of slavery as they themselves did.   Congress
and the President and the Courts had interpreted their
rights under the " Compact" as they themselves had
dictated.   But this was not enough.   The conscience of
the North must be forced, so as to make it certain that
the departments of the Government never would interpret and execute the " Compact " in any other way.
It is simply marvellous that the unnaturalness, the ab-
surdity, and the monstrous character of such a demand

did not appear to the minds of these able men of the South. If any of them saw it in the faintest degree in its true light, they did not give the slightest evidence of it. They all spoke with an air of sincerity, boldness, and patronizing condescension, which is produced by a consciousness of right and of power, mingled with an imperious disposition. Not one of them manifested the faintest suspicion that their project could fail. Not one of them had any adequate appreciation of the energy and determination which would be roused in the North in behalf of the Union by the attempt to destroy it. Senator Iverson, of Georgia, seemed to think that the North would be paralyzed by his declaration that it would cost the North one hundred thousand men and one hundred millions of dollars to make conquest of the South.

On the other hand, the Republicans were so honest in their assurances that they meant to obey the Constitution to the letter in regard to slavery as in regard to everything else, that they could not believe the secessionists were sincere in their imputation of abolition purposes to them, to be effected by any and every means. And they were incredulous in regard to the threats of breaking up the Union on such flimsy pretexts. Mr. Slidell said that, if the South should remain in the Union after the inauguration of Mr. Lincoln, the slaves would revolt in many parts of the South against their masters and cause bloodshed. He said they had been taught that Lincoln's Administration would lend them the hand in such work. The reply of the Republicans to this was that nobody but their own masters had taught them to expect such things from the incoming Republican Administration, and for that the Republicans could not be held responsible, especially when they had constantly disavowed any such purposes and had incorporated in their platform of 1860 a most scathing denunciation of the John Brown raid.

In fact it seemed that Mr. Rhett correctly represented the feelings of the secessionists when he affirmed that the secession movement had been in preparation for thirty years, and had at last only culminated on the occasion of the election of Lincoln to the presidency.

On the day that the Louisiana Senators made their adieus to the Senate, February 4th, the first step was The forma- taken in the formation of the Southern tion of the Confederacy. The conventions in the six Southern Con- federacy. "States," which had passed the secession or- dinance, had also elected delegates to meet in a general convention at Montgomery, Alabama, on the 4th of February following, for the purpose of forming a con- federation of these "States," establishing a provisional government for the confederation, and electing a pro- visional executive.

The Republican and Abolitionist historians have in- dulged in certain criticisms upon the forms and meth- ods employed by the secessionists in passing the seces- sion ordinances and creating the new confederacy. The gist of these criticisms is that these things were done by "State" conventions instead of by the direct act of the people, as our system of democracy would have required. The criticism is not, however, well founded. The Con- stitution of the United States was framed by delegates elected either by "State" Legislatures or by conventions within the "States," and ratified by conventions within the "States"; and its provision for future amendment speaks only of Congress, "State" Legislatures, and con ventions within the "States," as the bodies for effecting changes in the organic law. The Constitution of the United States knows nothing of a direct appeal to the people in any of these cases. The secessionists, there-

fore, followed our constitutional precedents in passing
their secession ordinances and establishing their new
Confederacy by means of conventions in their "States."
They argued that, as they had confided powers to the
United States Government by the acts of conventions
within the several "States," they could withdraw them
in the same manner—yea, that they must so withdraw
them, if they withdrew them at all ; and that, as they
had withdrawn themselves from the old Confederation of
1781 to form the Union of 1787, by the acts of conventions within the respective "States," they could withdraw themselves from the Union of 1787 in the same
manner—yea, must so withdraw themselves, if they
withdrew at all.   The demands of their critics that these
movements should have been submitted to the direct
suffrages of the people are thus seen to be based, not
upon the precedents and analogies of our constitutional
law and practice, but upon the theories of an advanced
democracy.   If the secessionists had any right to do
what they did do, the manner in which they accomplished it cannot be successfully assailed.

The first problem with which the delegates from these
"State" conventions had to wrestle was, of course,
confederation. It required, however, only   The provi-
three days to solve this problem. On the   sional Consti-
8th day of the month (February) they or-   Confederacy
dained and declared the union of the six "States"
represented in the convention under a provisional constitution, which was to continue in force for one year,
unless a permanent constitution should take its place
before the expiration of that period.   This provisional
constitution was, in substance, the Constitution of the
United States, altered in a few points to fit the conditions of a provisory organization, to make express those
particular interpretations which the secessionists had

put upon the old instrument, and to add such improvements as the experiences of these men under the working of the old system had suggested to them.

They naturally declared in the preamble that the provisory constitution was formed by delegates from sovereign and independent "States"; and they consistently changed the language of the provision of the Constitution of the United States in regard to the taxing powers of the Government so as to prohibit the enactment of a protective tariff, and also the language of the provision concerning the rendition of fugitive slaves so as to impose that duty upon the Governor of the "State" in which the fugitive should be found.

The reasons for these changes and modifications lie on the surface, and need no further examination. We find, however, in Section 7 of Article I. of this provisory instrument some divergencies from the provisions of the Constitution of the United States upon the same subject, for which the reasons are not apparent. This section of the constitution of the new Confederacy provides that, "the importation of African negroes from any foreign country, other than the slaveholding States of the United States, is hereby forbidden " . . . and "that Congress shall have power to prohibit the introduction of slaves from any State not a member of this Confederacy."

Apparently, the charge freely indulged in at the North, that the "cotton States" were planning and intriguing to reopen the African slave-trade, was here fully and completely refuted. These provisions can, however, be interpreted in another way, a less generous way indeed, but perhaps more in accordance with the intentions of their framers—that is, as an inducement to the other slaveholding "States," which furnished the "cotton States" with slaves, especially to Maryland and Virginia, to join the Confederacy which the "cotton States" were forming. The provisions were drawn, whether consciously or not, with most subtile adaptability to the production of that result. Here was a constitutional provision protecting the great profits of the slave-producing "States" in the domestic slave-trade against foreign competition, coupled with a provision giving the new Confederate Congress the power to destroy these profits altogether if these "States" should not enter the Confederacy. Once within the Confederacy, and the independence of the Confederacy won, that clause in the Confederate constitution prohibiting the foreign slave-trade might be repealed. Was this one of the reasons for making the process of amendment easier in the Confederate constitution than it was in the Constitution of the United States? One would think that the "State sovereignty" principle would have required it to be made much more difficult.

On account of the necessity for speedy action, the convention made itself the legislative body of the provisional government, and conferred upon itself in this capacity the power to elect the provisional President and Vice-President. There was not much question in the provisional Congress as to who should be the President. Mr. Davis stood head and shoulders above all the others. Besides being the prime representative of the doctrine of "State sovereignty," and the clearest mind among them, he had had the most varied experience in public life. He, as we know, had been soldier, legislator, and high executive officer. No one else was seriously considered except Mr. Toombs; and he, though a very brilliant man, was thought of more on account of the claims of his "State," as the "Empire State" of the Confederacy, than because of his own fitness for office. Of the two, Mr. Davis was far the calmer, more conservative, more prudent and judicious. The choice was the best that could have been made, although the downfall of the Confederacy under his leadership has made many Southerners feel that it was a mistake. The historian knows, however, that, in the great plan of history, there was not the slightest chance for the success of secession in these United States, and sees, from the point of view of the world's history, that Mr. Davis might have done better, if only he had not done so well.

Mr. Davis denied ever having made any effort to secure the presidency, or ever having entertained any desire for it. He declared that he preferred the military office, which had already been conferred upon him by Mississippi, that of commanding general of her army. He took no part in the convention at Montgomery, and was at "Briarfield," his plantation home, when he was elected President. He, however, accepted promptly the great burden, and started almost immediately for Montgomery to assume the functions of the office.

On the other hand, the selection made for the vice-presidency was more deserving of criticism. The chances for the succession of the Vice-President to the first office by an accidental termination of the life of the President, or by his capture in war, were much greater than the average of chances in such cases. The Vice-President ought, therefore, to have been a man of the same character, equipment, and experience as the President. Mr. Alexander H. Stephens, of Georgia, the man finally selected, was far from this. Physically he was weak, and appeared insignificant. He was also inclined to pedantry in his knowledge, and, therefore, little fitted for executive office. Moreover, he was an old-line Whig, and altogether half-hearted in his seces-

The Vice-President.

sionism. He had to prod himself continually to keep his courage up. The reasons for his selection were almost purely political. They were to attach the old Whigs to the secession movement, and to satisfy the claims of Georgia for office.

The selection of the members of the Cabinet was also governed too largely by political considerations. One portfolio was given to each "State" forming the Confederacy, except Mississippi, which had the presidency, and one was given to Texas, whose convention had passed the secession ordinance on the 1st of February, but on account of the irregular method of its assembly, and for other less honorable reasons, had submitted the ordinance to the people, who had not yet voted upon it. The first Confederate Cabinet.

In anticipation of the popular ratification of the ordinance, the Texas convention had voted to join the Confederacy, and had elected delegates to the Confederate convention-congress. Texas was, therefore, virtually a member of the Southern Confederacy, while her Representatives and Senators were still in Congress at Washington, doing what they could to embarrass the Government of the United States, and revealing to the Confederate Government at Montgomery everything taking place at Washington. The way in which the Texan secessionists proceeded was most dishonorable and reprehensible. They insulted, threatened, and bullied their grand old Governor, Sam Houston, the father of their country, and when he would not yield to their demand to call the Legislature together in extra session, they called it themselves, without any regard to the provision of the constitution of the Commonwealth vesting that power solely in the Governor. After having in this irregular manner assembled the Legislature, and then, through it, Texas joins the Confederacy.

the convention, they referred the secession ordinance,
passed by the convention, to the voters, but, as we have
seen, resolved in the convention to join the Southern
Confederacy, and elected in the convention delegates to
the Confederate convention-congress.   Finally, after the
voters had ratified the ordinance, the Senators and Representatives from the Commonwealth at Washington
still remained in their places, until the convention at
Austin could pass the formal act declaring the "State"
out of the Union.   A period of one month and four days
thus elapsed between the first passage of the secession
ordinance and the final act of the convention, during a
part of which period the "State" of Texas was represented both at Washington and Montgomery, and in
both places by secessionists, those at Washington keeping those at Montgomery fully informed of what any
honorable man would have regarded himself bound by
his solemn oath, as a member of the National Legislature, to have kept sacredly locked in his own bosom
against the enemies of the United States.

But to return to the composition of the first Confederate Cabinet.   The principle of selection, as we have
seen, was to give each "State" one place, and
then let the delegates from the "State" in
the convention-congress designate the man.
The first Cabinet composed in this manner consisted of
Mr. Toombs of Georgia, Secretary of State ; Mr. Walker
of Alabama, Secretary of War ; Mr. Memminger of
South Carolina, Secretary of the Treasury ; Mr. Mallory
of Florida, Secretary of the Navy ; Mr. Benjamin of
Louisiana, Attorney-General, and Mr. Reagan of Texas,
Postmaster-General.   Of these only two were men of
great ability, Toombs and Benjamin, and both of these
had grave faults.   Toombs was too impulsive and Benjamin was too much given to intrigue.

*The compo-
sition of the
Cabinet re-
sumed.*

On the 18th day of February, Mr. Davis was inaugurated and the machinery of the new Government put into operation. The inaugural address was short, and hardly equal to the average efforts of its author. It contained no statement The inauguration of President Davis. of grievances, but it pronounced the doctrine that the secession movement was an illustration of " the American idea that governments rest on the consent of the governed, and that it is the right of the people to alter or abolish them at will whenever they become destructive of the ends for which they were established." He claimed that the " seceding States" had merely asserted the right which the Declaration of Independence defined as inalienable, and that each of them, as sovereign, was the final judge for itself of the time and the occasion for the exercise of this right. He drew from these premises the conclusion that the act of secession was not revolutionary, but that the " States" forming the new Confederacy had simply changed "the agent through which they communicated with foreign nations," and that if the United States should still undertake to assert jurisdiction over the " seceded States" the act would be offensive war. He expressed the hope, but not the expectation, that they would be allowed to go in peace. He evidently looked for war, and recommended the creation of a regular army and navy of the Confederacy, and hinted at the advantages which the legalization of privateering might produce. At this day, the address impresses one as being weak and totally fallacious, as containing a theory of government little removed from anarchy, and a doctrine in reference to the offensive and defensive entirely reversed from truth and fact.

While these movements were in progress at Montgomery, the Union-savers were exerting themselves at

Washington both within and without Congress, and
the Union-destroyers were at work in the other slaveholding Commonwealths, those not yet in
the new Confederacy, upon their counter-
plan.

Continua-
tion of the ef-
forts to save
the Union at
Washington.

On the self-same day that the Confederate
convention met at Montgomery, a Union Peace conference assembled at Washington in answer to a call issued
by the Virginia Legislature on the 19th of January preceding. All the non-slaveholding Commonwealths, except Michigan, Wisconsin, Minnesota, California, and
Oregon, and all of the slaveholding Commonwealths
which had not passed secession ordinances, except Arkansas and Texas, were represented. That is, thirteen
non-slaveholding, and seven slaveholding, Commonwealths participated in the conference. The delegates
chosen by the Legislatures or Governors of these respective Commonwealths were all men of the highest character, and of great influence in all conservative circles.
Such men as Fessenden and Morrill of Maine, Chitten-
den and Harris of Vermont, Forbes, Crowninshield,
Boutwell, and Allen of Massachusetts, Hoppin and Arnold of Rhode Island, Baldwin and Battelle of Connect-
icut, Dudley Field, Curtis Noyes, Wadsworth, Corning,
Dodge, King, and Wool of New York, Stockton, Fre-
linghuysen, and Price of New Jersey, Wilmot and
Franklin of Pennsylvania, Chase, Groesbeck, and Ewing
of Ohio, Smith and Orth of Indiana, Palmer and Stephen
Logan of Illinois, Harlan and Grimes of Iowa, Rodney
of Delaware, Howard and Reverdy Johnson of Maryland,
ex-President Tyler, Rives, and Seddon of Virginia, Ruf-
fin of North Carolina, Caruthers and Zollicoffer of Tennessee, Clay and Guthrie of Kentucky, and Doniphan of
Missouri, were sent upon this great mission of pacification. Certainly if there were not intellect and character

enough in such an assembly to effect a compromise of interests between the warring sections of the country, and invent a *modus vivendi*, it was to be feared that the Nation did not possess them.

This body, under the chairmanship of the venerable ex-President of the United States, John Tyler of Virginia, wrestled with the mighty problem before it from the 4th to the 27th of February. They were able to agree upon a series of recommendations, which were offered to the two Houses of Congress on the first and second days of March.

The Peace Convention and its work.

These recommendations provided : that slavery should be prohibited in all the existing territory of the United States lying above the latitude of thirty-six degrees and thirty minutes ; that the existing slave status in the territory south of that line should not be changed ; that neither Congress nor a Territorial Legislature should forbid or hinder the taking of slaves from any State into the existing territory of the Union south of the latitude thirty-six degrees and thirty minutes ; that neither Congress nor a Territorial Legislature should pass any law impairing the rights arising from the relation of master and slave, but that the same should be subject to judicial cognizance in the courts of the United States, according to the course of the common law ; and that any Territory, north or south of said line, should, when its population equalled that required for a Congressional district within the " States," be admitted into the Union as a " State," with or without slavery, as its constitution might provide, on an equality with the original " States ":

That treaties by which territory should be annexed to the United States, except for naval stations and depots, or transit routes, must, to be valid, be ratified by a two-thirds vote of the Senate, and that this two-thirds vote must contain the votes of a majority of the Senators from the slaveholding "States," and also of a majority of those from the non-slaveholding "States" :

That Congress should have no power to legislate in regard to slavery in the "States," nor in those places subject to the exclusive jurisdiction of the United States, but lying within the boundaries of slaveholding "States," nor in the District of Columbia, without the consent of Maryland and the owners of the slaves within the District, and the payment of damages to the non-consenting owners ; that Congress should have no power to prevent masters from bringing their slaves into the District, retaining them while there, and taking them away again ; that Congress should have no power to prohibit the slave-trade between "States" and Territories recognizing slavery, nor, in case the traffic should be by water, prevent touching at points in non-slaveholding "States" and Territories ; and that Congress should have no power to impose a higher tax on slaves than on land :

That the States should have the power to return, through the operation of their own governmental instrumentalities, fugitives from labor to the persons to whom the labor was due ; and that Congress should pass efficient laws for carrying out faithfully the constitutional prohibition on the foreign slave-trade.

The conference recommended that all of these proposed provisions should be made amendments to the Constitution of the United States, and should be irrepealable and unchangeable, except with the consent of every "State" in the Union. The conference also recommended that the existing provisions of the Constitution in respect to fugitives from service or labor and in respect to the counting of slaves in the apportionment of Congressional representation and presidential electors should be made irrepealable and unamendable, except with the consent of every "State."

The conference recommended, finally, that the Constitution should be so amended as to require Congress to provide for payment out of the Treasury of the United States for escaped slaves whose rendition should be prevented by mobs or riotous assemblages, and to provide by law for securing to the "citizens of each State the privileges and immunities of citizens in the several States."

During the first sittings of this conference its membership had been increased by representatives from the new non-slaveholding Commonwealth of Kansas, the act for the admission of which was signed by the President on the 29th of January preceding the assembly of the conference. This made fourteen non-slaveholding Commonwealths that were represented in this body to seven slaveholding Commonwealths. The majority of the non-slaveholding Commonwealths voted in the conference against all of these recommendations, except only those relating to the prohibition of the foreign slave-trade and to the payment by the Government for slaves whose rendition had been prevented by the action of mobs or riotous assemblages. Delaware, Maryland, Kentucky, and Tennessee voted for all of them. North Carolina voted against most of them. Missouri refrained from voting on about half of them. And Virginia finally declared her dissatisfaction with the series as a whole, on the ground that it did not offer a sufficient guarantee for all of her rights.

On the 27th of February the resolutions of the conference were laid before the Senate by the Vice-President, Mr. Breckenridge. The Senate immediately referred them to a committee of five persons, Mr. Crittenden, Mr. Bigler, Mr. Thomson, Mr. Seward, and Mr. Trumbull, with instructions to report on the next morning. On the 28th, Mr. Crittenden reported to the Senate from the majority of

Resolutions of the Conference before the Senate.

this committee a resolution that the propositions of the Peace conference should be recommended by Congress to conventions in the several "States" for ratification as amendments to the Constitution. Mr. Seward and Mr. Trumbull offered an independent resolution that Congress invite the "States" to apply for the calling of a constitutional convention of the United States for the initiation of such amendments to the Constitution as would meet the existing emergencies. The resolution from the majority was made a special order for the next day, and when it was brought up Senator Douglas asked that the resolutions from the House of Representatives relative to amending the Constitution, just received in the Senate, should be considered along with it. These resolutions from the House of Representatives were the propositions of the committee of thirty-three of that body, already recited, which, with the exception of the one in reference to the immediate admission of New Mexico as a "State," and the one in reference to the rendition of fugitives from justice, the House had, with little change, adopted, on the 27th and 28th of February. The Senate allowed the House resolutions to be read, but laid them aside for the moment in order to give its whole attention to the propositions of the Peace conference and the resolution of its own committee in reference thereto. Whereupon Senator Hunter, of Virginia, immediately announced that he was not satisfied with these propositions and moved to substitute Mr. Crittenden's own series of resolutions, still on the calendar of the Senate, for them. Mr. Hunter's colleague, Mr. Mason, sustained Mr. Hunter in the assertion that the propositions of the Peace conference would not be satisfactory to Virginia. With this it became entirely manifest that their adoption by the Senate would be useless.

While, thus, it may probably be truthfully charged that Virginia rendered the work of the Peace conference nugatory, and blocked the work of pacifica- Failure of the proposi-tion upon that line, and while the motives the proposi- in the minds of her leaders for so doing may Peace Confer- have been reprehensible, still the historians ence. and publicists of this day are not disposed to find much fault with the result. The propositions of the Peace conference ought to have failed, because they meant, in the first place, the perpetuation of slavery as a perma- nent institution of the country, while the civilization of the world was and is working toward the liberation of all mankind ; because they meant, in the second place, the prevention of the nationalization of our people by confederatizing our political system, while the civili- zation of the world was and is making for the develop- ment of national states ; and because they meant, lastly, the destruction of political and moral progress upon many most important subjects, by withdrawing these subjects from a possible method of constitutional amend- ment, while political science demands that the real sovereign power in any political system shall be able to change the constitution, through regular forms of amendment, upon every subject. In a word, they would have turned back the clock of the world's civilization an entire century. They undertook to arrest the plans of Providence in the evolution of the world's history.

After the attitude of the Virginia Senators had caused the Senate to lay aside the propositions of the Peace conference, Mr. Douglas succeeded in induc- Last at-ing the body to take up the resolutions trans- tempts in the Senate to save mitted from the House the day before. The the Union by compromise. chief one of these was the proposed constitu- tional amendment which provided that no future amend- ment to the Constitution should ever give Congress the power to abolish, or interfere with, slavery within the "States." This was the form which the recommendation of the committee of thirty-three, that no future amendment touching slavery should be initiated except by a slave "State" or considered as ratified without the approval of every "State," had taken on in its passage through the House. It was now the 2d of March, and it seemed that the adoption of these House resolutions by the Senate was the only thing that Congress could do for the pacification of the country. It was well known that they did not satisfy the South. The Senators from the "border States" declared that they were next to nothing. Mr. Crittenden almost alone, under the persuasions of Mr. Douglas, felt that they might exercise some influence. These two patriotic men held the Senate together through the long hours of the night of the 3d of March, and into the morning hours of the 4th, in deliberation over the House resolutions, and, almost at the last moment of the existence of that Congress, secured their adoption by the Senate. The last hours of the Senate were passed in the attempt to pass the Crittenden resolutions also. This failed, as well as the attempt to pass the proposition of the Peace conference in the House.

What was offered to the South by Congress was a proposition to disable the Nation from ever putting into the hands of Congress the power to touch slavery within the Commonwealths. From any point of view enough, and from the point of view of sound political science altogether too much.

However careful and desirous the impartial historian may be to present the position of the secessionists in its most favorable light, and however anxious he may be to prevent the failure of their cause from prejudicing his views of their motives and their reasoning, still he will find it most difficult to understand why, in every sound mind to-day, the Republican leaders are not to be considered as having offered everything that could have been expected from wise, honest, and sincere men for the pacification of the country, and, from the point of view of a sound political science, more than they ought to have done. They always expressed themselves as ready to vote for the calling of a national convention to consider all grievances from whatever section coming, and thus give time for passion and excitement to cool down, and for misapprehensions to be corrected. They had not yet taken the government of the Union into their hands, and, therefore, they had *done* nothing to justify secession, rebellion, or revolution, and they wanted to be calmly heard as to what they proposed to do. The secessionists, however, treated this proposition as a mere subterfuge. It is difficult to believe that they were moved to reject it from the conviction that it was a subterfuge. It seems, rather, as if they wanted to escape a plain statement of reasons and policies, which the whole people might weigh and consider before choosing the course which would lead to disunion and war.

Republican attitude toward pacification summarized.

Again, the Republican leaders were ready to secure slavery in the "States" where it was by an unchangeable amendment to the Constitution, and they voted for the proposed amendment providing that no future amendment to the Constitution should ever be made, which would empower Congress to interfere with slavery in the "States," and voted for it in such numbers as to adopt it, by the requisite two-thirds majority, and that, too, after the Senators and Representatives from six of the Southern "States" had withdrawn from their seats.

Still further, when the Crittenden resolutions were before the Senate, Mr. Anthony, speaking for the Republicans, on the 16th of January, offered to allow New Mexico to be organized at once as a new slaveholding "State," if the people of the Territory should so will it. This Territory covered all the territory of the United States south of the latitude of thirty-six degrees and thirty minutes, except the Indian Territory, and its northern boundary ran up at some points to the latitude of thirty-eight degrees and a little higher. The Territory did not contain a population sufficient, under the existing law of apportionment, to send one member to the House of Representatives in Congress, but the Republicans were willing to waive this requirement. The Republicans thought this virtual offer of New Mexico a fair equivalent for the Crittenden measure dividing all the existing Territories of the United States between the North and the South by the line of thirty-six degrees and thirty minutes. They preferred this form, because they thought to escape thereby the reproach of having helped to extend slavery by Congressional legislation, a thing which they could not do without destroying the *raison d'être* of their party. But the Crittenden proposition was not acceptable to the secessionists, unless amended, as proposed by Mr. Powell, so as to cover all territory then possessed, *or thereafter to be acquired*, by the United States. From the point of view of the designs on Cuba and Mexico, with slavery or without it, as their inhabitants might decide, this did not appear to the secessionists an equivalent to the Crittenden-Powell proposition. The Republicans, however, considered such an incentive to foreign conquest as that contained in Mr. Powell's amendment to be highly immoral, as it certainly was.

Still further, the Republican leaders in Congress

agreed, during the month of February, to the organization of the Territories of Colorado, Nevada, and Dakota
without any provision in the bills excluding slavery.
These three Territories covered almost all of the territory of the United States north of the latitude of thirty-
six degrees and thirty minutes. They were therefore
open to slaveholders with their slaves, if they chose to
go into any of them; and the United States Supreme
Court had, in its Dred Scott opinion, positively declared
the right of the slaveholders to go with their slaves into
any Territory of the Union.

Lastly, the Republican leaders acknowledged the people of the North to be obligated by the Constitution to
return, or pay for, every fugitive slave that came into
their hands, and, also, acknowledged the duty of Congress to pass laws to punish the citizens of any Commonwealth for going into any other for the purpose of
exciting, or attempting to excite, insurrection therein.
They were not willing, as individuals, to aid in the
execution of the Fugitive Slave law, but they declared
that all Commonwealth laws which contravened the
pledge in the Constitution for the rendition of fugitive
slaves ought to be repealed, and they were ready to empower the Treasury of the United States to pay damages
to the slaveowner, whenever the officers of the Government should be prevented by popular violence from returning the fugitive.

To the historian, who regards the course of world
events from the vantage ground of the present, and to
the modern political scientist, these offered
concessions of the Republicans appear alto- *Criticism of the Republican attitude.*
gether too generous. They should never
have been willing to consent to the extension of slavery
over one foot of free territory, either by a positive act of
Congress, or an act omitting the restriction on slavery, or

by an act encouraging the people of any Territory where slavery already nominally and legally existed to make it real and permanent. And they never should have been willing to withdraw anything from the amending power in the Constitution. This meant nothing less than the confederatizing of the political system of the United States, and the prevention of political progress by lawful peaceable means. It meant a return to the system of 1781, as to the excepted subjects. It meant the reversal, in principle, of the chief advance which we had made in the development of our constitutional law from the system of 1781 to that of 1787. No publicist who has perceived the movement of modern political history toward the development of national states can, for one moment, approve of such a reactionary course. Instead of this, he would demand that existing exceptions from the amending power be expunged from the Constitution, and that the amending power itself should be so formulated as only to guard the sovereign power of the Nation from hasty and inconsiderate action, but never so as to thwart its deliberate and well-determined purpose.

When now we consider that there was another great party at the North, numbering almost as many adherents as the Republican party itself, which was ready to yield to almost any demand, as the price of union, that the secessionists might make, it is indeed difficult to explain the irrationality, as well as the passionate precipitancy, of the secessionists, except upon the old Greek maxim that "whom the gods would destroy they first make mad."

We know now that the spirit of civilization was working for much more advanced results than the Republicans themselves consciously intended. Immediate abolition of slavery in the Commonwealths, and thorough nationalization of our political system, were consummations far beyond their hopes. Their hearts had to be fired to these results by the madness of the secessionists, who, upon the basis of their "State sovereignty" theory, sought to destroy the Union for the sake of perpetuating and extending the institution of African slavery. Not until then did the Republicans see that both slavery and "State sovereignty" must go, and in their places universal freedom and national sovereignty must be enthroned.

This then was, in the plan of universal history, the meaning of secession : The hastening of emancipation and nationalization. The United States were lagging in the march of modern civilization. Slavery and "State sovereignty" were the fetters which held them back, and these fetters had to be screwed down tight in order to provoke the Nation to strike them off at one fell blow, and free itself, and assert its supremacy, forevermore.

While the Government at Washington was thus wasting its time and energies in fruitless efforts at compromise and conciliation, the Confederate Government at Montgomery was securing and preparing the sinews of war. Every fort, arsenal, navy yard, custom-house, post-office, and mint within the boundaries of the seven "States," which had by the 4th of March passed the secession ordinance, had been seized by the troops of these respective "States," except only Fort Sumter and Fort Pickens and the fortifications upon Key West and the Dry Tortugas. President Buchanan's Secretary of War, Mr. John B. Floyd, had sent large shipment of arms to these Southern arsenals, and had taken care to place the larger part of the regular army within the Southern "States." Consequently the "State" governments of the Confederacy, and the Confederate Government found themselves fairly well supplied at the outset with implements of war of the latest pattern possessed by the United States Government; and when, during the latter part of February, General Twiggs, in command of about half of the United States army, surrendered his troops, with all their arms, munitions, and equipments to the Texan military authorities, the seven "States" of the Confederacy had in their possession fully half of the military property of the United States. It was calculated that they had seized some thirty millions of dollars' worth of the property of the United States.

The North regarded this as sheer robbery. The secessionists said that they had only taken their share, and that they held it subject to future disposition by agreement with the Government of the United States. From the point of view of their doctrine, that the Government at Washington was only the general agent employed by the several "States" to administer the joint affairs and property of a confederacy of sovereigns, they had, perhaps, sufficient moral justification for calling it a division rather than a robbery, had they taken only a fair share, but they went far beyond that. From the legal point of view, on the contrary, they had not the slightest right to any part of it. From the legal point of view these seizures were pure and simple robberies, and could be cleared of the criminal character only by the successful maintenance of the possession. In most cases they had not even the justification of secession, since they were made before the Commonwealths in which the seized property was located or deposited had passed the secession ordinance. It was the separate "State" governments rather than the Confederate Government upon whom the immediate responsibility for these seizures rested, but the chiefs of the Confederate Government, while still in their seats, as members of Congress at Washington, had advised their "States" to do these things, and the Confederate Government became the subsequent receiver of most of the property which these "State" governments had seized. Throw the best light upon it we may, it is still a dark spot for the Confederates in the history of their movement.

The Government at Montgomery lost no time in working up its military preparations. It simply adopted the laws of the United States *en bloc*, except only such as were inconsistent with the constitution of the Confederacy, and continued the existing United States officials in office as Confederate officials, and then had free hand to attend to its finances and its military organization. Already before the end of March, it could have met the Republican Administration at Washington with a military power greater than the United States had under command, in better discipline, and possessed with a better understood and more resolute purpose. When Mr. Lincoln took his oath upon the Constitution, he found himself called upon to meet a condition instead of a theory.

CHAPTER V

THE INAUGURATION OF LINCOLN AND THE CONDITION OF THE GOVERNMENT HE WAS CALLED TO ADMINISTER

Laws Give no Special Protection to the President-elect—Mr. Lincoln's Journey to Washington—Mr. Lincoln in Washington as President-elect—General Scott's Preparations for the Safety of the Capital—The Inaugural Address—Review of the Address—Criticism of a Part of the Address—Faint-heartedness at the North—Democratic Attitude at the North—Lack of Support in the Cabinet.

THE Government of the United States does not concern itself in the slightest degree about the personal security of the President-elect of the country. It leaves him to find his own way to the capital and to the place of his inauguration. Before he is invested with the powers of the office to which he has been chosen, he must take care of himself like any private citizen. After he is so invested, he may, of course, take care of himself by public means. The theory of this is that the people will do no harm to him whom they have freely chosen to rule over them. If this theory is sound in ordinary times and under ordinary conditions in elective governments, it certainly is not so when passion runs to an extraordinary height, and when large numbers of men declare their purpose to resist the government of the chosen magistrate.

Mr. Lincoln could not but have felt that he took his life in his hand when he set out upon his journey from

Laws give no special protection to the President-elect.

138

Springfield to Washington. He was obliged to pass
through country where the inhabitants were, in large
numbers, intensely hostile to his election, and Mr. Lin-
to his accession to power. He knew well coln's journey
to Washing-
enough that Southern men had, in 1856, ton.
threatened, in the event of the election of Frémont, to
proceed in force to Washington, and prevent Frémont's
inauguration by any means necessary to the result ; and
before he had completed much more than the half of his
journey, rumors that an attempt of the same kind would
be made against his own inauguration reached his ears.
When he arrived in Philadelphia, he was met by the
skilful detective Allan Pinkerton, who told him that
there was evidence that an attack upon his person in
Baltimore had been arranged.   The President of the
Philadelphia, Wilmington and Baltimore Railroad, Mr.
Felton, had suspected that violence might be offered to
Mr. Lincoln in passing through Baltimore, because of
the secession spirit which prevailed there, and because
of the great opportunity which the slow passage of the
trains through the city, drawn, as they then were, by
horses, would offer.   He had put Mr. Pinkerton upon
the scent, and both he and Pinkerton had become convinced that there was great danger to Mr. Lincoln in
going through Baltimore at a known time.   They tried
to dissuade him from carrying out the announced plan
of his journey from Harrisburg to Washington, via Baltimore, on the 23d of February ; but he decided to ad-
here both to route and time.   A few hours later Mr.
Frederick Seward, son of the incoming Secretary of
State, arrived in Philadelphia, and sought an immediate audience with Mr. Lincoln.   He delivered to Mr.
Lincoln a message from his father, and one from General Scott, both of whom were in Washington, to the
effect that his life would be endangered in passing

through Baltimore at a known hour.   Mr. Lincoln was, however, a brave man, and he shrank from stealing into the capital into which he had the right of a triumphal entry.   He realized, however, that for the sake of the country he was in duty bound not to run any unnecessary risks.   He wanted still to go on, with an escort, but no escort was provided or volunteered.   At the last moment, he yielded to the persuasions of his friends, and took the night train of the 22d from Philadelphia instead of the day train of the 23d from Harrisburg.   This brought him to Washington in the early morning of the 23d, some five hours before he was expected in Baltimore.   During his night journey, he had worn a travelling-cap instead of his customary "beaver," and was attended only by his friend Colonel Lamon.   These were the facts upon which was founded the story that Mr. Lincoln had sneaked unannounced, terror-stricken and disguised, into the city which was the seat of the Government that he had been chosen to administer.

From the 23d of February to the 4th of March, he remained in his hotel as quietly as it is possible for a President-elect, within ten days of his inauguration, to do.   The most important event of his life during this period was a visit from the members of the Peace conference.   The Southerners especially were curious to see the strange creature from the "wild and woolly West," and divine, if they could, his governmental policies.   They found a homely man, a plain man, but a man who understood himself and the crisis which he had been called upon to meet.   He is reported to have said to Mr. William C. Rives, of Virginia : "My course is as plain as a turnpike road.   It is marked out by the Constitution.   I am in no doubt which way to go."   They had heard nothing with that kind of a ring from the outgoing President.   It had to them an

Mr. Lincoln in Washington as President-elect.

ominous sound. It gave them something to think about, and to talk about with their friends at home.

General Scott had made ample preparations for the safety of the capital on inauguration day. The old warrior had been a good deal angered by the rumors which had come to him of intended violent resistance to the inauguration of the lawfully elected President, and he proposed to crush any such movement with an iron hand. He had gotten together a couple of batteries of artillery, nearly a thousand men of the regular infantry and marines, and a good strong detachment of the city volunteers. He planted his batteries so as to control the grounds on the east front of the capitol, and marched his infantry in parallel streets with the presidential procession from Willard's Hotel to the Capitol. If any violence had been intended, this display of military power and vigor repressed it. The inauguration took place without any unusual incident, and Mr. Lincoln took possession of the official mansion as the lawfully elected and lawfully installed President of the United States.

General Scott's preparation for the safety of the capital.

The inaugural address was a calm, plain statement of the President's intention to preserve the Union, and to execute the laws of the United States throughout the whole country. It was not an anti-slavery address. It was not even an anti-slavery-extension address. Mr. Lincoln went even so far as to say in it that he would have no objection to an irrevocable amendment to the Constitution prohibiting the United States Government from ever interfering with slavery in the "States." And he repeated the assertion, which he had, as a private citizen, already made, that he had no purpose of interfering, directly or indirectly, with the institution of slavery in the "States" where it existed, and that he did not believe that he had any

The inaugural address.

lawful right to do so. Moreover he said nothing about what the policy of his administration concerning slavery in the Territories would be ; and he disclaimed any assault upon the Supreme Court of the United States in his views of the extent of its authority in determining constitutional questions.

Why Mr. Lincoln, whose reputation, and whose election to the presidency, rested upon his anti-slavery-extension principles, should have shifted the whole issue to the question of saving national unity and preserving the Government was a query in the minds of many of his party friends at the moment, and, too, of many of their successors. A broad view of the subject will, however, quickly and clearly reveal the reason. The situation required the power and universal supremacy of the Government to be well settled and maintained before the acts of the Government could be of any general value as laws of the land ; and Mr. Lincoln always went for one thing at a time and the big things first. There is no need of going any further than this in explanation of the tone of the address.

Review of the address.

It was certainly a very wise proclamation of policy. It was the only policy upon which he could hope to unite the North and divide the South, which was his well-considered purpose. A pronounced anti-slavery policy, or even anti-slavery-extension policy, would have produced the directly opposite effect. A much duller man than Mr. Lincoln could not have failed to see that. Mr. Lincoln knew he must speak strongly and in no uncertain language. This he could do in reference to the maintenance of the Union and the Government, and reckon upon general approval at the North and some approval at the South. He affirmed that the Union was older than the Constitution, and was not, therefore, the product of the Constitution, but was an historical development. And from this perfectly sound and true premise, he drew the conclusion that "no State upon its own mere motion" could "lawfully get out of the Union ; that resolves and ordinances to that effect" were "legally void ; and that acts of violence, within any State or States, against the authority of the United States" were "insurrectionary or revolutionary according to circumstances." He declared that the Union was, despite the secession ordinances passed in seven of the "States" and the formation of the Confederate Government at Montgomery, still unbroken, and that he should take care that the laws of the Union should be faithfully executed in all the "States." And he announced his determination to hold, occupy, and possess the property and places belonging to the United States Government, and to collect the duties and the imposts everywhere. Here was certainly a definite policy, and one in the support of which all but the secessionists could unite.

The secessionists understood well enough that it made the issue with them plain and direct, and that they must yield or fight. They seized, however, upon some unfortunate expressions in the address, and twisted them into a quasi admission of the correctness of their secession theory. The exact words of Mr. Lincoln which were subjected to this interpretation ran as follows : "Beyond what may be necessary for these objects,"— that is, holding the property and places belonging to the United States and collecting the duties and imposts— "there will be no invasion, no using of force among the people anywhere. Where hostility to the United States in any interior locality shall be so great and universal as to prevent competent resident citizens from holding the Federal offices, there will be no attempt to force obnoxious strangers among the people for that object.

While the strict legal right may exist in the Government to enforce the exercise of these offices, the attempt to do so would be so irritating, and so nearly impracticable withal, that I deem it better to forego for the time the uses of such offices. The mails, unless repelled, will continue to be furnished in all parts of the Union. So far as possible the people everywhere shall have that sense of perfect security which is most favorable to calm thought and reflection. The course here indicated will be followed unless current events and experience shall show a modification or change to be proper, and in every case and exigency my best discretion will be exercised according to circumstances actually existing, and with a view and a hope of a peaceful solution of the national troubles and the restoration of fraternal sympathies and affection."

This language was certainly a little confusing to the minds of Union men, and by so much encouraging to the secessionists. Mr. Jefferson Davis subsequently cited these passages of the address as among the things which encouraged the hope at the South that the North would allow the South to go in peace. Mr. Lincoln should never have used the word invasion to describe the presence of the National Government in any " State " of the Union, or the entrance, so to speak, of the National Government into any "State" of the Union. The National Government is as much at home in any " State " organized within the boundaries of the United States as the " State" government, and the idea that the entrance of the United States soldiers into any "State" is an invasion rests upon the most radical misconception of the distinctions between international law and constitutional law.

Mr. Lincoln also made a mistake in announcing that he would not, for the time being, fill the United States

offices, and cause the execution of the United States
laws, in the interior of hostile communities.   This encouraged still further the hope and belief among the
masses of the people in the Southern "States" that
peaceable disunion was even probable.   It would have
been far better for them to have clearly understood at
this critical moment, that all the dangers of rebellion
must be risked by them in their attempt to break up the
Government.   It is true that Mr. Lincoln put in a saving proviso, of which they ought to have taken more
distinct notice, but it was natural that they should mag-
nify what was favorable to them as they did.

Taken all together the address certainly shows that
even Mr. Lincoln's mind was not entirely clear as to the
national character of our political system, but it also
shows that it was clearer than that of any of his contem-
poraries.   The whole country, North and South, was
more or less tainted with the doctrine of "States-
rights."   The difference between almost all of the public
men of the day was a difference in degree more than a
difference of kind.   It is wonderful that Mr. Lincoln
should have been, in the midst of such surroundings, so
clear as he was.

It is difficult for the present generation to realize how
confused in mind and purpose and how faint-hearted the
men of the North were at the moment when
Mr. Lincoln assumed the reins of govern-   Faint-heart-
ment.   All through the winter preceding his   North.
inauguration the evidences of demoralization in the Republican party had become increasingly manifest.   It
seemed as if the party had become frightened at its own
victory and at the consequences entailed by it.   The
municipal elections following the National and Commonwealth elections showed a great falling off from its ranks.
Its journalists appeared utterly at sea without compass or

rudder. Mr. Greeley himself, the leader among them, seemed never to that moment to have considered what must be the principle of his party in regard to the question of sovereignty, the deepest question of any and every political system. The after-world will never cease to wonder at that famous editorial of his, of November 9, 1860, in the chief organ of his party, his own *Tribune*, in which he wrote : "We hold, with Jefferson, to the inalienable right of communities to alter or abolish forms of government that have become oppressive or injurious ; and, if the cotton States shall decide that they can do better out of the Union than in it, we insist on letting them go in peace. The right to secede may be a revolutionary right, but it exists nevertheless ; and we do not see how one party can have a right to do what another party has the right to prevent. We must ever resist the right of any State to remain in the Union and nullify or defy the laws thereof ; to withdraw from the Union is quite another matter. And whenever a considerable section of our Union shall deliberately resolve to go out, we shall resist all coercive measures designed to keep her in. We hope never to live in a Republic whereof one section is pinned to the residue by bayonets." In this view Greeley fraternized with Davis and Stephens instead of with Lincoln. In his work on the "American Conflict," published three years and a half later, he endeavors to explain that his object in this strangely inconsistent editorial was to induce the Southerners to go into National convention for the settlement of all grievances and differences. Be this as it may, the Southerners cared nothing about his purposes. They had here the indorsement of their secession doctrine by the leading journalist of the Republican party, and they made the most of it. Many of the Republican journals followed the lead of the *Tribune;* and it is needless to say that the Democratic newspapers of the North vied with each other in justifying the actions of the secessionists and throwing the whole blame for the situation upon the Republican party. It is true that in the chagrin of defeat, they said much that was not really meant. But the secessionists did not understand that, or would not. They were only encouraged thereby in their extravagant estimate of the injuries they thought they were suffering at the hands of the Republican party, and in their hope that a divided North would prevent the Republican Administration from attempting to exercise its jurisdiction in the "seceding States" by force.

Still further, the people themselves held meetings, in which many Republicans participated, where nothing but conciliation and compromise were preached. The existence of such a state of feeling in the metropolitan city of New York is nothing surprising, even to the men of this generation. It rose, however, to a higher degree than we, of to-day, can well understand. The secession of the city itself from the Commonwealth of New York was recommended by Mayor Fernando Wood to the Common Council; and Mr. Daniel E. Sickles, afterward one of the bravest of the Northern soldiers who fought for the maintenance of the Union by military power, declared, in his notorious speech of December 10, 1860, upon the floor of Congress, that, in the event of secession in the South, New York City would free herself from the hated Republican "State" Government of New York, and throw open her ports to the free commerce of the world. Not only Democrats spoke thus, in New York and for New York, but old Whigs lent their voices to the encouragement of disunion. At the peace meeting of the 31st of January, 1861, in New York City, Mr. James S. Thayer, one of the most respected and influential of the

old line Whigs, said : " If the incoming Administration
shall attempt to carry out the line of policy that has been
foreshadowed," *i.e.*, the policy of enforcing the laws in
" States " which had declared their independence of the
Union, " we announce that, when the hand of Black
Republicanism turns blood red, and seeks from the fragments of the Constitution to construct a scaffolding for
coercion, another name for execution, we will reverse
the order of the French Revolution, and save the blood
of the people by making those who would inaugurate a
reign of terror the first victims of a national guillo-
tine."

But if the attitude of Democratic New York at that
juncture is surprising, what is to be thought of Republican Philadelphia, whose Republican Mayor was highly
applauded, at a peace meeting, for saying that the criticisms upon Southern slavery indulged in at the North
should cease, that " the misplaced teachings of the pul-
pit, the unwise rhapsodies of the lecture-room, the exciting appeals of the press, on the subject of slavery,
must be frowned down by a just and law - abiding
people."

The Abolitionist wing of the Republican party was
never noted for strong Unionism, and it was only to be
expected that the attitude of its members, at this juncture, would be an additional embarrassment to the President. How disloyal they were can be, perhaps, best
illustrated by an extract from Mr. Wendell Phillips's
New Bedford address of April 9, 1861 : ' Here are,"
he said, " a series of States, girdling the Gulf, who
think their peculiar institutions require that they should
have separate government. They have a right to decide
that question without appealing to you or me. . . .
Standing with the principles of '76 behind us who can
deny that right. . . . Abraham Lincoln has no

right to a soldier in Fort Sumter." The Abolitionists seemed to have no conception that the great movement of the world's history which lay just in front of them was the solution of the problem of national sovereignty as well as that of personal liberty, and that the attainment of abolition was possible only through the vindication of the sovereignty of the Nation.

Of course the Breckenridge Democrats at the North gave Mr. Lincoln no support. Nor were the Douglas Democrats much more to be relied on at the moment. Mr. Douglas himself said that the United States Government could not be jus- *Democratic attitude at the North.* tified in holding forts in the " seceding States," much less in retaking them, unless the intention was to reduce these " States " to subjection, which, at that time, seemed to him not to be seriously considered.

And lastly, Mr. Lincoln found, at first, no adequate support in his own Cabinet of advisers for the policy expressed in his inaugural address. Mr. Seward was bent upon maintaining peace, at almost any sacrifice. So were Cameron, *Lack of support in the Cabinet.* Bates, and Smith. Chase had " States-rights " views that were troublesome. Only Welles and Blair were in nearer sympathy with the President. It was Seward who gave the President the greatest embarrassment. He, as the Secretary of State for Foreign Affairs, was the person to whom the Confederate Government, in its assumed character of a foreign nation, would address itself; and much, very much, almost everything, depended upon his discretion, firmness, and loyalty in meeting such approaches.

This was the situation in the Government, and among the people of the North, when Mr. Lincoln's Administration was called upon to face the demands of the Southern Confederacy for the recognition of its independence. The problem was one of so great difficulty, and the manner in which it was treated is so little understood, that the whole subject requires to be dealt with in considerable detail, and with no little patience and impartiality.

CHAPTER VI

THE ATTEMPT OF THE SOUTHERN CONFEDERACY TO NEGOTIATE WITH THE GOVERNMENT OF THE UNITED STATES

The Appearance of the Confederate Commissioners in Washington and Their Mission—Justices Nelson and Campbell at the State Department—The Sumter Situation—Justice Campbell and the Confederate Commissioners—The Alleged Pledge of Evacuation—Mr. Lincoln's Plan for Relieving Sumter—The Embarrassment of Mr. Seward—Rumors of the Preparations to Relieve Sumter—President Lincoln's Notice to Governor Pickens—Mr. Davis's View of the Alleged Pledges—The Departure of the Expedition from New York—The Confederate Commissioners and the Memorandum of Mr. Seward—The Demand for the Evacuation of Sumter.

MR. SEWARD had not been in office more than a week when he was confronted with the question of the attitude which the United States Government should take toward the Southern Confederacy. In compliance with a resolution of the Confederate Congress, passed in the middle of February, the Confederate President had appointed three highly respectable citizens of the Confederacy, as he called them, Mr. Martin J. Crawford of Georgia, Mr. John Forsyth of Alabama and Mr. A. B. Roman of Louisiana, as commissioners from the Confederate Government to the Government of the United States for the purpose of instituting negotiations with the United States Government for "the settlement of all matters between the States forming the Confederacy

The appearance of the Confederate Commissioners in Washington and their mission.

151

and their other late confederates of the United States, in relation to the public property and the public debt at the time of their withdrawal from them." One of these gentlemen, Mr. Crawford, had arrived in Washington several days before the expiration of President Buchanan's term. He was provided with a letter of recommendation to Mr. Buchanan from Mr. Jefferson Davis. Mr. Davis did not attach his official title to his signature, from which we may fairly conclude that the letter was meant to be quasi-confidential. Mr. Davis explained years afterward that Mr. Buchanan had intimated to him, through Mr. Hunter of Virginia, " that he would be happy to receive a commissioner from the Confederate States, and would refer to the Senate any communication that might be made through such a commission."

It is certainly difficult to believe that President Buchanan could have consciously authorized Mr. Hunter to make such a statement to Mr. Davis, after having refused to have anything to do with the South Carolina commissioners, and after the castigation applied to him by Mr. Davis, in the Senate of the United States, therefor. The President had, as we have seen, become stiffer in his Unionism after that event, rather than more limp. On the other hand, the attendant circumstances go to prove the correctness of Mr. Davis's statement of Mr. Hunter's communication to him. It is, of course, possible, not to say probable, that Mr. Hunter, in his great desire for a peaceable solution of the mighty question confronting the whole country, had put an exaggerated interpretation upon what Mr. Buchanan had said, persuading himself, if he was conscious of it at all, that it could do no harm, and might be productive of great good. Certain it is that President Buchanan promptly refused to see Mr. Crawford, or to have anything to do with his commission. Mr. Crawford considered this attitude of President Buchanan to be a violation of a promise, and attributed it to the fact that "he had become fearfully panic-stricken" between the date of "his promise" and the arrival of the commissioner. Despite this rebuff, however, Mr. Crawford waited around Washington, taking note of everything he saw, for the arrival of his colleagues.

About a week after the inauguration of Mr. Lincoln Mr. Forsyth appeared; and Crawford and Forsyth immediately applied verbally, through Senator Hunter, it is supposed, to the new Secretary of State, Mr. Seward, for an unofficial interview, which Mr. Seward promptly, but respectfully, declined to grant. Whereupon the two commissioners addressed to Mr. Seward a written request for the appointment of a time when they might present their credentials to the President of the United States and explain to him the object of their mission. The date of this letter was March 12th, and the contents of it explained the general purposes of the mission, which were, briefly, to officially inform the Government of the United States of the withdrawal of seven "States" from the United States and the formation by them of a new Confederacy, and "to secure a speedy adjustment of all questions growing out of the political separation," thus effected "*de facto* and *de jure.*"

Mr. Seward wrote his reply to this communication on the 14th day of March. He put it into the form of a memorandum, unsigned by him, and placed it in the State Department to be called for by the commissioners. The Confederate authorities professed to find Mr. Seward's methods in this transaction inexplicable; but if they had only reflected that Mr. Seward was cautiously seeking to meet them in a manner which could not in any possible way be tortured into an official recognition of them or their agents, they might have understood him.

Mr. Seward's memorandum contained a full *résumé* of the contents of the letter of the so-called commissioners, and then went on to decline to fix any time for receiving these gentlemen calling themselves commissioners of the "Confederate States," or to have any official intercourse whatsoever with them, on the ground of the nullity of the whole movement, which they professed to represent, from the point of view of the Constitution and the political system of the United States. Mr. Seward stated in his memorandum that he had submitted his views as expressed therein to President Lincoln, and that the President coincided with him in them, and sanctioned his refusal of official intercourse with Messrs. Forsyth and Crawford. He furthermore called the attention of the so-called commissioners to President Lincoln's inaugural address, a copy of which was enclosed with the memorandum.

On the same day that Mr. Seward filed this memorandum in the State Department, there to be copied, and the copy to be furnished to Messrs. Forsyth and Crawford, upon application, Mr. Justice Nelson of the Supreme Court of the United States, a citizen of New York, presented himself, of his own motion, before the Secretary of State, the Secretary of the Treasury, and the Attorney-General, Messrs. Seward, Chase and Bates, for the purpose of influencing them by argument toward a pacific policy, and of stating to them that, from a careful study of the Constitution and laws of the United States, he had reached the conclusion that, without very serious violations of the same, coercion could not be successfully effected by the Executive Department of the Government.

Returning from his visit to the State Department, we are told that he accidentally met one of his colleagues upon the Supreme Bench, Mr. Justice Campbell of Alabama, and communicated to him the fact and the purpose of his interview with the Secretaries and the gist of the conversation with them. Mr. Seward had, of course, regarded Justice Nelson as a friend to the Union, and had conferred with him very frankly. He told him that the Administration was face to face with the secessionist Confederacy upon two issues ; that the first was the question of holding or abandoning Fort Sumter, and the second was the question of receiving the Confederate commissioners ; and that the second question, if pressed at the moment, would embarrass the Administration in dealing with the first.

The situation in reference to Sumter was as follows : On the 3d of March' the Confederate General Beauregard had assumed command at Charleston The Sumter and had virtually invested Fort Sumter. On situation. the 4th of March word had been received by the President from Major Anderson that he had about one month's rations in the Fort, and if not relieved within that time, that he would be obliged to abandon the post or starve. Upon the receipt of this message the President immediately took counsel with General Scott, and was advised by the General that evacuation was almost inevitable, and that at least four months would be necessary to make ready an expedition to relieve the garrison.

Mr. Lincoln then turned to his Cabinet and put the following question to each of its members : "Assuming it to be possible to now provision Fort Sumter, under all the circumstances is it wise to attempt it ?" Chase and Blair replied affirmatively, but the other five thought it would be unwise. Seward especially so expressed himself. This occurred on the 15th of March, the very day that Mr. Seward filed his memorandum in answer to the letter of the Confederate commissioners in the State

Department, and the very day of Justice Nelson's visit to Mr. Seward. The Cabinet meeting had taken place only a few hours before Justice Nelson's visit, and, therefore, what had occurred at the meeting was fresh in Mr. Seward's mind. It is true that Mr. Lincoln himself had never expressed any other purpose than the one declared in his inaugural in reference to Fort Sumter, which was the determination to hold possession of all the places belonging to the United States, and that he did not, at the meeting on the 15th of March, commit himself, in the slightest degree, to any other course or view. But Mr. Seward had not yet learned that Mr. Lincoln was not to be directed by his Cabinet, even when the majority for or against a proposed policy was five to two, with Mr. Seward himself among the five. Knowing then what he did, at the moment of Justice Nelson's visit, Mr. Seward felt quite certain that the withdrawal of the troops from Fort Sumter would take place within a fortnight. He very probably told Justice Nelson what his impressions were in regard to the impending evacuation, and pointed out to him how the demands of the Confederate commissioners for official recognition, at that very juncture, had so crowded the Administration as to force it to take a stand, which might put an end to peace efforts altogether. That stand was the reply to the letter of the Confederate commissioners, which reply was, at the very moment, lying in the State Department awaiting the call of the messenger from the commissioners for it.

These were the facts and the impressions which Mr. Justice Nelson imparted to Mr. Justice Campbell when they accidentally met in the street just after Justice Nelson's interview with the Secretaries. On the spur of the moment Justice Nelson suggested that Justice Campbell might be of service in the cause of peace, and

Justice Campbell immediately expressed his willingness to do anything within his power. Whereupon Justice Nelson returned to the State Department, accompanied by Justice Campbell, and sought Mr. Seward again. Mr. Seward naturally supposed that Justice Campbell was a Union man, holding as he did one of the highest offices in the gift of the United States Government, and felt, therefore, no hesitation in repeating before him what he had already said to Justice Nelson. As a matter of fact, if we may judge from the course of subsequent events, Justice Campbell's heart was, at that moment, with the secessionists, and he was anxious to induce Mr. Seward to recognize the commissioners from the Confederate Government and treat with them as the diplomatic representatives of an independent nation. He saw, however, that what Mr. Seward had said to Justice Nelson was true, namely, that the hands of the Administration were full with the Sumter matter, and that if the commissioners should apply for the answer to their demand, that answer must be the memorandum which Mr. Seward had just filed in the State Department. It was also plain to Justice Campbell that any pressure brought upon Mr. Seward by the commissioners might result in a change of Mr. Seward's attitude on the question of evacuating Fort Sumter.

Justice Campbell then took it upon himself to see the Confederate commissioners, and persuade them to delay sending their messenger for Mr. Seward's answer to their letter. In the interview between him and them, the notion was evolved that the evacuation of Fort Sumter would be ordered by Mr. Lincoln's Administration, provided they would not ask for an immediate reply to their communication of March 12th. The connection between the two subjects having been thus established in their minds,

Justice Campbell and the Confederate Commissioners.

they apparently soon began to think, and then to say, that the evacuation of Fort Sumter had been promised them, pledged them, provided they would delay their demand for the answer to their letter to Mr. Seward. Justice Campbell in a letter to Colonel Munford, published in the year 1874, stated that he said to Mr. Seward, in the interview of March 15th, that he concurred with him in the view that the Administration could not undertake anything more at the moment than the evacuation of Fort Sumter, and that he would see the commissioners and write to Mr. Davis himself ; that he asked Mr. Seward what he should write Mr. Davis in regard to Forts Sumter and Pickens, and that Mr. Seward authorized him to say that before the letter could reach its destination Mr. Davis would learn by telegram that the order for the evacuation of Sumter had been given, and that no change would be made in the status of Fort Pickens ; that he communicated these "assurances" given by Mr. Seward to the commissioners and to Mr. Davis ; that Mr. Crawford objected to the delay in pressing for recognition, and finally yielded only upon the reduction of Mr. Seward's alleged statements to writing and the personal assurance of the Justice that, as written down by him, they were correct and accurate ; and, finally, that he (Justice Campbell) communicated in writing to Mr. Seward the fact that he had furnished Mr. Crawford with a written document, in which he had expressed entire confidence in the evacuation of Fort Sumter within ten days, and in the preservation of the existing status by the United States Government toward the "Southern Confederate States," and had advised against the commissioners pressing for an immediate reply to their note of March 12th to Mr. Seward as likely to be productive of evil results.

These are the elements out of which the Confederate

Government constructed a pledge by Mr. Seward, and through Mr. Seward by Mr. Lincoln, to evacuate Fort Sumter within ten days, provided the com- The alleged pledge of evacuation. missioners would not embarrass Mr. Lincoln's Administration by pressing for an answer to their demand for recognition.

Five days subsequent to these interviews between Mr. Seward and the Justices, and between the Justices and the Confederate commissioners, the commissioners, we are told by Mr. Justice Campbell, telegraphed to General Beauregard at Charleston to know if Sumter had been evacuated, or if anything indicating intention to evacuate had occurred ; and received immediate reply that Major Anderson was still strengthening his defences. Justice Campbell tells us, further, that he, accompanied by Mr. Justice Nelson, sought Mr. Seward again, and showed him the despatch from Beauregard, and that Mr. Seward assured him that the delay in evacuating Sumter was accidental, and promised that any change "in the resolution in reference to Sumter or Pickens" would be communicated to him. These statements by Mr. Seward were then written down by Justice Campbell and the paper was sent to Mr. Crawford, and Mr. Seward was informed in writing by Justice Campbell of these facts.

The Confederate Government regarded this episode as completely confirmatory of a pledge on the part of Mr. Lincoln's Administration to evacuate Fort Sumter. The actual facts did not warrant the conclusion, either in regard to the making, or the confirming, of a pledge, but they could easily be distorted so as to appear to do so, and it was not unnatural that, in that time of anxiety and confusion, this happened with good faith.

Down to this moment, that is, March 20th, the President had communicated his thoughts, much less his determination, if indeed he had reached any, to no one except Mr. Blair, who, he knew, agreed with him in opinion, and in whom he had perfect faith. The question of secession did not fall within the domain of any particular executive depart-ment, and the President felt himself at liberty to confide in that member of his Cabinet upon whose sympathy he could most fully count. Through Mr. Blair he came into communication with a brave and resourceful man, who had been in the naval service of the United States, Mr. G. V. Fox. Mr. Fox was a brother-in-law of Mr. Blair. He was the man who had proposed to Mr. Buchanan, during the preceding February, to undertake an expedition for the relief of Sumter. Mr. Fox laid substantially the same plan before Mr. Lincoln a day or two before the first interview between Mr. Seward and the two Justices occurred. Mr. Lincoln now acquainted General Scott with his communications with Mr. Fox, and then laid the proposition of Mr. Fox before the Cabinet for consideration. General Scott discouraged the plan, and only two members of the Cabinet favored it, Chase and Blair. The President then sent Fox to Sumter, and Hurlbut and Lamon to Charleston, to examine the condition of things on the spot before making his decision. Fox arrived in Charleston on the 21st of the month (March), and immediately applied to Governor Pickens for a permit to visit Fort Sumter, which was granted, according to the Governor's statement, upon the assurance that his purposes were pacific. Mr. Fox and President Lincoln undoubtedly considered a project for sending provisions to the hungry men in Fort Sumter as containing no hostile purpose. Governor Pickens also stated, in his message to the South Carolina Legislature, at the beginning of its session in November of 1861, that Mr. Lincoln's other emissary,

Mr. Lin-coln's plan for relieving Sum-ter.

Colonel Lamon, appeared in Charleston a few days after Mr. Fox, and told the Governor that he had come "to try to arrange for the removal of the troops" from Sumter, and that he hoped to return to Charleston in a few days for that purpose.

Colonel Lamon did not, however, return to Charleston, and at the end of the month, Governor Pickens sent an inquiry to the Confederate commissioners in Washington in regard to him and his mission. This despatch from Pickens reached Washington on the 30th. The day before it came, Mr. Lincoln had again laid the question of relieving Fort Sumter before his Cabinet. This time Chase, Blair and Welles expressed themselves in favor of making the attempt, and Bates wavered in his opposition to it. The President had still kept his own counsel, but Mr. Seward now saw that evacuation could no longer be counted on, although he still gave his voice for it. When, then, Justice Campbell brought Governor Pickens's inquiry of the Confederate commissioners to Mr. Seward, as he did so soon as it was received in Washington, Mr. Seward had been disabused of the idea that the evacuation of Fort Sumter was certain, or even probable. Mr. Seward immediately made known to the President the contents of Governor Pickens's despatch, and Mr. Lincoln promptly disavowed Lamon's authority to promise what Pickens claimed he did in the despatch.

On the 1st day of April Mr. Seward saw Justice Campbell and informed him what the President had said in regard to Governor Pickens's telegram of inquiry. Justice Campbell now began to reveal his sympathy with the secessionists, *The embarrassment of Mr. Seward.* and Mr. Seward became more cautious in his utterances. He fell back now on the President, and ceased to advance opinions of his own in regard to what the Administration would determine to do. President Lincoln allowed him to assure the commissioners, through Justice Campbell, "that the Government would not attempt to supply Fort Sumter without giving notice to Governor Pickens." This is the only assurance which President Lincoln ever gave, or authorized to be given, and it is an exaggeration to make a pledge even out of this.

During the next few days rumors of the preparations to relieve the beleaguered and hungry troops at Sumter began to float about Washington. On the 7th (April) Justice Campbell addressed another communication to Mr. Seward, asking if his assurances still held ; to which Mr. Seward replied : "Faith as to Sumter fully kept. Wait and see." On the next day, Mr. Crawford sent a despatch to General Beauregard at Charleston, which ran as follows : "Accounts uncertain because of the constant vacillation of the Government. We were reassured yesterday that the status of Sumter would not be changed without previous notice to Governor Pickens, but we have no faith in them. The war policy prevails in the Cabinet at this time." It would appear from this language that the only pledges or assurances which the Confederate commissioners considered as having been made to them by the United States Government were contained in Mr. Seward's communication to them, through Justice Campbell, on April 1st, viz., that the United States Government would not undertake to supply Fort Sumter without giving notice to Governor Pickens.

On the same day that Beauregard received this despatch, Mr. Chew, one of the subordinates of the State Department at Washington, accompanied by Lieutenant Talbot, appeared in Charleston, and sought both Governor Pickens and General Beauregard. When admitted to audience, Mr. Chew read to the Governor and the General the following notice : " I am directed by the President of the United States to notify you to expect an attempt will be made to supply Fort Sumter with provisions only ; and that if such an attempt be not resisted, no attempt to throw in men, arms, or ammunition will be made, without further notice, except in case of an attack upon the Fort."

In commenting upon this communication to Governor Pickens, the ex-President of the Confederacy wrote, twenty years later : " Thus disappeared the last vestige of the plighted faith and pacific pledges of the Federal Government." There is no doubt that the Government at Montgomery held this view at the time. Nevertheless it is difficult to understand how they could have done so. The Government of the United States gave but one assurance, namely, that it would not undertake to supply Fort Sumter without giving notice to Governor Pickens, and this it fulfilled to the letter. And President Lincoln gave this assurance, not for the purpose of delaying any answer to the Confederate commissioners on the question of recognizing them, but for the purpose of delaying an attack upon the Fort until he could get his relief expedition in readiness.

The transports bearing the means of relief to the Sumter garrison left port on April 7th, and if not hindered might have been expected to arrive in Charleston Harbor on the 9th or 10th. There was no war vessel with them. The Secretary of the Navy, Mr. Welles, intended to send the war-ship Powhatan from New York with them, but the President ordered the Powhatan, at the last moment, to go to Pensacola for the relief of Fort Pickens. The President issued this order through Mr. Seward without the knowledge of Mr. Welles, and saw his mistake too late to rectify it.

Mr. Davis's view of the pledges.

The departure of the expedition from New York.

When the Confederate commissioners at Washington learned of the notice to Governor Pickens and General Beauregard, they sent their secretary to the State Department for the official answer to their letter of March 12th. So soon as they received and read the memorandum of the Secretary of State, they immediately addressed a communication to him, in which they declared that they did not, in their letter of March 12th, "ask the Government of the United States to recognize the independence of the Confederate States," but that "they only asked audience to adjust in a spirit of amity and peace, the new relations springing from a manifest and accomplished revolution in the Government of the late Federal Union," and that the refusal on the part of the Government of the United States "to entertain these overtures for a peaceful solution, the active naval and military preparations of this Government, and a formal notice to the commanding General in the harbor of Charleston that the President intends to provision Fort Sumter by forcible means, if necessary, are viewed by the undersigned, and can only be received by the world, as a declaration of war against the Confederate States." They then declared that they, in behalf of the Confederate Government, accepted the gage of battle. They closed their communication with an explanation of the delay in demanding the reply to their letter of March 12th. They said in reference to this that their secretary called at the State Department for the answer on the 13th of March, and was informed by the Assistant Secretary of State that Mr. Seward had not had time to consider their note; that he was asked by the Assistant Secretary for the addresses of Messrs. Forsyth and Crawford, and was told by him that any reply which might be made to their note would be sent to their lodgings; that they

The Confederate commissioners and the memorandum of Mr. Seward.

consented to the delay of twenty-three days in receiving an answer " not of their own volition and without cause," but because of the assurances of Mr. Seward, communicated to them by Justice Campbell, that Fort Sumter would be evacuated, and no attempt would be made to provision it without previous notice to Governor Pickens ; and that " it was only when all these anxious efforts for peace had been exhausted, and it became clear that Mr. Lincoln had determined to appeal to the sword to reduce the people of the Confederate States to the will of the section or party whose President he " was " that " they " resumed the official negociations temporarily suspended, and sent ' their ' secretary for a reply to ' their ' official note of March 12th."

Mr. Seward made no reply to the propositions and assumptions of this document, beyond acknowledging its reception.   And the commissioners shook from off their feet the dust of the wicked capital, as they considered it, and turned their faces and their footsteps southward.

Meanwhile General Beauregard had telegraphed the Confederate Secretary of War at Montgomery word of the notice from President Lincoln to Govern- The demand or Pickens of the intention on the part of for the evacuation of Sum- the United States Government to provision ter. Fort Sumter.   Beauregard's despatch was dated April 8th.   The reply from the Confederate Secretary was not made until the 10th.   The Confederate Government is thus seen to have acted with deliberation.   The reply was an order to General Beauregard to demand the evacuation of Fort Sumter, and to reduce it, if the demand should be refused.   Beauregard immediately answered that the demand for surrender would be made at noon of the next day, the 11th.   The Confederate War Secretary replied to this by advising an earlier hour, but

Beauregard telegraphed him that he had special reasons for the hour designated.

Accordingly, at about two o'clock in the afternoon of April 11th, General Beauregard sent two of his aids, Colonel Chesnut and Captain Lee, to Major Anderson with the summons for evacuation. Major Anderson immediately replied, declining compliance. At about the same time that Beauregard received Anderson's answer, advices reached him from Montgomery directing him not to bombard Sumter, if Anderson would fix a time when he would evacuate, and agree not to use his guns against the Confederate forces in the meantime, unless first fired on by the Confederates.

In accordance with these instructions Beauregard sent a second demand to Anderson, at about eleven o'clock in the evening. Anderson replied to this in the early morning of the 12th, and offered to engage to evacuate the Fort at noon of the 15th, provided he should not receive prior to that time controlling instructions from his Government or additional supplies, and provided he should be furnished with necessary and proper means of transportation. These conditions of surrender were not acceptable to the Confederate commander, and his reply, dated at twenty minutes past three in the morning of the 12th, informed Major Anderson that fire would be opened upon the Fort by the Confederate batteries in one hour from that time.

Accordingly at half-past four o'clock in the morning of the 12th of April, the Confederate guns began to hurl their balls against the Fort covered by the flag of the Union. The gates of Janus were flung open, and the great question of the sovereignty of the Nation or the sovereignty of the "States" was appealed from the forum to the battlefield.

CHAPTER VII

THE CAPTURE OF FORT SUMTER AND THE CALL TO ARMS

The Offensive and the Defensive in the Sumter Affair—Rebellion
or War—The Surrender of Sumter—The Union Driven to
Take Up Arms—The Call for Troops—The Refusals to Obey
the President's Call for Troops—Prompt Action of the Gov-
ernors of the Northern States—The Attitude of Mr. Douglas
—The Peril of the Capital—Virginia Convention Passes the
Secession Ordinance—Seizure of Harper's Ferry and Gosport
Navy Yard—The Sixth Massachusetts in Baltimore—The Ef-
fect of These Events on the Country—The Attitude of John
Bell after the Fall of Sumter—Tennessee's Treaty with the
Confederacy—Tennessee's Secession—The Blockade Procla-
mations—North Carolina's Secession—Secession in Arkansas—
Secession in Missouri Attempted—Secession in Missouri Foiled
—Attempts at Secession in Kentucky—The Attitude of the
Government and of the People—The President's Policy toward
Kentucky—William Nelson—Major Anderson Sent to Cincin-
nati—L. H. Rousseau—Manifestations of Magoffin's Disloyal
Purposes—The Loyalty of the Legislature—The Unionists
Elect the Congressional Delegation—Northern Anger Aroused
by the Situation in Maryland—Rumors of Attack upon the Cap-
ital—General Lee's Conduct—The Exodus of the Secessionists from Washington—The Occupation of Maryland—The
Maryland Legislature at Frederick—The Isolation of Baltimore—Triumph of Union Cause in Maryland—The Defence
of Washington.

MR. GREELEY wrote in his "American Conflict,"
that the Confederacy had no alternative to an attack
upon Fort Sumter except its own dissolution. If he

meant by this that the Confederates acted defensively in attacking Sumter he was still laboring under that bale-ful confusion of mind which produced the strange editorial in the *Tribune* of November 9, 1860. Such a proposition could only be defended upon the principle that the Commonwealths were separately and completely sovereign under the Constitution of the United States; that the United States was nothing more than a central government, and that this central government was nothing more than a joint agent of these separate sovereigns, which each of them might dispense with at its own pleasure; and, finally, that when a Commonwealth should dispense with this agency, its presence thereafter within the original territorial limits of the Commonwealth, even in the places subject to its exclusive jurisdiction, was the presence of a foreign invader. This was the doctrine of the secessionists, but it found no warrant either in the history of the formation of the Constitution, or in any provision contained in the text of it, or in the practice of the Government during more than seventy years of existence under it. It was simply a revolutionary claim which stamped its upholders as rebels until they should succeed in establishing it by physical force.

The offensive and the defensive in the Sumter affair.

There can be no question in the mind of the historian and constitutional lawyer to-day that the "States" claiming to have seceded from the Union were the aggressors. The South Carolina authorities fired the first shot of the conflict when they opened their batteries upon the *Star of the West*, on the 9th of January, and the Confederate agent of the "States" claiming to have seceded fired the second shot in Charleston Harbor on the morning of April 12th, and in both cases the shot fired was against the supremacy of that law and authority to

which those who did the deed owed obedience and
allegiance.

The more puzzling query is whether the result of these
acts was rebellion or war.   It certainly was not a war between independent nations.   That was the   Rebellion or
deepest issue of the conflict, and the outcome   war.
proved the contrary.   Neither was it in a strictly correct sense civil war.   It was not a struggle between two
parties for the possession of the Government, each claiming to be legitimate ; nor were the belligerent parties
composed generally of adherents resident within the
same localities.   It was really the attempt of a section to
constitute itself a separate country, a separate nation,
a separate sovereignty.   And the first step in such a
procedure is, and must be, rebellion, which, if successful, is then termed, in political nomenclature, revolution.   From a strictly legal point of view, every person
engaged in it makes himself subject to the criminal law
of the Government against which he rebels, but when
the spirit of rebellion becomes so general throughout a
large section of a country as to take possession of the
vast majority of the people within that section, and
when the rebels constitute responsible government and
regularly organized armies, and proceed to battle for
the recognition of their claims according to the methods of regular war, then the practice of the world is
not to deal with them as traitors under the criminal
law, but as belligerents in quasi-war.   That is, while
the government against which the rebellion is directed
in such a case may, in strict legality, treat every rebel
as a traitor under its criminal law, international principle and good public policy recommend to the government, in such a situation, a quasi-international
treatment of the rebels, if not of the question of the
rebellion.

We arrive at truth and justice, the basis of law, only through the medium of human interpretation, and we determine, in democratic countries, the correctness of that interpretation by the power of conviction which it exerts over the minds of great numbers of the people. When, then, there is anything like a balance of numbers in a division of the whole country, the employment of criminal conceptions, and the application of the criminal law, by the party in possession of the original government against the other party results, usually, in barbarizing both parties.   There are conceivable situations, indeed, in which this must be done ; when, for example, the question is government or anarchy.   But when it is, as it usually is in these cases, a question of one government or another, then the world-ethic of a democratic age recommends toleration of differences so far, at least, as to ascribe a rational sincerity to all, and to treat those in rebellion more as belligerents than as traitors.

This is not an entirely logical position, from the point of view of either of the governments concerned.   Both are liable to confound the qualities of belligerency with the rights of independence.   And while one will deny belligerency as involving a recognition of independence, the other will claim independence as involved in a recognition of belligerency.   But if we regard the question from the point of view of the world's progress in civilization, a progress in which so much has been accomplished through antagonism, we may perceive the philosophy, if not the logic, of the proposition and the practice.

Major Anderson and his little band of loyal soldiers defended Fort Sumter for thirty-four hours against the shot and shell of the Confederate batteries, and when its walls were beaten down upon them, and the barracks set on fire by red-hot shot, surrendered the work on the condition of being allowed to withdraw in possession of their individual and company property, and to salute the flag of the Union in departing. The surrender of Sumter. The steamboat *Isabel* took them down the harbor, and transferred them to the *Baltic*, which was lying in wait for them outside the bar. On the 18th, they arrived at the port of New York, and Major Anderson immediately made his official announcement of the surrender to the Secretary of War.

If the Confederacy had no alternative to the attack upon Fort Sumter but its own dissolution, the Union had now no alternative to its dissolution but the overthrow of the Confederacy. It is true that no person had been killed on either side, The Union driven to take up arms. except by the bursting of a gun in the final salute to the flag, but the sovereignty of the Union had been forcibly expelled from territory which it had possessed for decades, and over which it still claimed the rights of property and dominion. That sovereignty must now repossess itself of this territory and reassert and re-establish the supremacy of its will, or else it must accept the proposition that "discontented individuals too few in number to control administration, according to organic law," may, under any pretence they may desire, break up their government by taking shelter under a claim of sovereignty in the localities or communities in which they reside, to which they may profess to owe a paramount allegiance. Verily, it was the question whether popular government should perish from the earth.

President Lincoln did not wait for Major Anderson's official report. He recognized that the time for deliberation and discussion had now passed, and the time for action had arrived. He saw clearly that he must now go forward with a firm hand and a determined purpose, if he would save the Nation from dissolution, yea, if he would even save its capital from those in rebellion against its sovereignty.

On the day after the fall of Sumter he issued the call to arms. This remarkable proclamation should be carefully studied, since it contained Mr. Lincoln's conception of the situation which confronted him. In it Mr. Lincoln first declared that the execution of the laws of the United States were, and for some time had been, " obstructed in the States of South Carolina, Georgia, Alabama, Florida, Mississippi, Louisiana, and Texas by combinations too powerful to be suppressed by the ordinary course of judicial proceedings or by the powers vested in the marshals by law." Mr. Lincoln thus distinctly indicated the view, at the outset, that he was dealing, not with nations or even with " States," but with private combinations of persons in rebellion against the sovereignty of the United States, and the constitutional and legal authority of the United States Government; that secession was an utter abortion; and that the claim of the rebels in South Carolina, Georgia, and the other communities, to be the " States" of South Carolina, Georgia, and the like, was an absolute impossibility in principle.

Dealing, according to this conception, with a domestic insurrection, and not with a foreign enemy, Mr. Lincoln derived his duties and his powers from those clauses of the Constitution which imposed upon him the obligation to see to the faithful execution of the laws of the United States, and conferred upon him the means of discharging the trust. There was no difficulty, from his point of view, in finding executive power to use the existing army and navy to maintain the authority of the Government

The call for troops.

Lincoln's theory of the situation.

against insurgents, but it was not so easy to find the executive power to increase the forces, and without this the arm of flesh would not be strong enough to deal successfully with the situation. The Constitution gave Congress the exclusive power to create armies and navies, and to provide for bringing the militia of the " States " into the service of the United States, that is, for bringing them under the command of the President of the United States. By a statute of sixty-five years' standing, however, Congress had conferred upon the President, under its power to provide for calling the militia of the "States" into the service of the Union, the authority to issue the call himself at his own discretion, and the Supreme Court had decided, more than thirty years before, not only that this statute was constitutional, but that any militiaman refusing to obey the command of the President calling him into the service of the United States was subject to the process of a United States court-martial. Here, then, was, without question, an executive power to increase the military forces under the command of the President to any extent which the population and resources of the country would bear, since every male citizen between the ages of eighteen and forty-five was, at that moment, by another congressional statute, subject to militia service. As a matter of fact, however, the general organization of the militia on the basis of this law requiring universal military service had fallen into desuetude. So far as actual organization was concerned, the militia of 1861, in the United States, was more a volunteer system than a compulsory service. As organized, therefore, at that date, its strength was far short of what the Congressional statute provided and required.

President Lincoln was, of course, obliged to take things as he found them. There was no time to spare in transactions with the "States," however loyally disposed they might be, for executing the Congressional act for the universal organization of the militia. The President must address himself, first of all, to the existing organizations. He despatched his commands to the Governors of all the "States," except those in which the insurrection existed. He addressed the Governors in their capacities as the highest officers of the militia in their respective "States." Good political science, and a sound construction of the Constitution itself, made them his military subordinates in the matter of bringing the militia into the service of the United States, if no farther, and a refusal by any one of them to obey his call ought to have been considered an offence of the highest character, to be dealt with by a court-martial of the United States.

The President stated that the first service to which the seventy-five thousand militia thus called into the service of the United States would probably be assigned would be the repossession of the "forts, places, and property" which the insurgents had seized. He did not appear from this to be especially anxious about the safety of the capital. The events of the next five days, however, made it manifest that the first duty of the new army must be the defence of Washington.

The proclamation contained, further, the command of the President to the insurgents to disperse within twenty days. And it closed with the summons to the two Houses of Congress to meet in extraordinary session on the 4th day of the following July. Whatever may have been the President's reasons for deferring this meeting for so long, it certainly showed strong nerve in him to be willing to carry the great responsibility alone for such a period.

The Governors of Virginia, North Carolina, Kentucky,

Tennessee, Missouri, and Arkansas flatly and insolently refused to obey the President's call for troops from those Commonwealths, and the Governors of Dela- *The refusals* ware and Maryland did not obey it.   No ordi- *to obey the President's* nance of secession had as yet been passed in *call for troops.* any of these Commonwealths, and no one of them claimed to be out of the Union.   From a true juristic point of view, as well as from the point of view of a sound political science, these men made themselves, by their military insubordination, subject to a United States court-martial.   They ought to have been arrested, tried, and condemned by a military tribunal for one of the most grievous offences known to public jurisprudence. It was the physical power to carry out such a procedure that was lacking ; and the fear of the effect of such an unprecedented course upon the inhabitants of these Commonwealths might have deterred the President from using it, had he possessed it.   At this day such an attitude on the part of "State" Governors would be regarded very differently from what it was then, and might be dealt with very differently.

The Governors of the non-slaveholding Commonwealths, on the other hand, all answered with alacrity. All of these Commonwealths east of the *Prompt ac-* Rocky Mountains, except only Rhode Island, *tion of the* had Governors of Mr. Lincoln's own party ; *Governors of the Northern* and the Democratic Governor of Rhode Isl- *States.* and, Mr. William Sprague, was as prompt as any of these. He even proposed to lay aside his civil functions and put himself at the head of the contingent from his Commonwealth.   And the great leader of the Northern Democracy, Senator Douglas, called immediately *The attitude* upon the President, and assured him of his *of Mr. Doug-* loyal sympathy and co-operation in the im- *las.* pending conflict.   This great patriotic act of Mr. Douglas made the North a unit substantially in the support of the Administration. *The divided* North, upon which the secessionists had counted, had now vanished like a will-o'-the-wisp before the rising sun. The North viewed the question now no longer as slavery against freedom, but as national existence, as the maintenance of government, as the suppression of rebellion against lawful authority. With this consolidation of the public opinion of the North in his support, Mr. Lincoln felt that the most important field had been won. For this he had worked and waited since the day of his inauguration, and he viewed the realization of his hopes with supreme satisfaction and sincere thankfulness.

The other chief object of his solicitude, however, the preservation of the border slaveholding Commonwealths against the passage of secession ordinances, was now placed in extreme jeopardy, and with it the safety of the capital was imperilled.

The peril of the capital.

We have seen that the Governors of all these Commonwealths except only Delaware and Maryland, had refused obedience to the President's call for troops, and in some cases had threatened to array themselves against the military power and authority of the Government, and that the Governors of Delaware and Maryland did not obey the call. While the action of these two functionaries was not positively hostile, it still gave the President more anxiety than the more pronounced attitude of the others, since these Commonwealths lay geographically between the capital and the loyal North. General Scott had collected a few companies of regulars, and seemed to think that he could hold out against any attack until the arrival of re-inforcements, provided they should be promptly forwarded.

There was a general belief in Washington that a well-matured conspiracy for the capture and destruction of the city existed, and the alarm over the situation for the first few days after the capture of Sumter was genuine and great.   If the Marylanders would furnish no troops for the relief of the city, and should resist the passage of troops from the loyal Commonwealths through their territory, it was manifest that such delay might be thus caused in receiving re-inforcements at Washington as to give the conspirators, if there were any, a fair opportunity to execute their purposes.   The Confederate Secretary of War, Mr. L. P. Walker, proclaimed in his speech of April 12th at Montgomery, that the Confederate flag would float over Washington City before the 1st of May. And the secessionist leaders in Virginia considered the capture of the city as one of the first movements which Virginia should undertake after deciding to join the Confederacy.   It was now conjectured in Washington that the plan of the conspirators was to have the Marylanders prevent the passage of troops from the North across their "State"; gather Virginia troops along the Potomac opposite Washington; effect the secession of Maryland; then have Maryland reclaim possession of the District of Columbia upon the same principle that South Carolina claimed Fort Sumter, viz., by virtue of her sovereign right to resume all of her grants to the United States Government at her own pleasure; and finally enforce the claim, if the United States Government should refuse to surrender the District, by the military forces of the two "States."

The events of the next five days after the fall of Sumter seemed to justify fully these conjectures.   On the 17th the convention at Richmond passed the secession ordinance by a secret vote.   Less than a fortnight before it had rejected the proposition by a majority of two to one.   It now resolved to submit its vote approving secession to

Virginia convention passes the secession ordinance.

the people for ratification. It appointed, however, a distant day for that purpose, the 23d of the following month, and long before that time the old Commonwealth was occupied by the forces of the Confederacy. The popular vote, when it was cast, was the merest farce.

The day following the passage of the secession ordinance by the convention, the Virginia secessionists seized Harper's Ferry, and sent their General Taliaferro to capture the great navy-yard of the United States at Gosport near Norfolk. This was also speedily accomplished, and therewith the Confederacy obtained possession of ships, cannon, arms, munitions, and military and naval stores to the value of some ten millions of dollars.

Seizure of Harper's Ferry and Gosport navy-yard.

The events of the 19th were even more exciting and threatening. Already in the afternoon of the 16th some four or five hundred Pennsylvania troops had made their way across Maryland, and had reached Washington without incident. A few more arrived on the 18th. On the 19th the Sixth Massachusetts regiment, uniformed and armed, undertook to go by rail to Washington, through Baltimore. The cars containing seven of the companies were drawn by horses from the Northern to the Southern station with safety. The mob had by this time, however, gathered in force, and began to obstruct the tracks in the streets, and the other four companies were compelled to march through the town. The mob fell upon them with all kinds of missiles, even firing pistols at them. The Mayor and the police endeavored to disperse the rioters, but were unsuccessful. The soldiers were obliged to take care of themselves. They at last cleared their way with bullets and fixed bayonets. Four of the soldiers were slain outright, a dozen or more of the rioters were

The Sixth Massachusetts in Baltimore.

killed, and a considerable number of them wounded. The regiment reached Washington in the afternoon of the same day, and with the eight hundred or more Pennsylvanians, some city volunteers, and General Scott's five or six companies of regulars, placed the capital out of danger of a surprise.

The events of the week from the twelfth to the twentieth set the whole country in commotion. A wave of passionate anger, presaging fearful war, swept over the North, the South, and the slaveholding Commonwealths which had not yet renounced their allegiance. From the vantage ground of the present, we can easily comprehend the deep indignation of all loyal hearts. The flag of their country had been shot down; the authority of their Government had been defied, and expelled by force of arms from a place which was the property of the Union; and loyal soldiers had been attacked, maimed, and killed upon the soil of a Commonwealth where they had every kind of right to be, and over which they were obliged to pass in order to defend the capital of the Union against capture and destruction. It would have been, indeed, a base and cowardly people who would not have been stirred to wrathful feeling and belligerent deeds by such events.

The effect of these events on the country.

It is more difficult to see why the secessionists should have experienced any increased resentment toward the Northern people and the Government of the United States on account of them. These were outrages committed by themselves. It is psychologically true that the committers of outrages usually become greatly excited against their victim in the execution of their work, but the rational mind can see no reason or justice in it, though it may discover the explanation of it. And it is almost impossible to comprehend the mental processes of

the professed loyal men, in the slaveholding Commonwealths that had not before these events passed secession
ordinances renouncing their allegiance to the Union,
which led them to participate sympathetically in the
newly excited feelings of the secessionists. One would
think now that those events ought to have increased their
aversion toward the destroyers of the Union and have
made them more determined in their loyal attitude. They
did do so in Kentucky and Missouri very generally, and
in some notable instances in Tennessee. The wonder is
that they did not do so in all cases. And the wonder of
wonders is the unaccountable apostacy of John Bell.

Bell was the acknowledged leader-in-chief of the
Unionists of the South. He had almost evenly divided
the popular vote of the slaveholding Commonwealths with Breckenridge in the election of
1860. He made his campaign upon a platform
whose only principle was : "The Union, the Constitution, and the enforcement of the laws." A firm and decided stand on his part would probably have rallied
most of his followers in the slaveholding Commonwealths
that had not then passed secession ordinances to more
determined efforts for upholding the cause of the Union
in their midst. At least, it would most probably have
prevented Tennessee from casting her lot with the Southern Confederacy. It was the grand opportunity of his life.
Had he clung to the principle of his platform, and used
his influence and his eloquence to inspire his friends and
followers with courage and patriotism, he would not now
be forgotten, as he is, but would be enthroned among
the heroes of our national history. Instead of this
he crept ignobly into the secessionist meeting in the
Court House at Nashville, just after the fall of Sumter,
and virtually gave in his adherence to secession, while
nominally disapproving it, and therewith sealed the fate

The attitude
of John Bell
after the fall
of Sumter.

of the Union cause in Tennessee and his own everlasting downfall. It was a sad ending of a noble career. He had stood firmly against the repeal of the Missouri Compromise—that is, against the extension of slavery into the Territories north of thirty-six degrees and thirty minutes. He had incessantly proclaimed that all differences must be fought out and settled by discussion and vote within the Union. And he had declared the Union, the Constitution, and the enforcement of the laws to be the fundamental principle of his political creed. But now he deserted the Administration and the Union at the very first attempt made by the new President, not even to enforce the laws against those defying them, but only to protect the soldiers in the military posts of the Union from starvation and capture. It is impossible to describe the chagrin and dismay which overcame the followers of this grand old man in his native Commonwealth and in many other quarters, when they learned that he had surrendered his proud leadership in Tennessee, and had himself become virtually a follower of the narrow-minded, passionate Governor of the Commonwealth who was bending all his energies to commit Tennessee to secession. They lost the courage to resist the social persecution, which was now inaugurated in Tennessee, as well as in Virginia, against all who would not declare themselves unreservedly for secession ; and it soon became the doctrine of the Tennessee secessionists that those who would not join hands with them in destroying the Union must leave the "State."

The theory of cowardice is hardly a satisfactory one upon which to account for the strange conduct of Mr. Bell. He was conciliatory in his habit of mind, but had not been considered cowardly. He undoubtedly reasoned that a neutral position on the part of the slaveholding Commonwealths, which had not yet declared secession, would avert war, and give opportunity for a peaceable reconstruction of the Union. He thought that successful war against the Union by the Confederacy would lead to permanent separation, and that successful war by the Union against the Confederacy would lead to a change of the Constitution, and the abolition of slavery in the Commonwealths. He was for the Union under the existing Constitution, not for the Union under any constitution which the necessities of war might require. We can see how he thus reconciled his conduct with the first two elements in his platform-principle : " The Union, the Constitution."   But how he made it harmonize with the third element—" the enforcement of the laws "— is not so easy to comprehend, that is, not so easy from a general point of view. If, however, we reflect that to the Southern mind in 1860, this phrase meant especially the enforcement of the Fugitive Slave law, and the Kansas-Nebraska Act as interpreted in the Dred Scott opinion, we may help ourselves to understand how Mr. Bell explained away, to his own satisfaction, that apparently loyal and patriotic principle for which he stood as a presidential candidate in 1860. We must do him the justice of believing he was convinced by his own sophistries.   We must also do the Tennessee secessionists the justice of believing that they thought themselves patriots in now establishing a reign of terror over Union sentiment in Tennessee. From the Governor down they were men of narrow mind and unlimited passion. Emboldened by the apostacy of Bell and the consequent timidity of those whom he had left in the lurch, they now trampled under foot every dissent from their own views, and every man who dared to express it.

A Confederate agent immediately appeared in Nashville, and the Democratic Legislature authorized Governor Harris to appoint commissioners to negotiate with him a military alliance between Tennessee and the Confederacy. The convention agreed upon between the two parties provided for the transfer of the command of the military forces of the "State" to the Confederate authorities, and for the ultimate transfer of all the munitions of war in the possession of the "State" to the Confederacy. This agreement was secretly ratified by the Legislature on the 7th of May.

Tennessee's treaty with the Confederacy.

On the day preceding this act, the Legislature passed a secession ordinance, appended to it a provision adopting the constitution of the Confederacy, and submitted both to a popular vote to be taken June 8th. When this day arrived, the "State" had been already a month in the grasp of the Confederacy, and the farce at the polls was proclaimed by the Governor to have been an overwhelming ratification of the ordinance and of the Confederate constitution. A few brave men among the Union leaders, such as Johnson, Etheridge, Maynard, Stokes, and Brownlow, stuck to their principles and left the "State," but the great majority of them felt compelled to seek service under the Confederacy in order to prove the sincerity of their ignominious conversion.

Tennessee secession.

The secessionist Governor of North Carolina, Ellis, also seized the opportunity offered by the excitement over the fall of Sumter to dragoon that Commonwealth into the secession movement. The people had elected a large Unionist majority to a convention on the 30th of the preceding January, and at the same time had voted against holding any convention. Nevertheless a convention of the disunionist minority assembled at Raleigh on the 22d of March, and waited for the course of events to open a way for the accomplishment of their purpose. It was probably

North Carolina secession.

with their approval, and perhaps upon their advice, that the Governor proceeded, on the 20th of April, to seize the United States mint at Charlotte, and, on the 22d, the United States arsenal at Fayetteville. He had already more than three months before taken possession of the United States forts near Beaufort and Wilmington. They were not, at the time, garrisoned, and he gave it out that he feared their occupation by irresponsible persons. Ostensibly he had held them for the United States Government, not against it. No such excuses, however, were now offered for the seizures of the mint and the arsenal. They were taken from the United States Government, and held against that Government. The "State" had not as yet pretended to have seceded from the Union. Nothing therefore distinguished the Governor in the commission of these acts from a common robber, except that they were executed by virtue of the abuse of his public powers, and for what he considered to be the advantage of the community over which he governed. On the 26th he proceeded to call the Legislature for the purpose of effecting the passage of a secession ordinance.

President Lincoln accepted these movements as putting the people of North Carolina in an attitude of rebellion to the Government of the United States, and, on the 27th, he issued a proclamation, supplementary to that of April 19th blockading the ports of the seven "States" in which conventions had passed secession ordinances, and extended this inhibition of commerce to the ports of Virginia and North Carolina.

The Blockade proclamations.

The President's proclamation of the 19th had been directly evoked by an order of the Confederate Government of the 17th proposing to use these ports for the fitting out and commissioning of privateers to prey

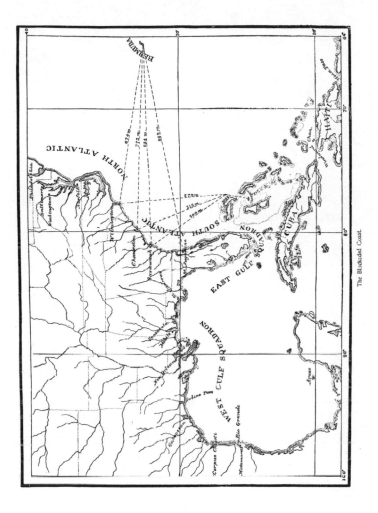

The Blockaded Coast.

upon the commerce of the United States. The Confederates represented Mr. Lincoln's proclamation as involving a recognition of belligerent rights and of independence. Mr. Seward, on the other hand, instructed the ministers of the United States to foreign nations to say that it was meant simply as a means of suppressing insurrection. The text of the proclamation supports this interpretation. It declares the amenability of persons acting under the letters of marque of the Confederate President to the laws of the United States in reference to the crime of piracy.

The North Carolina Legislature made a great ado over the supplementary proclamation of the 27th, extending the blockade to the ports in that Commonwealth. It immediately issued the *North Carolina secession.* call for a convention, ordered the election of delegates to the convention upon the 18th of the following month (May), and fixed the date of its assembly for the 20th. It sent a representative to the Confederate Congress, and the lower house of the body passed a resolution declaring that the President of the United States, in blockading the ports of North Carolina, had assigned North Carolina to the position of a foreign country, and had declared war upon her, and authorizing the Governor "to use all the powers of the State, civil and military," to protect its citizens and defend its honor.

The view which the leaders in North Carolina then imposed upon the people with every violence of speech and act was that Mr. Lincoln had overturned the Constitution of the United States, assumed a military dictatorship, expelled them from the Union and from the protection of its laws, and was proceeding to destroy them by means of the ravages of war and slave insurrection. The Union sentiment was thus suppressed and reduced to silence, and the convention accomplished its mad work on the very day of its assembly, and with perfect unanimity.

Arkansas was borne along even more swiftly by the force of this insane excitement. The convention called Secession in Arkansas. by her Legislature to consider secession had assembled in the early days of March, and after having listened to propositions from the Confederate President had voted not to pass a secession ordinance. It had resolved, however, to submit its action to the people at the polls on the first day of the following August. It had then adjourned to the 17th of August, to await the decision of the voters upon the subject.

Upon the fall of Sumter and the call for troops to suppress the rebellion, the convention immediately reassembled. The Union sentiment was suppressed by the same sophistries, expressed and impressed in the same violent and brutal ways as obtained in Tennessee and North Carolina. On the 6th of May the convention passed the secession ordinance, with only a single voice and vote raised against it.

It was the well laid, and, to a degree, well developed plan of the secessionists to secure the passage of secession Secession in Missouri attempted. ordinances in Missouri and Kentucky also by the help of the Sumter excitement. The Governor of Missouri and a majority of the Legislature were favorable to secession. They assisted in the development of the movement through January and February, and, when they thought the time was ripe, the Legislature issued, on January 16th, its call for the convention. To their great surprise an overwhelming majority of the delegates chosen were Unionists. In fact when the convention assembled, on the 28th of February, not a single one of the members declared for secession. It passed a resolution against secession, elected delegates to the "border States" convention proposed by the Legislature of Kentucky, and, on March 22d adjourned to meet again in the following December, unless called together earlier by the committee chosen by it and vested by it with this power in any emergency which might seem to its members to require immediate action.

During all this time the Governor, Mr. Jackson, had been devising a scheme for getting hold of the United States arsenal at St. Louis. But fortunately for the Union cause there was a stanch loyalist in St. Louis at this time who more than equalled the Governor in the craft of politics, as well as in intelligence, courage, and resoluteness. This was Francis Preston Blair, Jr., the brother of Montgomery Blair, Mr. Lincoln's Postmaster-General.

As far back as January the Governor began an attempt to corrupt the commandant of the arsenal. This was quickly reported in Washington with the result that the commandant was changed and the garrison at the arsenal re-enforced. Then the secessionists began the organization of armed clubs, under the title of "Minute Men," for the purpose of capturing the arsenal. Blair and the Unionists formed, in counter movement, a committee of safety and proceeded to organize companies of "Home Guards," for the defence of the arsenal.

Upon the incoming of the new Administration, with his brother in the Cabinet, Mr. Blair was able to have a most capable and patriotic man, Captain Nathaniel Lyon, appointed commandant in St. Louis, and with Lyon in authority over the military of the United States in the city, and his committee of safety, and his influence in Washington, Blair was able to foil the Governor and the Legislature and their secessionist support in all their schemes for the

Secession in Missouri foiled.

capture of the arsenal, and the commitment of Missouri
to the Confederate cause.

The Unionists had, however, a very serious struggle
to maintain their ground when the excitement over the

The strug-
gle between
the Unionists
and the Seces-
sionists after
the fall of
Sumter.
fall of Sumter and the call for troops swept
over the land. As we have seen, the Govern-
or refused the call in terms of insult to the
President, as well as disloyalty to the Union.
Blair and the committee of safety went to
work, however, enlisting volunteers. The Governor, on
his part, began the establishment of a " State " camp in
the suburbs of the city under the direction of his " State "
Brigadier-General Frost. His purpose from the first
was, undoubtedly, the seizure of the arsenal. During
the last week of April he was in communication with
the Confederate President, asking for arms with which
to attack the troops of the United States in the arsenal.
In the night of the 8th of May, cannon, muskets, and
ammunition sent by order of the Confederate President
actually arrived in St. Louis by steamer from New Orleans. Blair and the committee of safety allowed them
to be taken without opposition to Camp Jackson, in order to have certain proof of the treasonable designs of
the Governor and his General.

Meanwhile President Lincoln had authorized Blair
and his committee to proclaim martial law in St. Louis,
if they deemed it necessary, and to create a military force
of not more than ten thousand men under their command, to act with Lyon and his regulars in the arsenal.

The day following the arrival of the arms, Captain
Lyon went out to Camp Jackson *incognito*. He saw
the arms sent by the Confederate Government, and other
most convincing proofs of the disloyalty of the Governor
and General Frost. On the next day, May 10th, Lyon
proceeded with his forces to surround the camp, and

demand its surrender. He had planned his attack so well and so quietly that success was certain. Frost surrendered without the firing of a single musket. On the way back to the arsenal, however, with his prisoners, Lyon was set upon by a secessionist mob, and it became necessary to allow his troops to fire in self-protection. Ten or fifteen persons were killed, and quite a number wounded. The excitement in the city became very intense. Unfortunately in the height of it, General Harney, the commander of the military department in which St. Louis was situated, arrived upon the scene.

General Harney was a genuinely loyal man, but he was one of those mild, conservative, urbane gentlemen, who are very slow to suspect deceit and treachery, and very prone to attribute to all men the uprightness of which they themselves are conscious in their own hearts. Harney was Lyon's superior in command, of course, and was a favorite with General Scott, the Commander-in-chief of the United States army. He immediately manifested his disposition to listen to the representations of Frost, Price and others of the opponents of Blair and Lyon, who declared that they had no disloyal purposes in assembling the militia around St. Louis.

Blair and Lyon knew that Harney was being deceived, and when he began to speak of disbanding the "Home Guards" which the President had authorized them to organize, they sent a deputation to Washington to confer with the President. The other side also sent representatives. Blair's brother in the Cabinet espoused the cause of the one faction, while Bates, the Attorney-General, also a Missouri man, was inclined to favor the other. Mr. Lincoln, with his unfailing sagacity, saw the situation as it was, and determined to sustain Blair and Lyon. He relieved Harney, raised Lyon to the rank of a brigadier-general, and put him in command at St. Louis. The President did not announce his determinations to the public immediately, but sent them in confidence to Mr. Blair, and wrote him to allow Harney to remain in command unless or until it should become necessary in his judgment to remove him. Mr. Blair held the President's order from the 18th of May until the 30th, during which period it became entirely manifest to Blair and his friends that Jackson, Frost, Price, and the Missouri Legislature, then assembled at Jefferson City, were preparing for armed rebellion, and that Harney was almost oblivious to the fact, and was allowing the moments during which their plans might be frustrated to slip by unimproved. On the 30th of May Blair determined to delay no longer, and delivered to Harney the President's order of the 16th, relieving him and putting Lyon in command.

Jackson and Price now sought an interview with Blair and Lyon. This occurred at St. Louis, on the 11th of June. Jackson demanded that the "Home Guards" should be disbanded, and that no more United States soldiers should be placed in Missouri. Lyon on the other hand demanded the dissolution of the "State Guards" and the abandonment of the project for organizing the military dictatorship of the Governor over the Commonwealth. He also declared that the United States Government would not yield its constitutional rights to march its soldiers into or through the Commonwealth, and station them therein, according to its own discretion. The Governor and his attendant, General Price, pronounced the attitude assumed by Blair and Lyon to be a declaration of war upon Missouri. They returned in haste to Jefferson City, ordering the railroad bridges to be burned behind them. Arriving there, the Governor published the results of the interview at St. Louis and called for fifty thousand men to take arms in the service of the "State" against the United States Government. The Governor drew a distinction between the constitutional requirements of the Federal Government, which it was the duty of the citizens of Missouri to obey, and " the unconstitutional edicts of the military despotism " enthroned at Washington, which they were obligated to resist. But no Unionist was deceived by such contradictions, however much the Governor might deceive himself by them. Lyon followed them with a strong force by steamer up the Missouri River, and, on the 15th (June), took possession of the capital of the Commonwealth. Missouri was now in the hands of the United States army.

The convention which had adjourned, as we have seen, the preceding March, after having appointed a committee with power to call its members together again upon an emergency, was now summoned by this committee. It assembled on the 22d of July and before the end of the month it had established a loyal Commonwealth government in Missouri. With this the position of Missouri was definitely determined, and the danger of the enactment of a secession ordinance by any body of men entitled to claim to represent the " State " was entirely averted.

It was the attitude of Kentucky, however, which, next to that of Maryland, gave Mr. Lincoln the greatest concern. Besides its inestimable value from political and strategic points of view, it was the "State" of his nativity, and his strongly sentimental nature made him regard its soil and its inhabitants with particular affection.

Attempts at secession in Kentucky. The attitude of its government and of the people.

The government of the Commonwealth, in both the legislative and executive branches, was in the hands of the Breckenridge Democrats at the moment of the attack upon Sumter, and the Governor, Beriah Magoffin, refused, in insulting language, President Lincoln's call upon him for Kentucky's quota of the militia to suppress insurrection and enforce the laws. The President had faith, however, that the feeling of the great mass of the people was with him, and he determined so to act as to give time and opportunity for the Union sentiment to develop into intelligent opinion and settled purpose.

The prevailing notion in Kentucky, at the moment, was that the "State" should remain neutral in the impending struggle, and refuse to allow the troops of either the United States or the Confederate States to enter its limits. Even the strongest Unionists did not seem to perceive, at the moment, that this would mean aid to the Confederacy, by defending the secessionist "States" against the approach of the authorities of the Union. Even John J. Crittenden reasoned, at first, that, if Kentucky and the other "border States" should assume this attitude, war between the two sections would be averted, and the "Confederate States," after a few years of trial with their experiment, would return voluntarily to the Union. He went so far, at first, as to approve of the Governor's refusal of the militia on the President's call, although he took pains to explain his position, and that of those who thought with him, to the Government at Washington, with very different reasons from those advanced by the Governor. He wrote to General Scott that while Kentucky regretted the language of her Governor's answer to the President, she "acquiesced in his declining to furnish the troops called for, and she did so, not because she loved the Union the less, but she feared that if she parted with those troops, and sent them to serve in your ranks, she would have been overwhelmed by the secessionists at home and severed from the Union; and it was to preserve substantially and ultimately our connection with the Union that induced us to acquiesce in the partial infraction of it by our Governor's refusal of the troops required." The confusion of the thought in this proposition is made very manifest in the confusion of the grammar in which it is expressed. Still it held sway over the minds of most, and of many of the best.

The President's policy toward Kentucky was, if not dictated, very largely determined by these views of the prominent Unionists in the Commonwealth. The President's He saw that he must so shape the course of policy toward Kentucky the Administration as to force the disloyal tucky. men in Kentucky to show their hands. When they should reveal their purpose, which the President fully understood, of making Kentucky a bulwark and a battle-ground for the Confederates, Mr. Lincoln had full faith that the Unionists would then, themselves, call the armies of the Union to their rescue. His idea was simply to put himself in a position to answer the call, promptly and vigorously. He did not, of course, consider himself under any legal obligation to await the call, but only thought best to do so, unless it should be too long delayed. Early in May, he selected a brilliant young Kentuckian, William Nelson, at the William moment a capable naval officer, and, giving Nelson. him leave of absence from duty in the navy, sent him to Louisville, with the understanding that he should undertake the military organization of the Unionists in central Kentucky. Arms were sent to him for distribution among them.

The President also sent another noted Kentuckian, Major Robert Anderson, the late commander at Fort Sumter, the best known military character Major Anderson at Cincinnati. in the country, at the moment, to Cincinnati, with the authority to receive volunteers from Kentucky and Virginia into the United States service.

A little later the President commissioned the brilliant
young Unionist of the Kentucky Senate, L. H. Rous-

L. H. Rous- seau, to raise and organize a brigade of Ken-
seau. tuckians for the United States army.   General Rousseau established his camp, "Joe Holt," across
the Ohio River on Indiana soil.

While these movements were in progress the Legislature was again in session, upon the call of the Governor,

Manifesta- who now showed his disloyalty with distinct-
tions of Ma- ness to all who would see it.   He declared
goffin's disloy-
al purposes. that the Union was already dissolved, and
that the Government at Washington was a usurpation.
He again recommended the arming of the militia, under
the "State Guard" organization, commanded by his
military man, Simon B. Buckner, and the calling of
the "sovereign convention" of the "State," the body
which should determine, in his view, the attitude which
the "State" would take in the impending conflict.   It
was charged that he applied to the Confederate Government at Montgomery for arms.

The Legislature, however, remained loyal; repudiated
his pronunciamento against the Washington Govern-

The loyalty ment; refused to call a convention; rejected
of the Legis- his demand for three millions of money with
lature. which to purchase arms, accoutrements, and
ammunition for his "State Guards"; and passed a law
requiring the oath of allegiance to the Union from every
member of the "State Guards," and authorizing the
organization of the loyal "Home Guards."   It still proposed to use these only in defence of the neutrality of
the "State," it is true; but these measures had the effect
of preventing the success of any attempt to pass a secession ordinance, and of purging the "State Guards" organization, and of organizing the militia in the loyal
"Home Guards."

The month of May passed while these movements were being accomplished. The "border State" Peace conference, presided over by Mr. Crittenden, was held. The Legislature adjourned. The secessionists were gathering in the south-western portion of the Commonwealth, and the Unionists were getting complete control in the other portions. *The course of events during May.* Still no United States troops were on Kentucky soil, but many Kentuckians had volunteered their services to the Union, and were organizing and drilling in the camps just across the Ohio. The conservative Unionists were becoming convinced that the neutrality of Kentucky would be an impossibility, and that Kentucky would be obliged to fight on the one side or the other.

The election of members of Congress from Kentucky for the special session of that body called by the President to meet on the 4th of July was now at hand. All felt that the crisis in Kentucky's affairs had arrived. The Unionists went *The Unionists elect the Congressional delegation.* boldly into the contest, and, after a three weeks' campaign of a most exciting character, won nine of the ten seats. Kentucky might still, by the fortunes of war, be made a temporary battle-ground, but there was now no further danger of a secession ordinance, or of the disloyalty of her inhabitants. If any of them should choose to throw in their lots with the Confederates, they would have to do it without the justification or excuse of "going with their State," that is, they would have to accept the character of unmitigated rebels against their own *de facto* and *de jure* "State" government, as well as against the National Government. Mr. Lincoln was profoundly gratified with the result, and now felt certain that the northern boundary of the Confederacy could not be further advanced. He could now, at last, clearly estimate the territorial extent of the rebellion.

When the Massachusetts regiment left Baltimore in the afternoon of April 19th, the city was virtually in the hands of the secessionist mob.   At about four o'clock they held a mass-meeting and manifested such strength and determination that the authorities, both of the city and the Commonwealth, were terrorized into obedience to them, where they were not already in sympathy with them. Even the Governor, Mr. Hicks, though loyal to the Union and the Government, gave way before the storm of disunion so far as to address the meeting, and to say : "I bow in submission to the people. . . . I will suffer my right arm to be torn from my body before I will raise it to strike a sister State."   The Mayor had gone even further, and had informed the crowd that an understanding had been concluded between the Maryland authorities and the president of the Philadelphia and Baltimore Railroad company to the effect that no more troops would be brought over the line without the consent of these authorities.

The situation in Maryland.

About midnight the Mayor, Mr. Brown, the Police Marshal, Mr. Kane, and the Police commissioners held a conclave, and resolved upon the destruction of the railroad bridges on the lines between Baltimore and the North.   Before daylight three bridges on the Philadelphia line and three on the Harrisburg line had been burned by their emissaries. The party which did the work on one of the lines was led by the Police Marshal himself, who in the midst of his nefarious work sent a telegram to the notorious secessionist of Frederick, Bradley T. Johnson, exhorting him to "send expresses over the mountains and valleys of Maryland and Virginia for the riflemen to come without delay," and declaring that "further hordes will be down upon us to-morrow," and that "we will fight them, and whip them, or die."

The burning of the railroad bridges.

The burning of these bridges, severing the National Capital from the source of its defence against capture, was an act of veritable treason, committed by the municipal authorities of Baltimore, and not simply by private persons. These authorities claimed that Governor Hicks joined in the resolution. He denied it. If, however, he did, then the Commonwealth government was involved in the treason. Exact political and legal logic would have required the immediate seizure of the city, and all other necessary points by the troops of the United States, the establishment of martial law over them, the arrest of all persons concerned in the treasonable act, and the trial of them under the processes of the criminal law of the United States, if not under the processes of martial law. But the Government at Washington did not have, at the moment, the necessary physical power to assert its just authority.

On the day following the rebellious outbreak in Baltimore, Governor Hicks telegraphed to the Secretary of War that the secessionists had the upper hand in the city, and that he thought it prudent to decline, for the time being, the President's call for the four regiments of Maryland militia. He had no more power to do that than a general in the regular army had to decline the order of the President to bring his detachment to Washington. His refusal to obey the President's command in regard to this matter, no matter how mildly and tentatively expressed, made him subject, in sound jurisprudence, to the jurisdiction of the court-martial. The demoralization, the perfect bewilderment, of thought upon this subject, as well as upon almost every other public relation, which obtained in the so-called "border States," as well as in the "States" that had passed secession ordinances, are a speaking testimony of the growth of the Confederate theory of the Constitution during the forty years between 1820 and 1860. It is doubtful if Mr. Lincoln himself and his chief advisers realized the enormity of the offence which these " border State " governors had committed in refusing to obey the President's order to send forward the troops under their respective commands, and in assuming to declare their respective " States " neutral in the struggle of the Government to maintain the Union and enforce the laws. And it is also doubtful if he and they realized the character and extent of the President's power in dealing with such conduct. The widespread demoralization in thought and reasoning had not left them entirely untouched. The President did, however, upon hearing of the measures taken by the Maryland authorities to prevent the passage of any more troops across the Commonwealth, order a despatch to be sent to the president of the Philadelphia and Wilmington Railroad, instructing him that Governor Hicks had no authority to forbid the soil of Maryland to troops coming to Washington under the orders of the President of the United States, and commanding him to send them on prepared to fight their way through, if necessary.

On the same day, the 20th, a committee of Baltimoreans appeared in Washington bringing a request to the President from Hicks and Brown that no more troops should be led through Baltimore. The President consulted General Scott and then replied that he would make no point of marching the soldiers through Baltimore, but would order them to proceed around the city. The committee apparently assented to this proposition, but upon the return of its members to Baltimore, they were repudiated by the secessionists for not having refused their consent to the march of the

The request of Governor Hicks to the President that troops should not be brought through Baltimore.

troops through any part of Maryland.   The secessionists then sent two new men to Washington to make further demands of the President.   Mr. Lincoln preferred to deal with the highest authorities, and sent a despatch to Hicks and Brown requesting their presence at the White House.

In the meantime the loyal and capable presidents of the Philadelphia and Wilmington and the Pennsylvania Central Railroads, Felton and Thomson, had   The Presidevised a route by rail to Perryville, at the   dent's answer. head of the Chesapeake Bay, thence by water to Annapolis, and thence by rail again to Washington ; and when Brown with three friends, Hicks having excused himself, arrived in Washington, the President told them that the troops must come to Washington ; that they would be brought either by the Perryville-Annapolis route, or from Harrisburg and marched around Baltimore, provided no obstacles should be placed in their way, but that if any should be, they would be ordered to select their own route, and fight their way through, if necessary.   Brown and his friends were thus compelled to assent to the President's proposition.

This interview took place in the forenoon of the 21st, and these gentlemen left the White House to return to Baltimore.   In less than two hours they were   Brown's back again with the story that three thousand   second visit to the President. troops were at Cockeysville, some fifteen miles north of Baltimore, on the railroad to Harrisburg, and that the people were rising to attack them.   The President sent an order to these troops to return to Harrisburg, despite the fact of their sore need in Washington.

By this time the people of the North had become thoroughly angered by the treasonable threats and deeds of the Marylanders.   The idea that the loyal soldiers should be forbidden to pass over any route in going to the defence of the capital against seizure by rebels was in-

Northern anger aroused by the situation in Maryland.

tolerable. The people were fast approaching the resolution to go in a mass, of their own motion, and march rough shod over any opposition which might be placed in their way.

Already, however, on the 19th and 20th, the Eighth Massachusetts regiment under Butler, and the Seventh

The Eighth Massachusetts and the Seventh New York on the way to Washington.

New York under Lefferts, both crack regiments of good fighters, led by brave and capable commanders, had arrived at Philadelphia. Butler proceeded with his men to Perryville, took possession of the ferry-boat *Maryland*,

and, embarking his soldiers upon her, steamed down the bay to Annapolis. Lefferts procured the steamer *Boston* at Philadelphia, and went with his regiment down the Delaware intending to proceed to Fortress Monroe and up the Potomac to Washington. He found, however, that the ascent of the Potomac might be hazardous, and steamed up the Chesapeake to Annapolis. He arrived in the harbor on the morning of the 22d, and found Butler and his men there. They had been there for more than twenty-four hours, but had not attempted to land. Governor Hicks was in the city, and he and the Mayor were endeavoring to dissuade Butler from landing. Hicks wrote again to President Lincoln requesting that no more troops be brought through Maryland, and that those on the boats in the harbor of Annapolis be ordered away. The President received this letter just after he had learned that the secessionists in Baltimore had taken possession of the telegraph offices in that city, and had cut Washington off from telegraphic communication with the North. At this same juncture another Baltimore committee called upon him, and proposed to him to solve the difficulties by acknowledging the independence of the Southern Confederacy. The President's indignation was roused to a high pitch. He refused promptly Hicks's requests, and told the committee that he should bring the troops through Maryland, and that if they should be attacked they would return the blow with severity.

On the afternoon of the 22d, Butler and Lefferts disembarked their troops at Annapolis without resistance. They remained in the neighborhood of the city during the next day, when four more regiments arrived in the harbor. On the same day messengers from General Scott made their way through to Annapolis. They brought orders to Butler to hold possession of Annapolis, but to send most of the troops to Washington.

In the morning of the 24th, the Eighth Massachusetts and the Seventh New York regiments started for Washington by way of Annapolis Junction on the Baltimore and Washington railroad line. The railroad from Annapolis to the Junction had been destroyed by the secessionists, and the troops marched this distance, repairing the road as they went. It was barely twenty miles, but they were so delayed by their work upon the road that twenty-four hours of time were consumed in the movement. Upon reaching the Junction a train of cars was found in waiting. Colonel Lefferts and his men boarded it, and by three o'clock that afternoon they were marching with flying colors and martial music up Pennsylvania Avenue, to the great relief of the President, the officials, the scanty garrison, and the loyal population of the city.

For three days before their arrival rumors of attack from Virginia had been rife. General Scott had reporteb to the President that two thousand rebels were said to be at a point some four miles below Mt. Vernon, that two thousand more were opposite Fort Washington, and that still two

Rumors of attack upon the capital.

thousand more were marching from Harper's Ferry. It was believed that Washington might be attacked at any moment by a force of from eight to twelve thousand men. The General thought that he could defend the city against the entrance of the rebel troops, but did not feel hopeful of his ability to protect it against bombardment from the heights across the Potomac. It is difficult to say what might have been the result of a vigorous advance of the rebels upon the city at any time before the 25th. There was a strong party in Richmond in favor of it. The commander-in-chief of the insurgent forces in Virginia, General Lee, on the contrary, issued an order, dated the 23d, forbidding an attack on Washington, and commanding his officers to act on the defensive, and to collect men and provisions along the line of the Potomac. Whether he did this from the belief that such an attack would be unsuccessful, or from the point of view that the South must act upon the defensive in self-justification, is not positively known. It is certainly probable, however, that the latter consideration had much weight with General Lee, at the moment.

Only five days before the issue of this order Lee was the Colonel of the First regiment of United States Regular Cavalry, and was in Washington conferring with General Scott. Scott had fixed his eye upon him for commander-in-chief of the Union army in the field, and the President virtually offered him the position on the 18th. The person through whom the President made the offer thought that Lee accepted it. Lee said subsequently that he declined it. He went over to Arlington, his home, in the morning of the 19th, and, on the 20th, wrote to General Scott resigning his position in the regular army. In this letter he wrote : " Save in defence of my native State, I never desire again to draw my sword." On the

22d, he was chosen by the secessionist Governor and convention at Richmond commander-in-chief of the Virginia militia. On the 23d he assumed command, and issued this order restraining the Virginians from attacking Washington or crossing the Potomac. After the arrival of the troops from Annapolis, on the 25th, an attack upon Washington could hardly have succeeded, and in a few days more it was out of the question.

The secessionist sympathizers among the officials and in the departments at Washington now gave up the hope of seeing their friends in possession of the city, and quickly resigned their positions and went southward. Among them were the commandant of the Washington Navy Yard, Commodore Franklin Buchanan, and Captain John B. Magruder of the Regular Artillery. *The exodus of the secessionists from Washington.*

The route from the North, by way of Perryville and Annapolis, was now fully open and in the firm possession of the Union troops. Butler was assigned to its defence. A military department was now created by order of the President covering the country for twenty miles upon each side of the railroad line from Annapolis to Washington. It was called the Department of Annapolis, and Butler was placed in command of it. *The occupation of Maryland.*

At the same time troops were being gathered at Philadelphia and Harrisburg under the command of General Patterson for an advance upon Harper's Ferry and Baltimore. General Patterson held his commission, at the moment, from the Governor of Pennsylvania, but was soon recognized by the President and General Scott as being in command of the Department of Pennsylvania, which was considered as comprehending, besides Pennsylvania, all of Maryland north of the Department of Annapolis.

Governor Hicks had called the Maryland Legislature to meet at Frederick, instead of Annapolis, because of the presence of the Union troops in the latter place. The body convened at Frederick, only about twenty miles distant from the rebel forces at Harper's Ferry, on the 26th (April). President Lincoln decided not to oppose the assembly of the members, but ordered General Scott to watch their movements, and to check any such as might appear hostile to the Union by any means he should consider proper and necessary.

The Maryland Legislature at Frederick.

The President also authorized General Scott to suspend the privileges of the writ of Habeas Corpus upon any of the military lines opened, at the moment, or subsequently, between Philadelphia and Washington. By the end of the month, the Baltimoreans found themselves isolated from the rest of the world, and surrounded by Union armies. On the 4th of May, General Butler moved up to the Relay House with two regiments of soldiers, and severed the connection between Baltimore and Harper's Ferry. The Maryland Unionists regained courage to speak and to act.

The suspension of the privileges of the writ of Habeas Corpus, and the isolation of Baltimore.

Governor Hicks now declared his attachment to the Union cause, and dismissed the secessionist militia gathered in Baltimore. The railroad bridges were rebuilt and the telegraphic lines repaired. The Legislature broke down in its attempt to introduce measures looking toward secession. On the 9th, troops were led through Baltimore without interruption. On the 13th, Butler took possession of the city, and entrenched himself permanently on Federal Hill. With this, railroad and telegraphic communication between Washington and the North, through Baltimore, was completely restored. On the 14th the dis-

Triumph of Union cause in Maryland.

heartened Legislature adjourned *sine die*, and Governor Hicks now issued his call for the four regiments of militia required of him by the President for the United States service. The rebellion in Maryland was crushed, and the Commonwealth was brought back to its proper position as a participant in the struggle for the preservation of the Union. It had played a disgraceful part, but it had served the National interests by rousing the anger of the North to the fighting point.

During the remainder of the month troops to the number of about fifty thousand poured into Washington, and were organized and equipped for action. At last on the 24th (May), they crossed the Potomac, took possession of Arlington and Alexandria, and began establishing the chain of fortifications reaching in semicircle from above Georgetown to the mouth of Hunting Creek, which made Washington impregnable from the south-west. It was agreed, on all sides, that Washington must be made safe before any forward movements should be undertaken. All felt that the capture of Washington by the Confederate forces would be about the greatest disaster which could befall the National cause. It would dishearten the Unionists, raise the courage of the Confederates to the highest pitch of enthusiasm, give the Confederacy prestige abroad, and transfer the scene of the contest from rebellious to loyal soil. To avoid such results everything else must, if necessary, be held in abeyance. Consequently the first real advance was made elsewhere, and the first real blow was struck in a different quarter.

The defences of Washington.

CHAPTER VIII

THE THREE MONTHS' WAR

ON the 23d of April, when all railroad communication between Washington and the West had been severed, the Governor of Ohio, Mr. Dennison,
appointed George B. McClellan commander-
in-chief of the Ohio militia, called into the service of
the United States, with the rank of Major-General.

McClellan had been a captain of artillery in the regular army, had had the experience of the Mexican War,

206

had witnessed the movements and operations of the Cri-
mean War, as a member of the military commission
sent to Europe for the purpose of gathering military
knowledge, had resigned his captaincy in 1857, and was,
at the moment, president of the Ohio and Mississippi
Railroad company, with residence at Cincinnati.   He
was well born, highly educated, only thirty-five years
of age, brave, capable and loyal.   Upon receiving his
appointment from Governor Dennison, he immediately
resigned his railroad presidency, and addressed himself
to the work of organizing and equipping the Ohio troops.
Camp Dennison, near Columbus, was his centre of operations, but he gathered troops along the north bank of
the Ohio River from Cincinnati to a point nearly opposite Wheeling.

Before Governor Dennison had appointed him to the
command of the Ohio troops, prominent citizens of Cincinnati had requested the Washington Government to
put him in command at Cincinnati with authority
to raise and organize an army.   On the 3d of May, the
President appointed him Commander of the Military
Department of the Ohio, which was made to consist of
the Commonwealths of Ohio, Indiana, and Illinois.
Finally, on the 14th of May, the President made him a
major-general in the regular army.

McClellan's first work after the organization of his
forces was naturally the defence of the Ohio line, and
then the rendering of aid to the Unionists in   McClellan's
Kentucky and Western Virginia.   At the   operations in
                                           Western Vir-
moment his chief forward movement must   ginia.
be in Western Virginia.   This part of Virginia was in-
habited by a loyal population, and contained but few
slaveholders or slaves.   It ran up like a wedge between
Ohio and Pennsylvania, commanding the great lines of
rail and telegraphic communication between the middle

Atlantic section and the West, and lastly it had, by the action of the secessionist convention at Richmond, been declared out of the Union. The occupation of this portion of Virginia was thus immediately seen to be both a military and a political necessity.

The West Virginians themselves took the initiative in inviting the movement. So soon as the convention at
The Wheeling Convention. Richmond passed its secret secession ordinance on the 17th of April, most of the members from the western counties went immediately to their homes, and began an agitation for the assembly of a convention of loyal men at Wheeling. They succeeded in bringing representatives of thirty-five counties together at that place on the 13th of May. This body immediately opened communication with President Lincoln, on one side, and General McClellan, on the other, and received assurances of assistance from both.

Governor Letcher was soon made aware of the Unionist movements in Western Virginia and sent Colonel
Attempts of the Virginia authorities to suppress the Unionist movement in the western counties. G. A. Porterfield with some East Virginia militia to Beverly, a spot well protected on the north-west by the line of the Rich and Laurel mountains, to organize an opposition to it. The secessionist forces soon advanced northward to Grafton, the point where the Baltimore and Ohio Railroad line bifurcates, one branch running to Wheeling and the other to Parkersburg.

The Wheeling convention adjourned on the 15th, after having called for the election of members to another
The delay of McClellan in crossing the Ohio. convention, the election to be held on the 26th, and the convention to assemble on the 11th of June. The vote of the people on the secession ordinance passed by the Richmond convention was to be taken, as we have seen, on the 23d of May. General McClellan desired to have these two

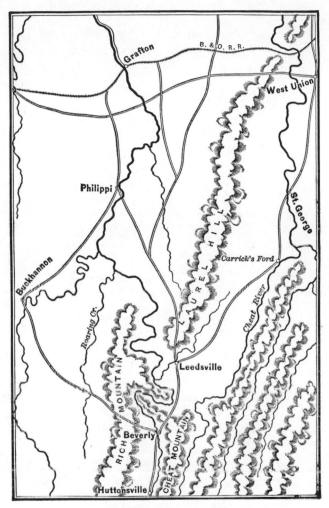

The West Virginia Battles.

elections take place in Western Virginia without the presence of Union soldiers therein. He felt sure of the results in both cases, and he did not wish them falsely attributed to the presence of his troops. The West Virginians themselves, who had volunteered in the Union service, were for this reason organized and encamped in Ohio at Camp Carlile opposite Wheeling.

On the evening of the 26th McClellan at length issued his orders to Colonels Kelly and Stedman to cross the Ohio and occupy Wheeling and Parkersburg. These orders were success- McClellan's advance. fully executed in the morning of the 27th. On the 30th they advanced to Grafton, Porterfield's troops having retired to Philippi, about fifteen miles to the southward. The railroad lines from Grafton to Wheeling and Parkersburg were quickly put in order, and by June 1st an army of six or eight thousand men was collected at Grafton under the command of General Morris.

General McClellan now ordered Morris to press on to Philippi and surprise Porterfield. On the morning of the 3d of June the attack was made, and the rebel forces, numbering from six to eight The engagement at Philippi. hundred men were beaten and dispersed. Porterfield with a few followers escaped to Beverly, and then continued their flight to Huttonsville, where they found refuge with another detachment of rebel troops.

The President of the Confederacy had, immediately after the adjournment of the Confederate Congress in the last days of May, repaired to Richmond, at which place the Confederate Congress had voted to reassemble on the 20th of July. Confederate troops had already been sent into Virginia and were gathered at Harper's Ferry, under the command of General Joseph E. Johnston ; at Manassas, under the command of President Davis at Richmond now assumed the direction of the military movements of the Confederates in Virginia.

General P. G. T. Beauregard ; and at Yorktown, under the command of General John B. Magruder. President Davis found General Lee in command at Richmond. He immediately sent Generals H. A. Wise and R. S. Garnett into Western Virginia to succor Porterfield and reorganize the secessionist forces there.

While they were engaged in this work at Lewisburg and Beverly the Unionist convention assembled, according to appointment, at Wheeling. Representatives from forty counties were present. The convention restored loyal "State" government in Virginia by electing Francis H. Pierpont Governor, and constructing a legislature composed of the existing members of the Virginia Legislature who would take the oath of allegiance to the United States and of such other persons as might be chosen in the places of such of the existing members as would not do so. The convention adjourned, on the 25th of June, until August, and the newly constructed Legislature of loyal Virginia met almost immediately. On the 9th of July it elected W. T. Willey and J. S. Carlile United States Senators, in the places of J. M. Mason and R. M. T. Hunter ; and Messrs. Willey and Carlile were on the 13th of July admitted by the Senate of the United States to seats in that body as the Senators from Virginia.

Reassembly of the Unionists in convention at Wheeling.

Virginia's loyal Legislature, and its election of United States Senators.

Already on the 21st of June, Governor Pierpont had made a regular demand upon the President for a force to suppress the rebellion in Virginia. This was well enough, but such juristic punctiliousness was unnecessary. Thousands of United States troops were before that date in Virginia, and many more were on the way thither. General McClellan arrived in person at Grafton on the

Governor Pierpont's call for aid to suppress rebellion in Virginia.

23d of June, and by the 4th of July he had assembled
an army of thirty thousand men at that point. To meet
this force the Confederate General Garnett had concentrated in and around Beverly from six to ten thousand
men.

Garnett threw forward, in the last days of June, a
detachment to the pass over Laurel Hill, between Beverly and Philippi, and another to the pass
over Rich Mountain, between Beverly and
Buckhannon; entrusting the command of
the latter to Colonel John Pegram, while leading the
former in person. He also left troops at Beverly to
cover his rear. The passes were thus held by not more
than five or six regiments, and the larger part of this
force was at Laurel Hill.

Laurel Hill and Rich Mountain.

General McClellan now sent General Morris with five
regiments to attack Garnett, and led the expedition
against Pegram at Rich Mountain in person. He found
Pegram strongly entrenched on the western face of the
mountain, and decided to send General W. S. Rosecrans
around the Confederate forces by the south, with the
purpose of falling upon their rear and cutting them
off from their base at Beverly. The manœuvre was not
so immediately successful as was hoped, but it finally
resulted in the dislodgment of Pegram and the surrender of his troops. The battle occurred on the 11th of
July, and the surrender on the 12th.

Meanwhile General Morris was advancing upon Garnett at Laurel Hill. Upon learning of the disaster to
Pegram at Rich Mountain, Garnett retreated toward
Beverly; but McClellan was too fast for him, and
reached Beverly from Rich Mountain before he had
made half the march from Laurel Hill. Garnett was
thus compelled to flee to the north-eastward. Morris
was in hot pursuit and overtook his rear guard about

noon of the 13th of July, at Carrick's Ford over Cheat River, some twenty-five miles from Laurel Hill. The Union troops immediately began the attack, dispersed the enemy and killed General Garnett himself.

Carrick's Ford.

In these several engagements the Union army had lost only about a dozen killed and forty wounded, while the Confederates lost about ten times as many, together with about one thousand taken as prisoners. The first stage of the Western Virginia campaign was thus entirely successful, and the Confederate forces were swept out of all parts of Western Virginia north of the Kanawha Valley. Viewed from the standpoint of subsequent events these battles were mere skirmishes, but at the time they were regarded as great victories, and the results of them were certainly most important and substantial. They gave Western Virginia to the Union throughout the entire course of the great struggle, made it possible to create the new Commonwealth of West Virginia, placed the direct line of railway from Washington through Virginia to the West in the hands of the Government at Washington, and turned all eyes upon McClellan as the coming man in case the war should continue.

General McClellan himself was not in the engagement at Carrick's Ford. He had, on the day of the affair, turned his face southward. His purpose was to form a junction with General J. D. Cox, whom he had ordered to cross the Ohio at Guyandotte and advance up the Kanawha Valley. With this movement he expected to drive the Confederates out of the whole of Virginia west of the Alleghanies. He had, however, already developed in his own mind a far more comprehensive plan than this, a plan with the correctness of which it is difficult to find

McClellan's movements after the battle of Rich Mountain.

any well-grounded fault. It was, in a word, after his junction with Cox, to cross the mountains to Wytheville on the railroad running from Lynchburg in Virginia to Knoxville in Tennessee, deliver East Tennessee and Northern Georgia from the secessionists, and attack Richmond from the rear. This would have been a masterful stroke. It would have put a Union army of fifty thousand men into the heart of the South, where it would have been protected by the natural fortresses of the mountains, nourished by a friendly population, and increased to double its strength by the voluntary enlistment of the hardy inhabitants of this loyal region. The objection to the movement would have been that he would be getting too far away from his base. But would he not have had his base right under him in this loyal region, which could have supplied his army easily for at least a year, at that time, and would most gladly have done so? It is true that his way to the Ohio would have been through a broken country and over poor roads, but it would have been, all the way, through a friendly population. If the authorities at Washington could only have contented themselves with the defence of the city, and have waited for the consummation of the developments in the rear as planned by McClellan, it does seem as if Richmond might have been taken, and the backbone of the Confederacy broken, in the summer and autumn of 1861.

The authorities at Washington were, however, not so much to blame for the haste of the Manassas campaign as the people of the North. The people were indignant at the bold effrontery with which the Government of their choice had been treated and defied, and were restless under the patience of the Government in dealing with it. They had answered the call of the Government promptly and generously, and had offered far more than the Government had asked. Their representatives were now in Washington in Congress assembled, and were urging the Administration to strike a speedy and decisive blow. The Confederate Congress was to meet on July 20th at Richmond, and the Confederate President with his Cabinet was already there, directing the military movements of the Confederate forces in front of Washington and elsewhere in Virginia. The meeting of that Congress in that place must be prevented, and Virginia, which had restored its loyal "State" government, must be rescued. "On to Richmond!" was the universal cry, and the Government was obliged to yield to the popular clamor. The military reason was obliged to give way to the political reason. There was, indeed, a military reason for the advance, but it was not tactical. It was the fact that the term of service of the militia called April 15th would soon expire, and many of the men desired to return to their homes. If any blow was to be struck with them, it must be done at once.

The military situation in the beginning of July on the Potomac and the lower Chesapeake was briefly as follows : General Patterson had marched down from his camp at Chambersburg with an army of twenty thousand men, and had threatened the Confederate General J. E. Johnston at Harper's Ferry. Johnston's force did not equal Patterson's and he, recognizing the weakness of the Harper's Ferry position on the north-east, abandoned the place and concentrated his army at Winchester, some twenty-five miles to the south-west. Whereupon Patterson crossed his forces over to the Virginia side, and fixed his headquarters at Martinsburg, about twenty miles north-west of Harper's Ferry. The two armies were, in a direct line, about twenty-five miles apart.

The military situation on the Potomac.

The army at Washington, and encamped on the Virginia side of the river from Alexandria to the bend above Georgetown, numbered about forty-five thousand men, under the command of General Scott and his chief subordinate in the field, General Irvin McDowell. It was confronted by a Confederate army of about fifteen thousand men, under the immediate command of General Beauregard. Beauregard's base of operations was Manassas Junction, a place some thirty miles from Washington, where the railway from the lower Shenandoah Valley joins the line leading from Alexandria to Richmond and to Lynchburg. The two Confederate armies had thus the advantage of what is termed in military language the interior lines of communication.

Finally, General Butler's force of about ten thousand men, which had occupied York peninsula with headquarters at Fortress Monroe, was opposed by Magruder's army of about the same strength.

Two slight collisions had taken place, one at Big Bethel, near Yorktown, on June 10th, and the other at Vienna Station, some fifteen miles west from Washington, on the 17th, in both of which the Union troops were worsted, results which greatly increased the impatience of the North.

Big Bethel and Vienna Station.

On the 29th of June, the President held his council of war upon the subject of the advance of the Union army from Washington upon Manassas. General Scott opposed the movement, but expressed the opinion that the Union army could vanquish the Confederates in a battle. His objection was based upon the consideration that a victory upon so small a scale would not amount to anything. The politicians in the council, that is, the President and the members of his Cabinet, felt that the people of the North could not be satisfied without a military effort on

The council of war of the 29th of June.

the part of the Government, and the President decided that the campaign must be undertaken. General Scott had foreseen the result, and had caused General Mc-Dowell to draw up the plan for the movement. General Scott now presented the plan to the council, with his approval of it from the tactical point of view.

The main points of the plan were that General Mc-Dowell, with a force of thirty thousand men and a re-serve of ten thousand, should attack the main position of the Confederates at Manas-sas, and turn it upon the south, that is, upon the Confederate right flank, while Patterson should hold Johnston's army at Winchester, and Butler should occupy the attention of Magruder before Yorktown.

The plan of the campaign.

Scott and McDowell thus calculated that Beauregard would be able to call to his assistance only the forces under General Holmes around Aquia Creek. McDowell thought that he would be obliged to fight not over thirty-five thousand men. He estimated Beauregard's army then at Manassas at twenty-five thousand. In fact, Beauregard did not have over twenty-five thousand after calling up all that Holmes could furnish him.

Butler detained the forces in front of him by his feints and manœuvres, and had Patterson done his duty, the Confederates under Beauregard might have been overwhelmed by McDowell's army.

Patterson moved forward from Martinsburg to Bunker Hill on the 15th (July). He was now directly north of Winchester and only nine miles away. He had a fine army of fifteen thousand men, while his adversary had not more than fifteen thousand, if so many.

On the 16th McDowell marched his forces out of the entrenchments in front of Washington, and headed them for Centreville, which place was to be his base of

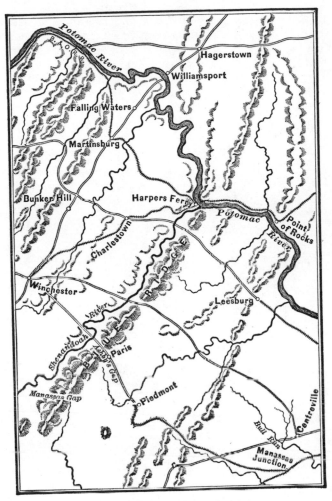

The Manassas Campaign.

operations. The Confederate Commander at Manassas and the Confederate President at Richmond were immediately informed of the advance by kind friends in or about Washington, and, on the 17th, Mr. Davis informed Johnston, at Winchester, that Beauregard was about to be attacked, and ordered him to march his forces to Manassas if possible. The advance on Manassas.

At the very moment when Johnston received this despatch, Patterson was making it possible for him to execute safely the fateful movement ordered by Mr. Davis. On the day before the order Patterson's blunder. arrived in Winchester, General C. W. Sandford in command of Patterson's left wing, which was composed of some eight thousand of his best troops, had advanced from Bunker Hill some three or four miles in a south-easterly direction, with the purpose of placing this force between Winchester and the Shenandoah River. Had this movement been followed up, Johnston would have been compelled either to remain in Winchester, or to come out of his entrenchments there and fight Sandford in the open field, with Patterson upon his exposed left flank. In either case Johnston could not have made his march to Manassas.

In the evening of the 16th Sandford had his troops in line for the advance toward the south-east, when a little after midnight, to his surprise and indignation, he received an order from Patterson to move toward Charlestown, a place some ten or fifteen miles due eastward from his position, and about twenty-two miles north-eastward from Winchester. On the 17th, Patterson's whole army abandoned its position on the north and north-east of Winchester, and virtually retreated to Charlestown. Patterson gave out, as his reason for this strange movement, that he had received reliable information that twenty thousand Confederate troops from

Manassas had joined Johnston, and that Johnston was about to fall upon him with an army of forty thousand men. General Sandford, who was nearer to Winchester than Patterson, declared that he had received no such information, and was almost in a mood to disobey Patterson's order, and risk a battle between Winchester and the Shenandoah without any support from Patterson, and upon his own responsibility.

Johnston learned of Patterson's unaccountable blunder on the 18th and immediately started with about two-thirds of his army, some eight thousand men, for Manassas. He marched eastward, forded the Shenandoah, passed through the gap in the Blue Ridge, turned southward to Piedmont Station on the Manassas railroad, took cars there, and on Saturday morning, the 20th, effected his junction with Beauregard at Manassas.

Johnston's march to Manassas.

Meanwhile McDowell's army had reached Centreville, driving the Confederate pickets before them. General Tyler, in command of the first division of the army, pursued the retreating enemy to Blackburn's Ford over Bull Run Creek, some three miles southward from Centreville, and became engaged in a sharp skirmish in which the Union troops were rather worsted. Tyler withdrew his detachment, instead of supporting it, because McDowell had commanded him not to bring on a battle at that juncture. The strong resistance which the Confederates made here to the farther advance of the Union army made it evident to McDowell that they had taken position on the west bank of Bull Run from the railroad bridge at Union Mills, on the south, to the Stone Bridge, over which the Centreville and Warrenton turnpike crossed the creek on the north, a distance of seven or eight miles. The creek was quite a formidable obstacle to the further ad-

McDowell's movements.

vance of the Union army, since it was not generally fordable, and since the bridges were few and easily defendable, and the west bank was higher than the east bank and covered with woods.

As we have seen, McDowell started out with the plan of turning the Confederate right, but by a personal examination of the roads in that direction, made on the 18th, he decided that the plan of the battle must be changed, and that he must undertake to turn the enemy's left. He immediately gave notice of this change to his division commanders, Tyler, Hunter, Heintzelman, Miles, and Runyon, and had he been able to make his attack on the morning of the 19th, he would in all probability have gained a decided victory. He could not, however, find an unfortified ford or bridge. It was nearly forty-eight hours before his engineers found the Sudley Ford only three or four miles above the Stone Bridge.

Neither Patterson nor McDowell was aware of Johnston's march from Winchester to Manassas, and of the increase thereby of the Confederate forces on the west side of Bull Run. Consequently McDowell did not call for any of Patterson's troops as a reserve in case of necessity, and planned his battle with reference to Beauregard's army only. In the night of the 20th, he assembled his division commanders again and gave them their instructions. Tyler, with the first division, was ordered to advance to Stone Bridge, and make a strong demonstration at that point, while Hunter and Heintzelman, with the second and third divisions, should march to Sudley Ford, cross Bull Run there, come down on the west side, strike the Confederates at Stone Bridge in their left flank, and open the way for Tyler to cross the bridge. Miles, with the fifth division, was commanded to remain in reserve at Centreville, while Runyon, with the fourth, should guard the communication with Washington.

McDowell ordered the movements from Centreville to begin in the darkness of the night, and expected the

three divisions which were to fight the battle to be at the Stone Bridge and Sudley Ford by six o'clock in the morning. Tyler's division was prompt and commenced pressing the Confederates around the bridge at about that hour. On the other hand, the divisions marching to Sudley Ford were so slow in their movements that they did not reach their objective point until about nine o'clock. This delay not only occasioned the disadvantage of fighting the battle in the heat of the July day, but it revealed the plan of the battle to the Confederates. Beauregard sat in his saddle for two hours on a hill top and watched the clouds of dust moving toward Sudley Ford. He divined at once that Tyler's attack on the bridge was only a feint, and he hurried his regiments northward to meet Hunter and Heintzelman at the Ford. Naturally Johnston's men, in coming from Winchester, had stopped on Beauregard's left, and the very first Confederate troops to come into the battle on the side next to the Ford were the men whom Patterson had engaged to hold fast at Winchester.

The divisions commanded by Hunter and Heintzelman crossed the creek successfully soon after nine

o'clock, and the wearied soldiers, who had been moving since three o'clock in the morning, went eagerly into the battle. They soon drove the Confederates back across the Warrenton turnpike, and opened the way for Tyler's division across the Stone Bridge. Two of Tyler's brigades rushed across, and about eighteen thousand victorious troops were now driving the Confederate left out of the valley, through which the Warrenton turnpike ran at this point, across Young's creek, and up the southern ascent from the valley.

Upon the crest of this ascent, called Henry Hill, the fleeing Confederates succeeded, at last, in making a halt behind General T. J. Jackson's fresh brigade, which stood, as they said, like a stone-wall, to cover them. Beauregard himself hurried to this point and took command in person. He soon gathered some ten thousand men and several batteries of artillery upon this very advantageous position, and prepared to make desperate resistance against the Union advance. It was evident that the fate of the day was to be decided at this point. For an hour and a half the battle raged with great determination on both sides. The scales of victory which, in the forenoon, had dipped so decidedly in favor of the Union forces now hung nearly even in the balance, inclining, if anything, to the advantage of the Confederates. One brigade of Tyler's division had not yet engaged in the struggle and was just preparing to advance, when a large column of Confederates was discovered moving upon the right flank of the Union forces. It was the remainder of Johnston's army from Winchester led by Kirby Smith. They had come down from Piedmont Station by train, and, on hearing the sounds of the battle, had jumped from the cars, and, forming quickly, had rushed upon the field exactly at the right moment and in the right place to give the day to the Confederates, and carry rout and panic through the Union ranks.

The Union forces now knew, for the first time, that they had Johnston's army upon them, and seeing no re-enforcements approaching with which to meet it, they gave up the fight, and fled in confusion and dismay from the field. Down

The rout of the Union Army.

the slope of Henry Hill, across Young's creek to the

turnpike, over the Stone Bridge, through Centreville, back to the Potomac, they poured, a disorganized, terrified mob, carrying and spreading consternation and fright as they went.

The Confederates followed them across Bull Run, but did not attempt to enter Centreville. Two fresh divisions of Union troops were at Centreville, and between that place and the Potomac, and the Confederate commanders were certainly justified in thinking that the retreating forces might reform behind these and return to the battle. They did not realize the extent of the demoralization which had so suddenly seized the Union army. Their own army was also badly crippled and exhausted, and in no condition to pursue. President Davis, who arrived on the field just in time to see his forces victorious, was anxious for an advance, but, in deference to Johnston and Beauregard, left the decision in their hands. They preferred to rest their troops through the night, and go forward by daylight, especially as the weather of the night following the battle was most inclement. On the next day they had free and open way clear back to the fortifications in front of Washington. The Union commanders had not thought of renewing the struggle, but had marched the reserves back to the entrenchments from which they had gone out on the 16th.

It had been a sanguinary battle. Nearly two thousand men were killed and wounded on each side. The number of prisoners taken was not great. As the Confederates were victorious they naturally had the advantage in this respect. Beauregard claimed to have captured between fourteen and sixteen hundred men, many of whom, however, were wounded.

General McDowell had planned the battle well, and

up to the moment of the appearance of Smith's division of Johnston's army on their right flank, the Union forces had fought the battle well. The fates, however, seemed to be on the Confederate side. First, Patterson let Johnston give him the slip; then the battle was delayed at least one day by the stupidity of the engineers in not finding an unfortified crossing; then the delay in the march of the divisions of Hunter and Heintzelman from Centreville to Sudley Ford revealed to Beauregard the plan of attack; and lastly the appearance of Kirby Smith and his division, at the most critical moment and in the most dangerous quarter, turned a hard-fought victory into a sudden and terrible defeat. In view of this course of events, it is certainly not surprising that religious natures among the Confederates should have concluded that Providence was smiling upon their cause, nor that such natures on the other side should have felt that the wrath of the Higher Powers was being poured out upon them.

It must be said further that the Confederate commanders showed themselves skilful, energetic, and courageous, and that they fought a good battle and won a great victory. The movement of Johnston from Winchester to Manassas was excellent strategy, and the successful defence of Henry Hill by Beauregard and Jackson was a splendid achievement. The master-hand of them all, however, was the Confederate President, who planned the combination of the two Confederate armies, and gave the order for the execution of the plan at exactly the right moment.

The immediate effects of this sudden and crushing defeat of the Union army were most deleterious to the Union cause. McClellan was called away from Western Virginia to Washington, and his plan for seizing the Knoxville and Lynchburg railroad, delivering East Tennessee, and approaching Richmond from the south-west, was abandoned. The loyal men of East Tennessee, Western North Carolina and Northern Georgia were thus deprived of the hope of assistance in their movements for resisting the jurisdiction of the Confederacy over their section, and were compelled to succumb to a long and galling oppression. Confederate camps were established at Cumberland Gap, Nashville, and Union City, and preparations were made for occupying Kentucky from these points, so soon as the disunionists in Kentucky could mature their plans. These leaders assembled and agreed upon the main points in their programme. In Missouri, Jackson and Price, who had been driven by Lyon into the south-western portion of the Commonwealth, took new courage, and began the organization of a strong force in that section for the purpose of regaining control over the "State" and making it a member of the Southern Confederacy. The Foreign Powers, which had been led by the anti-coercion policy, or rather the non-coercion policy, of President Buchanan into a partial recognition of the Confederacy, but had begun to see more clearly after hearing Lincoln's instructions to his diplomatic agents and reading his message to Congress, were again thrown into doubt and bewilderment in regard to the position which they should assume between the belligerents ; while panic reigned in Washington, and despair rested its black cloud over the North.

It was now evident to all that a long and terrible war would be necessary to quell the giant rebellion, and that the Government must choose between such a war and the dissolution of the Union. Not very many favored the latter alternative. More were wavering and undecided. The Government, however, and the great mass of people at the North, soon recovered sufficiently to express the determination that the last man and the last dollar should be expended in the defence of the Union and of national existence. With stern resolve they set about the colossal preparations for the three years' war now about to follow.

The Confederates, upon their side, never seemed to have considered at all that the victory placed them in a most advantageous position to offer peace for a Union reconstructed upon their own ideas, with half of the Territories for slavery, and guarantees in the form of unamendable amendments, which would secure them forever, in so far as law could do it, in the possession of their slave property. Their exaltation knew no bounds. Their President told them that their enemy numbered two to their one upon the field of Manassas, and they naturally concluded that every battle in which the Unionists would dare to engage could have only the same result. They resolved to persist, or rather they did not think of discontinuing to persist, in their work for complete and permanent separation. Nothing, in the long run, proved more disastrous to them than this first great victory. It blinded them to the dangers which lay before them. It maddened them for their own destruction.

CHAPTER IX

PREPARATIONS FOR THE THREE YEARS' WAR

Convictions as to the Length of the War after Bull Run—The Call
for Volunteers and Enlistments in the Regular Army and
Navy—The Powers of the President in Raising Armies and
Navies—Congressional Acts Enabling the President to Deal
with the Rebellion—The President as Military Dictator—The
Habeas Corpus Question—The Merryman Case—Mr. Bates's
Opinion on the War Powers of the President—The Raising,
Organizing, and Equipping of the Great Military Force Author-
ized by Congress—McClellan at Washington—Frémont in the
West—Halleck at St. Louis—Increase and Organization of the
Navy—The Production of the Materials of War at the North—
Preparations for War in the Confederacy—The Centres of
Confederate Military Organization—The Problems Confronting
the Confederate Leaders.

THE effect of the Confederate victory at Bull Run, as
to convictions concerning the length of the struggle,
was one thing at the South and the directly
opposite thing at the North. In the South
the mass of men believed that one Southerner had actually whipped five Northerners,
could do it every time, and that the Northern cowards
would hardly dare to try another bout. In a word, they
thought that the war was practically over, and secession
practically established, and that, therefore, no further
preparations on their part were necessary.

On the other hand, the people of the North were
made to realize the magnitude of the undertaking in
which they were engaged, and which they must prose-

226

cute to a successful end. While deeply humiliated by the disaster, they came quickly to understand that it was no reflection upon the valor of Northern soldiers, since the combatants were nearly evenly matched, as to numbers, in the last hours of the battle, and the Confederates had greatly the advantage as to position, and to appreciate the fact that not one-third of the army under the command of General Scott, on the Virginia border, had participated in the engagement. While, therefore, they lost no courage, they were forced to the conviction that the struggle was to be protracted, obstinate and bloody, and they immediately set about making preparations on a scale sufficient to accomplish the result upon which they were more firmly resolved than ever. On the day following the defeat, the House of Representatives voted : " That the maintenance of the Constitution, the preservation of the Union and the enforcement of the laws are sacred trusts which must be executed ; that no disaster shall discourage us from the ample performance of this most sacred duty ; and that we pledge to the country and the world the employment of every resource, national and individual, for the suppression, overthrow and punishment of rebels in arms." And this sentiment was quickly and distinctly echoed back from every city, village, hamlet and homestead of the North.

The President had already in his message of July 4th asked Congress to place at the disposal of the Government four hundred thousand men and four hundred millions of dollars. At the same time he informed Congress of his call of May 4th preceding for enlistments in the regular army and navy, and for volunteers to serve during the war, and directed the attention of Congress to the report of his Secretary of War that the regular army contained

The call for volunteers and enlistments in the Regular Army and Navy.

at that date, July 4th, in consequence of the call of May 4th, forty-two thousand men, and the volunteer force one hundred and eighty-eight thousand men, and also to the report of the Secretary of the Navy that the navy contained, in consequence of the increase of force so provided, eighty-two vessels, carrying eleven hundred guns, and manned by some thirteen thousand men. Here was a vast military force already at hand. It had been recruited in response to calls, issued May 4th preceding, for about eighty thousand men—forty-two thousand volunteers, twenty-two thousand regulars, and eighteen thousand seamen. The President acknowledged, in his message, doubts as to his constitutional power to make these calls, and said they "were ventured upon under what appeared to be a popular demand and a public necessity." He took the ground, however, that while he might have usurped the powers of Congress, he had not gone beyond that, and expressed the hope that Congress would ratify his acts.

There is no question that, in increasing the army by any other means than a call for militia, and in increas-

The powers of the President in raising armies and navies.

ing the navy by any means whatever, the President had assumed powers not expressly conferred upon him either by the Constitution or the laws. It is certainly a fair query, however, whether the President may not, in accordance with the spirit of the Constitution, in time of invasion or rebellion, and when Congress is not in session, ask his fellow-countrymen to come to the armed support of the Government and the country. It is certainly good political science to acknowledge such a power to him, and very bad political science not to do so. And he certainly would be a bad President who would refuse to assume such a responsibility under exigencies which, in his own honest opinion, required him to do so. A Pres-

ident who would let the Government go to pieces in an
armed attack upon it, either by foreign or domestic foes,
before he would ask the people to assist him in its armed
defence and in the maintenance of its supremacy, would
be a pitiable object, would be a President far more mer-
iting to be impeached and driven from office than the
President who should exceed his regular constitutional
powers in defending the country and maintaining the
enforcement of the laws.

It might be a dangerous thing to vest such a power in
the President by the express terms of the Constitution.
It might prove a strong temptation to ambitious and
imperious natures to expand unduly and unnecessarily
the executive power and prerogative.   It is perhaps best
that the Constitution should recognize the power as
belonging to the President in so general and vague a
manner as to make him feel the great weight of the responsibility which he assumes in its exercise, and thus
secure him against temptation to assume it lightly ;
but the constitution which permits the executive, under no exigencies, to call the people to his aid in upholding government is an unscientific and an unpracti-
cable instrument of public law, one which invites, and
even requires, infraction in the most critical moments
of a nation's existence.

The Congress which assembled on the 4th of July,
1861, was evidently inclined from the outset to interpret the Constitution from its whole spirit rather than
from the letter of express provisions.   On the very first
day of the session, Mr. Wilson of Massachusetts gave
notice in the Senate that he should ask leave to introduce a bill for ratifying the President's acts.   On the
next day he proposed to the Senate a joint resolution
which provided that all of the acts of the President in
increasing the army and navy, and in calling the militia

and volunteers should be legal and valid, "with the same effect as if they had been issued and done under the previous express authority and direction of the Congress of the United States." This precise resolution, though reported back to the Senate favorably and without change by the committee to which it was referred, was never voted on; but by separate acts Congress adopted substantially its contents and put the Administration upon the war footing.

By the acts of July 22d and 25th, the President was authorized to call for and accept volunteers to the
Congressional Acts enabling the President to deal with the rebellion. number of five hundred thousand men for a maximum service of three years, or for the period of the war, to fix the number of general officers necessary to command this vast force, and by and with the consent of the Senate to appoint them, and to arm these troops according to his own discretion. By the Act of July 29th he was authorized to increase the regular army by nine regiments of infantry, one regiment of cavalry, and one regiment of artillery, and to use any part of the military power, militia, volunteers, regulars, and marines, for suppressing rebellion against the Government of the United States, and removing obstructions to its operations which, in his opinion, could not be dealt with by the ordinary course of judicial proceedings. By the act of August 5th, he was authorized to enlist, through the Secretary of the Navy, and for the period of the war, any number of seamen and other persons necessary to place the entire navy in a state of utmost efficiency for active service. And finally by the Act of August 6th, all the acts, proclamations, and orders of the President relating to the army, navy, militia, and volunteers, issued after March 4th preceding, were approved and legalized.

In the second place, by the Act of July 13th, Congress empowered the President to collect the customs at the ports of delivery instead of the regular ports of entry ; and, if he should find it impossible to enforce the customs laws either at the ports of entry or of delivery, to cause the custom-houses at such ports to be removed to other places in the respective customs districts of these ports, or to be established on shipboard within these ports or near them ; and if he could not enforce these laws in either of these ways in such districts, to close the ports of entry therein, and blockade such ports against the entrance of any foreign vessels, and make capture of any vessel undertaking to enter.

In the third place, by the Act of July 17th, Congress authorized the Secretary of the Treasury to borrow the sum of two hundred and fifty millions of dollars, on the credit of the Government, by the issue of bonds and treasury notes in such proportion as the Secretary might find beneficial ; and by the Act of August 5th, Congress increased the duties on imports, levied a direct annual tax of twenty millions of dollars, and apportioned it among the Commonwealths, and an annual income tax of three per centum upon all incomes over eight hundred dollars, increased to five per centum in case the citizen assessed resided abroad, but reduced to one and one-half per centum, in all cases, upon income derived from the securities of the United States.   It was calculated that these provisions would place very nearly one million of dollars a day in the hands of the Government for the suppression of the rebellion and the re-establishment of the supremacy of the laws of the United States ; and to these ends Congress appropriated the vast sums to be thus raised to the equipment and maintenance of the army and navy.

In the fourth place, by the Act of August 6th, Congress authorized the President to seize, confiscate, and condemn any property employed, or intended to be employed, in aiding and abetting insurrection against the Government of the United States or resistance to the laws of the United States. This Act also declared any slave emancipated who should be employed by his master, or be permitted to be employed by his master, in any service hostile to the Government of the United States.

Finally, by the Act of July 13th, already referred to, Congress authorized the President to declare the existence of insurrection in all parts of the United States where he could not execute the laws by the ordinary processes, and to forbid commerce and intercourse between the inhabitants of such parts and the rest of the United States, and seize and confiscate to the United States all property employed in such illicit traffic and commerce.

With these several enactments Congress placed the Government on the war footing, ratified the President's *The President as military dictator.* assumption of war powers, and, on the 6th of August, adjourned, leaving the President practically in the position of a military dictator. This was good political science, and good public policy. It was also sound constitutionally. In periods of extreme peril to the political life of a nation, individual liberty, federalism in government, and even co-ordination of governmental departments must give way temporarily to the principle of executive dictatorship. It is a desperate remedy, a remedy of last resort, but it is one which every complete political system must contain, and under certain proper conditions employ. The two most modern constitutions of federal government, those of the German Empire and of Brazil, make express provision for it. They authorize the Executive in periods of extreme public danger to suspend the ordinary law and establish martial law. There is no question that the Constitution of the United States authorizes the Congress and the President, acting together, to do the same thing. The clauses of that instrument which vest in Congress the power to raise armies, provide for calling the militia into the service of the United States for repelling invasion and suppressing insurrection, and to declare war, and in the President the powers of a commander-in-chief, certainly contain the principle of the dictatorial power of the whole Government, if not of the President alone, and it is altogether gratuitous to concede that the Government of the United States overstepped its *constitutional* powers, and acted on the principle that necessity knows no law, in preserving the Union by force against dissolution. It overstepped its ordinary limitations, but it had, and has, the *constitutional* right to do that in periods of extraordinary danger.

The root of the error in denying this right lies in the claim that the Constitution made the Union. The truth is that the Union made the Constitution, and that the physical and ethnical conditions of our territory and population made the Union. The Union was, and is, the Nation, and men did not make the Nation by the resolutions of a convention. Men undertook to interpret the requirements of the Union in political and legal organization and to give them objective form and authority, but behind all that they did, or could or can do, was and is the Union, the Nation, whose preservation is the supreme principle back of the Constitution, and the supreme law within the Constitution. Any other view of these relations is unspiritual, is purely arbitrary and mechanical. Any other view leads, as it led in the South, to the loss of the ideal in our politics and jurisprudence, and consequently to dissolution, anarchy, and ultimate barbarism.

Congress passed, at this session, no formal resolution in regard to the suspension of the privileges of the writ of Habeas Corpus by the President's command. It was doubtful whether the President needed any approval of his action in this matter by Congress, or whether a disapproval by Congress would have been of any consequence from the point of view of a sound interpretation of the Constitution. The Constitution simply provides that "the privilege of the writ of Habeas Corpus shall not be suspended, unless when in cases of rebellion or invasion the public safety may require it." It is not expressly designated by whom the privilege of the writ may be in these events suspended. The provision is found in the article of the Constitution which treats of the powers of Congress, and it was argued that, from the textual connection, it must be concluded that Congress is vested with the power. But, from the point of view of a correct political science, it is easily perceived that the power belongs more properly to the Executive, at least when it is to be called into exercise upon or near the theatre of hostile operations. It is the President who must meet, and conquer or suppress, such movements, acting in his capacity of commander-in-chief of the military power. The Congress may not be in session at the time when these exigencies arise. Everything may depend upon the President's promptness and vigor. There is no question that a sound public jurisprudence would attribute such a power to him under such circumstances; and where the constitutional provision may be interpreted in more than one way, the dictate of a sound political science ought to determine which interpretation shall prevail. The then Chief Justice of the United

States, Mr. Taney, took the view, however, that Congress alone had the power to suspend the privilege of the writ, and that the power to suspend the privilege of the writ did not carry with it the power to make arbitrary arrest.

He gave this opinion in the Merryman case.   One John Merryman, accused of holding a rebel commission and recruiting a rebel military force in Mary- *The Merry-* land, was seized under a military order and *man case.* incarcerated in Fort McHenry.   Merryman applied, through counsel, to Chief Justice Taney for a writ of Habeas Corpus.   The Chief Justice issued it.   General Cadwalader, the commander of the Fort, declined to respond to it, on the ground that he had been authorized by the President to suspend the privilege of the writ, and had done so.   The Chief Justice then issued a writ of attachment for the body of General Cadwalader, but the United States marshal, who undertook to serve it, was stopped by the sentinel at the entrance to the Fort, and sent away with no answer.   The Chief Justice then filed the opinion, referred to above, in the office of the clerk of the Circuit Court of the United States for the district of Maryland, and directed a copy of the same to be transmitted to the President.   These events occurred during the latter part of May.   The President did not, however, order any return to be made to the writ of Habeas Corpus, nor command the execution of the writ of attachment, nor did he command the release of Merryman.   He submitted the question of his powers and duties in regard to these things to his Attorney-General, Mr. Bates, and, on the 5th of July, Mr. *Mr. Bates's* Bates instructed the President that he had *opinion on the* *War powers* the constitutional power to make military *of the Presi-* arrests, and suspend the privilege of the writ *dent.* of Habeas Corpus, in times of great public danger.   The

President followed the view of Mr. Bates, rather than
that of the Chief Justice, and the Congress, then in session, tacitly acquiesced in the President's course of action.   Mr. Bates's doctrine was and is sound jurisprudence, but Mr. Taney's propositions were, and still are,
the law of the land.   The development of constitutional
law on the side of the temporary dictatorial powers of
the President is still an unsolved problem in our system.

After the adjournment of Congress, the Washington
Government, the Northern Commonwealth governments

The raising,
organizing
and equipping
of the great
military force
authorized by
Congress.

and the people of the North settled down to
the work of raising, organizing, arming,
equipping and disciplining a military and
naval power of colossal proportions for the
purpose of suppressing the giant rebellion
against the Union and the Government.   The chief
centres of activity, if we may speak of chief centres
when every city, town, and hamlet was astir with martial life and animated with a stern and resolute purpose, were Washington, Cincinnati, Louisville, Cairo,
and St. Louis.

In the latter part of July General McClellan was
called to Washington, and given command of the new

McClellan at
Washington.

military department of Washington and
North-eastern Virginia.   He left General W.
S. Rosecrans in command in Western Virginia.   General
John C. Frémont had already been appointed to the
command of the military district of the West, composed

Frémont in
the West.

of Kentucky, Illinois, Missouri and Kansas,
and arrived in person at his head-quarters in
St. Louis at about the same time that McClellan assumed command in Washington.   Subject to Frémont's
orders, General Robert Anderson was placed in command at Louisville, General Benjamin M. Prentiss at
Cairo, and General Nathaniel Lyon at Springfield, Mis-

souri. General Anderson was superseded by General W. T. Sherman early in October, and General Sherman by General Don Carlos Buell in November. General Prentiss was superseded by General U. S. Grant early in September. General Frémont was superseded by General David Hunter early in November, and ten days later General Hunter was removed from command in St. Louis and General Henry W. Halleck was appointed in his stead. It was under the superior direction of these great chieftains that the vast army of six hundred thousand volunteers was assembled, organized, and disciplined during the late summer and autumn of 1861. Halleck at St. Louis.

The navy was organized in three squadrons. The North Atlantic Squadron, which was authorized to operate to the southern line of North Carolina, was placed under the command of Captain L. M. Goldsborough. The South Atlantic Squadron was placed under the command of Captain S. F. Du Pont. And the Gulf Squadron was entrusted to the command of Captain W. W. McKean. By the 1st of December (1861), the navy had been increased to two hundred and sixty-four war-ships, carrying two thousand five hundred and fifty-seven guns, and manned by over twenty thousand seamen. Increase and organization of the Navy.

The people throughout the Northern Commonwealths went earnestly and vigorously about creating the materials of war. Their genius for, and their experience in, manufacture enabled them to produce clothing, accoutrements, arms, ammunition, etc., without limit, while their great grain fields and prairies furnished food without stint. The only difficulty felt was in a sufficiently rapid manufacture of arms at the outset. At the outbreak of the war there was only one Government establishment at The production of the materials of war at the North.

the North for the construction of these implements, the armory at Springfield in Massachusetts. This plant could at that time produce only about ten thousand guns annually. There were, however, so many private establishments for the manufacture of weapons of all kinds that no need was felt for relying to any great extent upon governmental production. The arsenals at the North had been somewhat depleted by the orders of Mr. Buchanan's Secretary of War, Mr. Floyd, and the Washington Government found it necessary to send to Europe in the summer of 1861 for muskets. A few rather poor ones were purchased, but were soon thrown aside for the better models invented and manufactured at home. Many of the iron and steel foundries were changed into factories for the making of the heavy ordnance, and the new naval armaments were chiefly created at home.

Among the Confederates the preparations were by no means so earnest, active, and productive. As has been said, they generally thought that the struggle had been virtually ended by their victory at Bull Run. There was, however, at least one among them who was not thus deceived, and that one was Mr. Davis himself. He was continually saying that the contest would be long and bloody, and was continually urging his Congress and the people of the South to make adequate preparations to meet it.

Preparations for War in the Confederacy.

Already before the battle of Bull Run, the Confederate Congress had authorized the raising of sixty-six millions of dollars by loans, and had laid an export tax of one-eighth of a cent a pound upon cotton for the purpose of securing sufficient specie to pay the interest on the debt to be thus created. Before the end of the year the raising of about one hundred and twenty-five millions more by loan was authorized. According to the statement of President Davis the expenditures of the Confederate Government up to the beginning of February, 1862, amounted to one hundred and seventy millions of dollars. These loans were chiefly in the form of Treasury notes, convertible into twenty-year eight-per-cent. bonds, the interest upon which was to be paid in coin, the coin to be procured by customs duties and internal taxes.

Down to the date of the battle of Bull Run, the Confederate Congress had authorized the enlistment of one-year men only, and to the number of one hundred thousand. As a fact there were more than two hundred thousand men in the field before the 1st of August. By the Act of the 8th of August that Congress authorized the enlistment of four hundred thousand men to serve for a maximum period of three years, and also authorized, a little later, additional volunteer forces for local defence and special service.

The centres of organization around which these forces were being gathered in the late summer and autumn of 1861 were Yorktown and Centreville in Eastern Virginia, Winchester in the Shenandoah Valley, Lewisburg and Valley Mountain in Western Virginia, Knoxville, Nashville, and Memphis, in Tennessee, Little Rock in Arkansas, and the section of Missouri lying south-west from Springfield. The military chieftains to whom the work of organization and discipline was entrusted were Generals J. E. Johnston, P. G. T. Beauregard, T. J. Jackson, R. E. Lee, H. A. Wise, F. K. Zollicoffer, G. J. Pillow, S. B. Buckner, A. S. Johnston, Leonidas Polk, Benjamin McCulloch, and Sterling Price. There is no question that here was a great array of military talent, as subsequent events fully proved.

The immediate problems which they had to face

were certainly more difficult than those confronting the Union Generals. The South was poor in manufactures and in talent for invention. It was

The problems confronting the Confederate leaders.

also a second-rate food-producing section. Speaking generally, it bought both food and clothes, tools and arms, and all of the finer products of civilization from the North or from Europe, and paid for them in cotton. |How to arm, equip and provision the first large armies from the existing store of material in the South was a most serious problem for the Southern statesmen and generals ; and, then, how to change the agriculture of the South from the raising of cotton to the producing of food, and divert part of the labor of the South from agriculture altogether and employ it in the development of manufactures were almost equally difficult undertakings.

The first necessity was, of course, for arms. The Confederate President estimated the number of muskets and rifles in the arsenals of the "States" of the Confederacy in the spring of 1861, at about one hundred and fifty thousand. Of these, according to his statement, about fifteen thousand were Mississippi rifles, and the rest old muskets, recently altered from flintlocks to percussion locks. The United States officials, from the President down, and the Unionist historians, have maintained that the number of small arms in the "States" that claimed to have seceded from the Union was, at that time, much greater than this, owing to the treasonable acts of Mr. Buchanan's Secretary of War, Mr. Floyd, in sending too large a proportion of the arms belonging to the United States into that section. It is

The sending of arms to the South by Mr. Floyd.

probable that an exaggerated view of Mr. Floyd's doings has prevailed at the North, but, after making allowance for that, one cannot help feeling that Mr. Davis's estimate was conservative. He was not in the habit of overstating things, and he knew better than anyone else in the Confederacy that the Southern people would be very apt to estimate their wealth in military equipment much too highly. Whatever may be the exact truth as to these points, the seizure of Harper's Ferry, and the Navy Yard at Norfolk with its two thousand pieces of artillery, the capture of arms at Bull Run and Ball's Bluff, and in Missouri, and the purchases in Europe in 1861, placed the Confederates in a fair condition to meet the armies of the United States, in so far as the weapons of war were concerned. It must also be remembered that the people of the South owned and kept arms to a far greater extent than the people of the North, except perhaps in the extreme West. In 1861, it would have been rather difficult to find, in the country districts of the South, a man, or even a boy of sixteen, who did not possess a rifle, a double-barrelled shot gun and a pistol. There was much greater poverty in ammunition than in arms. Mr. Davis estimated the amount of powder on hand on the 1st of June, 1861, at two hundred and fifty thousand pounds, about one-fourth of what he thought would be necessary for a single year. He stated further, that, with the exception of two little private mills in East Tennessee, there was no manufacture of the article in the Confederacy. He also estimated the number of percussion caps to be had at about two hundred and fifty thousand, and claimed that there was almost no lead to be found. Copper for the manufacture of caps was, he stated, just beginning to be obtained in East Tennessee, and there were a few lead mines in Virginia, which were being worked in an indifferent manner. There was no saltpetre and but little nitre in store, but some four or five hundred tons of sulphur were found in New Orleans. As to the accoutrements of an army, such as uniforms, blankets, knapsacks, bridles, saddles, harness, wagons, etc., the Confederate President figured these at zero.

During the late summer and autumn of 1861, the Confederates went earnestly about the manufacture of *Beginning manufacture of arms in the Confederacy.* the implements of war. Powder mills were established in Virginia, North Carolina, South Carolina, Georgia, and Louisiana. Eight arsenals and four depots were supplied with machinery for the manufacture of arms, munitions, and equipments. Several good chemical laboratories were put into operation. Foundries for the casting of artillery were established at Richmond, Nashville, and New Orleans. And cloth factories, tanneries, etc., were springing into existence in many places. The blockade runners were also at work almost uninterruptedly between Wilmington, North Carolina, and Bermuda, bringing in a vast quantity of war material. By the end of the year 1861, the Confederates had between two and three hundred thousand men in their armies, and were fairly armed and equipped, in most places, for battle. They were, moreover, in good spirits and were confident of success. A majority of the engagements following their signal victory at Bull Run had resulted, as we shall see, favorably to them, and they generally felt that the ultimate triumph of their cause was not far off.

CHAPTER X

THE MILITARY MOVEMENTS IN THE LATE SUMMER AND AUTUMN OF 1861

AFTER the affair at Booneville, in Missouri, on the 18th of June, General Price had retired hastily with his forces toward the Southwest, gathering recruits as he went, and expecting to meet Confederate reinforcements as he neared the Arkansas line. On the 3d of July Lyon had, with a force

The military movements in Missouri.

of some three thousand men, begun pursuit. He had before this sent two regiments of infantry and a battery of artillery, under the command of Colonel Franz Sigel, to Rolla, and on the 23d of June this force had entered and taken possession of Springfield, the most important town in Southwestern Missouri. Sigel had immediately conceived the plan of intercepting Price on his retreat from Booneville to Arkansas. On the 28th he had advanced to Sarcoxie, and had found that Price had already passed by with a part of his men, but that two detachments were still to the north of him. These he sought, and, on the 8th of July, found, some eight or ten miles north of Carthage ; and on the next day he attacked them, although they more than doubled his force numerically, with the result that he was defeated and compelled to retire to Springfield. Meanwhile Lyon was advancing to his aid by forced marches. The junction of their forces was effected at Springfield on the 13th of July.

Lyon's total strength, after the junction with Sigel, was only about six thousand men, while Price, reinforced by McCulloch with a regular Confederate division, assembled at Cassville a force of about twelve thousand men and fifteen guns.

On the 1st of August, this army of Confederates and Missourians, under the command of McCulloch and Price, began the advance on Springfield. On that day the two armies were only thirty miles apart, and Lyon felt that it would be most hazardous for him to undertake the long retreat to the railroad terminus at Rolla, nearly one hundred miles away, since one-half of his enemy's force was mounted and could easily overtake him. He moreover feared the moral effect of a retreat without a struggle upon the population of Southern Missouri. He, therefore, resolved to risk a battle, and he put his army in motion toward Cassville on the same day that McCulloch and Price began their advance in the opposite direction.   On the second day of his march he encountered Rains's detachment at Dug Springs and drove it back upon McCulloch's division at Cave Springs.   The Confederates, believing Lyon to be much stronger than he really was, moved toward the northwest in order to effect a junction with another column coming from Sarcoxie, and Lyon returned to Springfield with the hope of finding there reinforcements from Rolla.   In this he was disappointed, and he soon learned that his enemy, in full force, had resumed the advance upon Springfield.

Lyon now saw that his only chance of victory, and perhaps of safety, was in surprising his adversaries, and in inflicting such losses upon them as to dis- _The battle_ able them, at least, from making pursuit. _of Wilson's_ On the evening of the 9th of August, he set _Creek._ out again from Springfield to fall upon his enemy encamped, at the moment, on the west bank of Wilson's Creek, ten miles to the south-west of Springfield.   His plan of battle was to send Sigel, with about a thousand men and a battery of artillery, around the Confederate right, with the order to assault their right flank, while he, with the rest of his force, about four thousand men, should attack in front.   Both movements appear to have been well executed in the beginning.   At daybreak, on the 10th, the Confederates were surprised, at about the same moment, in front and on the right flank, and the battle seemed to be turning in favor of the Union army.   The demoralization of Sigel's troops, however, when they found themselves within the camps of the Confederates, the treacherous use of the United States colors by the Confederates, and at last the fall of General Lyon, reversed the order of victory, and gave the triumph in the bloody battle of Wilson's Creek to the Confederates. About one-fourth of the Union army had been slain, wounded, or captured. The Confederates lost an even greater number, though not so great a proportion of their force. Lyon's death was a most serious disaster to the Union army. Colonel Sturgis, however, upon whom the chief command now devolved, brought the army back to Rolla in a successful retreat. The Confederates had been so badly crippled by the battle that they did not undertake any serious pursuit.

As the news of the defeat and death of Lyon spread through Missouri, the secessionists were greatly encouraged, and prepared themselves anew to join the standard of the Confederacy, whenever the opportunity should offer. The check, however, which the Confederates and Missourians had received at Wilson's Creek, and the misunderstandings between McCulloch and Price, the one holding commission from the Confederacy, and the other from the routed government of Missouri, caused McCulloch to retire with his troops into Arkansas. Whereupon Price, thus left in full command of all the troops in Missouri operating against the United States, began to move northwestward instead of pursuing the retreating Federals to Rolla. On the 2d of September, he encountered a body of Kansans under General Lane, at Drywood Creek, near the boundary between Kansas and Missouri, and drove them back into Kansas, taking possession of Fort Scott.

The Secessionists in Missouri encouraged to new efforts.

Meanwhile Frémont had appeared in St. Louis, as we have seen, and was gathering, equipping, and disciplining a large force for the rescue of Missouri and the holding of Cairo in Illinois at the junction of the Ohio River with the Mississippi, a place, therefore, of great strategic importance. Frémont's

The securing of Cairo.

opinion was that the holding of Cairo and of the river communication between St. Louis and Cairo were matters of much greater moment than sending aid to Lyon at Springfield. He had therefore left Lyon to shift for himself, as we have seen, and had sent reinforcements to Ironton, Cape Gerardeau, and Cairo, going himself, the 1st of August, to Cairo. He found that he had not acted any too promptly. The Confederate General Pillow had already appeared in New Madrid, not many miles below, with a force estimated by Frémont at twenty thousand men. Having secured Cairo, Frémont had returned, on the 4th of August, to St. Louis, in order to see what could be done for Lyon. Before he could relieve Lyon, however, the battle of Wilson's Creek was fought and lost, and Springfield had to be temporarily abandoned.

The news of the disaster reached St. Louis on the 13th. Frémont immediately resolved to establish a belt of fortifications reaching from Cape Gerardeau on the Mississippi, through Ironton and Rolla, to Jefferson City on the Missouri, and set to work in good earnest upon the execution of his plan.

Frémont's line of fortifications through Missouri.

Besides being thus pressed by the enemy, Frémont was harassed by difficulties with the new loyal "State" government just established by the convention at Jefferson City. The Governor chosen by the convention, Mr. Gamble, was a Democrat, and disposed to be quite conservative. Frémont, on the contrary, was a radical Republican, if not an outright Abolitionist. It was not unnatural, under the circumstances, that he should come quickly to the conclusion that he could save Missouri to the Union only by the assumption of dictatorial power. On the 31st of August, he issued his noted order proclaiming martial

Martial law proclaimed in Missouri.

law throughout the "State" of Missouri; designating the line of military occupation as extending from Leavenworth on the west, through Jefferson City, Rolla, and Ironton, to Cape Gerardeau on the Mississippi; commanding all persons taken with arms in their hands within this line to be tried by court-martial, and, if found guilty, to be shot; pronouncing the property of all persons in the "State" who should be convicted of having taken up arms against the United States, or of having taken active part with the enemies of the United States in the field, confiscated to the public use; and declaring the slaves of such persons, if any, to be free men.

It was a drastic measure. It created great excitement. In fact, it overshot the mark in one respect at least, viz.,

Lincoln's disavowal of part of Frémont's proclamation.

in declaring the emancipation of the slaves of all persons in rebellion against the United States. As we have seen, Congress had, by the Act of August 6th, ordained the emancipation of such slaves only as were employed, by command or permission of their owners, or the lawful agents of their owners, in any kind of military or naval service against the United States. President Lincoln himself was not prepared, at that moment, to go any further than this, if indeed he had the power to do so. He, therefore, promptly disavowed this part of Frémont's order, and the misunderstandings between Frémont and the Washington Government were thus begun, which terminated two months later in the removal of Frémont from the command of the military department of the West.

Frémont now sent Colonel Mulligan with a force of three thousand men and a battery of artillery to occupy and fortify Lexington, a place about one hundred and twenty-five miles up the Missouri River from Jefferson

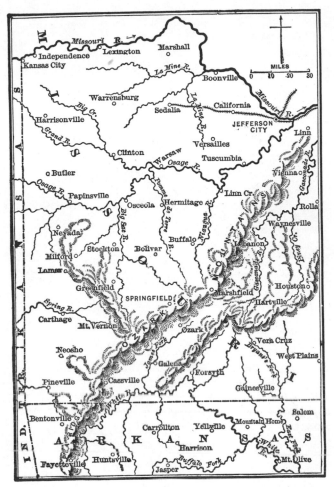

The Field of Operations in Missouri and Northern Arkansas.

City. Mulligan reached the place on September 9th, and immediately began fortifying College Hill. So soon as Price learned of this movement he determined to attack Mulligan before he could be reinforced. He appeared before Lexington on the 12th, with a large force which was soon increased to about twenty thousand men. General Frémont at St. Louis and General J. C. Davis at Jefferson City were deceived by the manœuvres of the enemy into the belief that Jefferson City was the point to be attacked. They, therefore, failed to undertake the relief of Mulligan at Lexington until it was too late. Price began the assault on the 18th, and pressed forward so vigorously that Mulligan was compelled to surrender on the 20th.

The Union defeat at Lexington.

So soon as Frémont learned of the disaster at Lexington, he started in pursuit of Price with an army of about twenty thousand men. The old Missourian was too wary to be caught, however, and on the same day that Frémont set out from St. Louis, he began his retreat southward. He reached Neosho and formed a junction with McCulloch, who had entered Missouri again with a strong Confederate division.

Price's retreat.

He also found Governor Jackson here, with a number of the secessionist members of the old "State" Legislature. This rump assembly went through the farce, at last, of voting Missouri out of the Union.

Secession in Missouri.

Frémont's army pursued slowly, and reached Springfield on the 27th of October. He established his headquarters here, while Price occupied Cassville. His plan was to push the war into Arkansas. His chief solicitude in regard to making this movement sprang from the consideration that the Con-

Frémont's advance to Springfield.

federate General Polk might send a force across from the Mississippi River, and strike him in the left flank. He, therefore, ordered General Grant, who had superseded General Curtis at Cairo, to make a demonstration from Cairo sufficiently strong to hold Polk's forces on the Mississippi.

The people of Kentucky had elected in August a strong Unionist Legislature and were gradually abandoning the idea of neutrality in the conflict and preparing to fall into line against the Confederacy. The secessionists in the Commonwealth had observed this change of temper and undertook to anticipate the occupation of Kentucky by Union troops. On the 3d of September, General Polk crossed the Kentucky line from West Tennessee and took possession of Hickman, and on the 4th he occupied Columbus. Just above this place is a high bluff commanding the Mississippi River and the Missouri shore opposite. Polk proceeded to occupy this bluff, and boastfully called it "the Gibraltar of the West."

So soon as General Grant, at Cairo, learned of Polk's advance, he sent detachments of Federal troops across the Ohio to Paducah and Smithfield, at the mouths of the Tennessee and the Cumberland. With these movements, the farce of Kentucky's neutrality was played to the end. It was now evident that her soil must furnish the first battle-grounds between the Ohio and the Tennessee lines.

At about the same moment when Polk entered Kentucky, the Legislature of the Commonwealth assembled, and the Senate sent a committee to Western Kentucky to investigate the violation of Kentucky's neutrality by both parties, and make report thereof. This committee repaired to Columbus immediately, and, on the 9th of

September, requested Polk to withdraw his forces from Kentucky. Polk answered at once, and offered to comply with the request, provided the " State " would agree to the simultaneous withdrawal of the Federal troops, and would engage to keep them out. He proposed to give the like guarantee for the Confederate Government in respect to the Confederate troops.

When Polk's answer was communicated to the Legislature, both Houses of that body immediately passed a series of resolutions, declaring that Kentucky's peace and neutrality had been wantonly violated, her soil invaded, and the rights of her people grossly infringed by the so-called Southern Confederate forces ; requesting the Governor to call out the military forces of the Commonwealth to expel the invaders ; invoking the United States Government to come to their aid and protection ; calling upon General Anderson to enter upon the active discharge of his military duties in Kentucky ; and appealing to the people of Kentucky to stand firm in their patriotism and in their devotion to the Union, and to assist in the expulsion of the lawless invaders of their soil. The Governor vetoed these resolutions, but they were passed over his act by overwhelming majorities. The relations of Kentucky were now entirely distinct. The Confederacy must reckon with her as an enemy.

The Confederate General Zollicoffer, who had been collecting troops on the line between East Tennessee and Western Kentucky, now crossed the line and occupied Cumberland Gap. On the 19th of September, he advanced to Barboursville, and dispersed a regiment of Kentucky Unionists.

The Confederates at Cumberland Gap.

On the 20th, General Anderson established his headquarters at Louisville and began the organization of the Federal forces in Northern Kentucky. The Legislature issued a call for forty thousand volunteers, and passed an Act making every Kentuckian who had voluntarily joined the rebel forces invading the Common-wealth incapable of inheriting any property in Kentucky, unless he should return to his allegiance to the United States within sixty days. The prompt action of the Legislature, and the arrest of one of the most outspoken of the secessionists, ex-Governor Morehead, and his confinement in Fort Lafayette, drove the disunionist leaders, such as John C. Breckenridge, William Preston, Humphrey Marshall, and John Morgan, into the Confederate ranks in Tennessee.

General Anderson at Louisville.

At last General Albert Sidney Johnston, appointed September 10th Confederate commander-in-chief in Tennessee, Missouri, and Arkansas, ordered General S. B. Buckner to advance from Middle Tennessee into Kentucky, and occupy Bowling Green on the south bank of the Barren River. This movement was consummated in early October, and General Johnston himself established his head-quarters at Bowling Green in the last days of the month.

A. S. Johnston at Bowling Green.

General W. T. Sherman had meanwhile superseded General Anderson at Louisville, and was demanding of the Washington Government two hundred thousand troops for the rescue of Kentucky from the Confederate occupation. All Northern Kentucky was in great excitement and apprehension, and the Legislature at Frankfort felt keenly that its own safety was imperilled.

Such was the situation in Kentucky when General Frémont ordered General Grant to threaten Columbus in order to prevent Polk from sending a column to the aid of McCulloch and Price.

Grant prepared an expedition during the first days of November, and although Frémont was superseded by Hunter before the preparations were completed, proceeded to carry out the instructions of Frémont. He ordered General C. F. Smith to threaten Columbus with a land force from Paducah, while he, with about four thousand men, dropped down the Mississippi in transports to a landing on the Kentucky shore some five miles above Columbus, and the next morning, the morning of the 7th of November, crossed over to Hunter's Landing on the Missouri shore. Grant's purpose, as thus revealed, was to attack a small Confederate garrison at Belmont, a hamlet directly across the river from Columbus.

Polk was immediately informed of the debarking of the Federal troops at Hunter's. He rightly concluded that the threat from Paducah was a mere feint, and promptly sent General Pillow across to Belmont with three regiments of troops. They arrived at Belmont in time to meet the Federal advance in front of the works. The Federals had, however, gained such a momentum of victory that they drove right on over the fortifications into the camps of the Confederates and scattered the enemy in every direction. Thinking the triumph complete the Federal regiments now virtually disbanded to plunder the camps and hold high revel over their success. General Polk was by this time relieved of any anxiety about the approach of General Smith from Paducah, and he sent General Cheatham across to Belmont with three more regiments, and then followed himself with two or three more. These all landed above Belmont, where Pillow's scattered troops had begun to collect.

Grant now found himself threatened by a force double his own, and in imminent danger of being cut off from his transports at Hunter's Landing. He succeeded, however, in reforming his men, and in cutting his way successfully through to the boats. He embarked his troops under the fire of the Confederates, and steamed back to Cairo in the evening after the battle.

The Federal loss in the battle was between five and six hundred, killed, wounded, and captured. The Con-

Belmont a Confederate victory. federate commander stated officially the Confederate loss at six hundred and forty-one men. Belmont was certainly a Confederate victory. It was claimed as such at the South, and recognized as such at the North, in which section the event created great depression of spirits. Still Grant had accomplished the purpose for which he had set out. It was now practically certain that Polk would not dare to weaken his force at Columbus in order to aid Price and McCulloch.

It was, however, also true that Price and McCulloch no longer needed his aid. Hunter did not share Frémont's sanguine views of the results of a campaign in Arkansas. He found that he had

Hunter abandons Frémont's plan of a campaign in Arkansas. great difficulty in subsisting his troops at Springfield, and he imagined that he did not possess the confidence of his soldiers. He determined to fall back upon Rolla, where he could re-provision the army through railway communication with St. Louis. While Grant was fighting the battle at Belmont, Hunter was executing this movement, and Price was advancing to Springfield, which now became his head-quarters. He occupied the valley of the Osage for the purpose of gaining both recruits and supplies for his army in that fertile and more populous district.

McClellan had now, by the executive order of November 1st, succeeded General Scott in the chief com-

Halleck at St. Louis. mand of all the armies of the Union. By his advice, General Henry W. Halleck was sent, about the middle of November, to St. Louis to take command of the department of the West. While

Halleck was something of a martinet, he had a good military education, and had formed a more adequate conception of the magnitude of the work before him than had any of his predecessors at St. Louis. He did not, therefore, deem it wise to carry on a petty war with Price, but rather to prepare himself for great movements, making it a point, however, to prevent Price from receiving recruits from Northern and Middle Missouri. He was entirely successful in the latter purpose, and this of itself forced Price to retire again to Springfield, where, with an army of some ten thousand men, he now established winter quarters, holding thus about one-half of that part of Missouri which lies south of the Missouri River.

As we have seen, the successes of McClellan at Laurel Hill and Rich Mountain, had caused the Confederate General Wise to fall back to Lewisburg in the valley of the Greenbrier River, in order to protect his right flank against the possible advance of McClellan southward. After Bull Run, and the call of McClellan to Washington, the Confederate President resolved to make another attempt to occupy Western Virginia. He sent General John B. Floyd to reinforce Wise and assume command in the Kanawha Valley, and General Robert E. Lee to take command of the remnants of Garnett's forces at Valley Mountain, and to exercise superior direction of the campaign in all of Western Virginia. *The military movements in Western Virginia after the battles of Laurel Hill and Rich Mountain.*

Lee soon saw that he must give up operating so far to the north as Valley Mountain, in order to maintain communication with Floyd and Wise, on the head waters of the Kanawha. He, therefore, moved southward, and took position in the upper part of the Greenbrier Valley in front of the defiles of Cheat Mountain. General Rosecrans, who had succeeded McClellan in command of the

Federal forces, had retired with the main body of his troops to Clarksburg on the Baltimore and Ohio Railroad, leaving the single brigade of General J. J. Reynolds to guard the passes of Cheat and Greenbrier Mountains.

Floyd began the offensive movement. His forces greatly outnumbered those of General Cox in front of him, and he easily compelled the Federals to fall back upon New River, the south branch of the Kanawha. He then left General Wise with a sufficient force to hold Cox's little army in check, and marched northwestward to Carnifex Ferry on the Gauley River, with the purpose of intercepting any reinforcements coming from Rosecrans at Clarksburg. After crossing the river successfully, he surprised the Seventh Ohio regiment at Cross Lanes, a few miles from the Ferry, and scattered it, after inflicting great loss upon it. This little battle took place on the morning of the 26th of August, and after his success, Floyd proceeded to fortify the heights about Carnifex Ferry in order to be able to resist any force coming from the North.

So soon as Rosecrans learned of Floyd's movements, he set out from Clarksburg with about ten thousand men, and, in about a week, he appeared before Floyd's intrenchments. This was the 10th of September. Rosecrans immediately ordered Benham's brigade to assault the works. The Federals were repulsed with considerable loss, and before McCook's brigade could come to their assistance, darkness intervened, and the battle was suspended. During the night, Floyd, who had only about two thousand men, and had asked aid from Wise in vain, slipped away. He retired to Sewell's Mountain and took up a strong position there. Rosecrans did not, however, follow. His troops were tired out by the hundred miles march from

Carnifex Ferry.

Clarksburg, and their exertions in the battle. He had driven the Confederates back into the mountains, and cleared the Kanawha Valley, and seemed to feel that he had accomplished all that was practicable or necessary at the moment.

So soon as General Lee learned of Rosecrans's march to the Kanawha Valley, he resolved to capture the passes into the middle section of Western Virginia Cheat Mounheld by the single brigade of General Rey- tain. nolds. On the 11th of September, he advanced northward from Huntersville with nearly ten thousand men. From the 12th to the 15th, he manœuvred about Reynolds with very great exertions to his troops, and with no results. On the 15th, he made a feeble attack upon Cheat Mountain, which was vigorously and successfully repelled. Lee now drew his forces back into the valley of the Greenbrier, leaving General H. R. Jackson with a single brigade to guard the passes through the Alleghanies into Eastern Virginia against Reynolds. Jackson intrenched himself on Buffalo Hill, from Greenbrier which he could command, with his artillery, River. the main road eastward over the Alleghanies. Reynolds, having been reinforced, attempted to dislodge him by an assault upon his works, October 3d, but failed.

General Lee had, meanwhile, proceeded southward, and had joined Floyd and Wise, assuming command of the entire force of about twenty thousand men. He did not, however, attempt to meet Rosecrans, although his army was much superior in point of numbers to the Federal force. He sent a small detachment across New River to Chapmanville, where, on the 25th of September, they were surprised and routed by a small body of Federals.

In addition to these discouragements in the field, General Lee had to deal with the quarrel between Floyd and

Wise, which was presently appealed to Richmond, with the result that Wise was withdrawn from his command.

Close of the campaign of 1861 in Western Virginia. Lee himself was recalled a little later, and sent to South Carolina, and a part of the army about Lewisburg was marched into the Shenandoah Valley, to reinforce General Stonewall Jackson at Winchester. Floyd made one more effort to regain the Kanawha Valley, but accomplished nothing more serious than inflicting annoyance upon the Federal supply trains. He was finally driven back into the mountains about the middle of November. And the expulsion of the Confederates from Huntersville, in the Greenbrier Valley, a month later, closed the campaign in Western Virginia, and left this section in the hands of the Federals.

General Stonewall Jackson inaugurated a little campaign further to the northeast, with the purpose of re-

The capture of Romney. capturing Romney, occupied by the Federal General Kelley for the protection of the Baltimore and Ohio Railroad line. It was for the purpose of this movement that Loring's brigade had been sent from Floyd to Jackson, as we have seen. Jackson succeeded in retaking Romney, but the troops with which he garrisoned the place, coming as they did from a more southern climate, found the winter in the mountains too rigorous for them, and were finally allowed to abandon the post and return to Winchester.

In Eastern Virginia the military movements during the late summer and autumn were even less active than

The military movements in Eastern Virginia after Bull Run. in Missouri, Kentucky, and Western Virginia, and resulted more unsatisfactorily to the Federal cause than those executed in these quarters. Of course the discouragement of the defeat at Bull Run was more keenly felt around Washington than elsewhere, and the necessity for thorough preparation before making another trial was more distinctly realized. The Administration and the people of the North accepted promptly the situation, and with practical unanimity settled down to the work of organizing, equipping, and drilling a vast army. They gave their new General, McClellan, *carte blanche* in almost every respect. It is true that McClellan complained of obstacles being thrown in his way, but it is now well known that McClellan magnified difficulties and underestimated advantages. The months of August and September and the half of October were passed in organizing, equipping, and drilling the new army, and in fortifying Washington upon all sides.

By the middle of October McClellan's army numbered over one hundred and fifty thousand men, with two hundred pieces of artillery. Deducting one-half of this number for the garrisons at Washington, Baltimore, and Annapolis, and on the upper and lower Potomac, and for the disabled and absent, McClellan had a force of at least seventy-five thousand men and one hundred and fifty pieces of artillery with which to begin active operations, while his enemy had not fifty thousand with which to meet him.

During the first days of October the Union army, in eleven divisions, lay along both sides of the Potomac from above Georgetown to below Alexandria. They were commanded by Generals Banks, Stone, McCall, Smith, Fitz John Porter, McDowell, Blenker, Franklin, Heintzelman, Keyes, and Hooker. The Confederates were stretched along from Leesburg to Aquia Creek. Evans's division was at Leesburg. The main army, under Johnston, was at and around Centreville. Their right occupied Aquia Creek, under the command of General Holmes. And Magruder, with a small force, still faced Butler on York peninsula.

The Confederate outposts opposite Washington, on Munson's Hill, were in plain view from the city during August. The growth of the Federal army, so to speak, on the west side of the river during September and October, caused the withdrawal of the Confederates from these advanced points. A few petty skirmishes had taken place, in which both sides usually retired unpursued.

The Confederates had planted batteries along the west bank of the lower Potomac, and had virtually cut Washington off from commerce by water with the North and the outside world. The people of the North blamed the authorities for allowing this to be effected, but it was soon understood that the only way in which this could be successfully dealt with was the driving of the Confederate army at Centreville and Aquia Creek back into the interior.

Situation opposite Washington and down the Potomac.

The temper of the Northern people began by October to change again, and a decided impatience for another advance became manifest. The weather was magnificent, the army was well organized, equipped, and drilled, and in fine spirits, and the condition on the lower Potomac was insufferable. McClellan, though still exaggerating in his own mind and in his representations the strength of the enemy, was made to feel that he must begin operations. On the 19th of October, he ordered a general reconnoissance along his front in the direction of Centreville. General McCall, who commanded the extreme right of the army on the west bank of the river, marched his division through Dranesville to within fifteen miles of Leesburg without discovering any signs of the enemy. He returned to Dranesville under order from McClellan, who feared that Johnston might sally forth from Centreville and strike the division in its exposed left flank.

The North demands now a new advance.

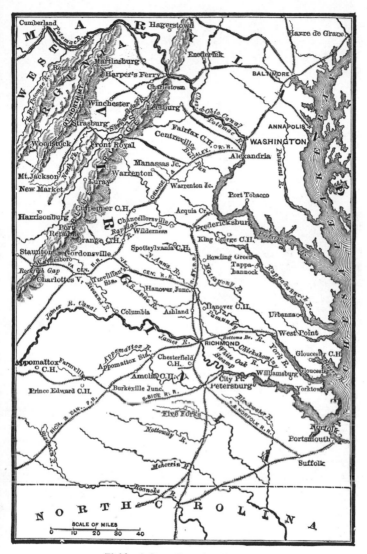

Field of Operations in Virginia.

On the next day, McClellan's Assistant Adjutant-General, A. V. Colburn, sent the following despatch to General Stone at Poolesville on the Maryland side of the river above Georgetown : " General McClellan desires me to inform you that General McCall occupied Dranesville yesterday and is still there. Will send out heavy reconnoissances to-day in all directions from that point. The General desires that you keep a good lookout upon Leesburg, to see if this movement has the effect to drive them away. Perhaps a slight demonstration on your part would have the effect to move them." General Stone very naturally concluded from the language of this order that he was commanded to send a detachment of his troops across the river in the direction of Leesburg. Leesburg was some miles back from the river, and was concealed from Poolesville by a high point on the Virginia bank, called Ball's Bluff, and by heavy intervening forests. There was, consequently, no way for Stone to keep any lookout upon Leesburg, except by sending troops across the river, and he certainly could make no demonstration against the enemy there without crossing the river. In a word, McClellan's order was too vague and left too much to Stone's discretion.

In execution of McClellan's instructions, General Stone ordered Colonel Devens of the Fifteenth Massachusetts regiment to take his regiment over to Harrison's Island which lies about midway, in the river, between Poolesville Landing and Ball's Bluff, and to send a scouting party over to the Virginia shore to look for the Confederates. Colonel Devens promptly executed these orders, and at about nine o'clock in the evening received a report from Captain Philbrick, the leader of the scouting party, that he had discovered, a short distance back from Ball's Bluff, a camp of Confederates which did not seem to be guarded at all. Devens immediately transmitted this information to General Stone. An hour or so later he received a written order from Stone to cross over, at once, from the island to Ball's Bluff with five companies of his regiment and surprise the camp discovered by Philbrick. Stone, at the same time, ordered Colonel Lee of the Twentieth Massachusetts to occupy Harrison's Island with four companies of his regiment, and to throw one company over to Ball's Bluff and hold it there after Devens's advance, as a cover for his return. The exact order to Devens was to attack the Confederate camp at daybreak, rout the enemy, pursue them as far as he deemed prudent, destroy the camp if possible and return to Harrison's Island, unless he should discover a position on the Virginia side near the river, which he could surely hold against large odds until reinforced, in which case he should occupy such position and report.

Despite the facts that the waters were high and swift, and that Devens had but three little boats at his command, not enough to carry over a single company at a time, the brave Massachusetts Colonel had his five companies upon the top of Ball's Bluff before daylight in readiness to advance. He marched forward toward Leesburg, but found no camp and no enemy. Philbrick's discovery was evidently nothing but the lights and shadows produced by a brilliant October moon. Devens advanced to within a mile of Leesburg before he saw any signs of his enemy. It was about seven o'clock in the morning of the 21st, when he got his first sight of them. He immediately sent back word to General Stone, and fell back to the open space of some ten acres on the top of Ball's Bluff. He reached there about nine o'clock without incident. He had now about six hundred and fifty men, in a greatly exposed position, surrounded as it

was by woods on all sides except the river side, and the
Confederates were advancing upon him, under the protection of the forest, in numbers unknown to him.   He
ought, in accordance with General Stone's directions, to
have recrossed immediately to Harrison's Island.   Instead
of this, he remained quietly on Ball's Bluff waiting for
reinforcements.   About noon the Confederates began to
fire upon his exposed troops from the woods, which were
within musket shot all around.

Meanwhile General Stone had gone down in person
to Edward's Ferry, a crossing of the Potomac some two
miles or more below the lower extremity of Harrison's
Island, and had ordered General Gorman to throw a
small force across the river at that point.   He also sent
an order to Colonel E. D. Baker of the California regiment, in command at the moment of a brigade, to either
throw the California regiment across the river, or call
back the troops of Devens and Lee, as he might deem
the wiser movement.   The order also authorized him to
assume the chief command on reaching the Virginia
side.   On receiving these directions, Baker, who was at
Conrad's Ferry, a crossing at the upper extremity of
Harrison's Island, immediately crossed over with his
entire brigade, composed of the California regiment, the
New York Tammany regiment, and the remaining companies of the regiments of Lee and Devens.   He arrived
at Ball's Bluff about two o'clock in the afternoon, when
Devens was being sorely pressed.   Baker was a brave,
impulsive man, filled with glowing patriotism, but
void of prudence.   He determined at once, without regard to the unfavorable character of the situation, to
fight.   He was the ranking officer on the scene, and
also had Stone's order to assume the superior command.
This he did immediately, and formed his line of battle, the
Fifteenth Massachusetts with two little pieces of artillery

on the right, the Twentieth Massachusetts with a small rifled cannon in the centre, and the California regiment on the left, with the New York regiment in reserve. He had not quite two thousand men. By this time the Confederate General Evans had brought up his entire brigade, consisting of four full regiments, numbering about three thousand men. Protected by the woods, the Confederates could simply shoot the Federals down, without exposing themselves. They picked off the officers, and the troops were thus soon thrown into inextricable confusion. At about four o'clock, Baker fell pierced through the head by a musket ball. Cogswell, the Colonel of the New York regiment, succeeded to the chief command, and tried to execute a movement for cutting his way out by his left flank toward Edward's Ferry, where he thought he might find reinforcements. But the Confederate Commander had anticipated this, and had blocked the way. It became now simply a matter of *sauve qui peut*. The Federals fled in every direction they could find open. Many jumped, or were pitched, over the Bluff. A few reached the little boats, which were soon overcrowded and sank. More crept along the shore under the cover of the now falling night, and straggled up to Conrad's Ferry, or down to Edward's Ferry. The slaughter was appalling. About a thousand men of the little force of less than two thousand were killed, wounded, or captured. The Confederate loss was reported by Evans at less than two hundred. Gorman, Stone, and even McClellan hastened to the scene of action. They arrived, however, too late. The work was over, and the Confederates had safely retired.

The whole army was dispirited and the whole North humiliated by the disaster, which everybody could see had resulted from the blunders of the commanders.

The public opinion seemed to demand a sacrifice, or more vulgarly speaking, a scapegoat. Who should it be? Baker was dead. Devens was not high enough in rank to satisfy. It was obliged to be Stone or McClellan. And so Stone, who certainly seems to have been the least culpable of the four, was arrested by order of the Secretary of War, confined secretly in Fort Lafayette for six months, and then released without trial or explanation.

The effect of the disaster on the Army and the people, and the sacrifice of Stone.

McClellan, on the other hand, was, ten days later, appointed commander-in-chief of all the armies of the Union, and now claimed further indulgence in military inactivity in order to plan an advance for all the armies at the same time. A little unintentional brush at Dranesville, on the 20th of December, between Ord's brigade and J. E. B. Stuart's Confederate brigade, in which the Federals won the field, was all that happened of any importance to disturb the quiet of the Potomac during the remainder of the year.

McClellan made commander-in-chief of all the armies of the United States.

The operations of the United States navy during this period were, on the other hand, quite uniformly successful. At the beginning of May the navy was as much disorganized as the army. Many of the ships were far away. Those caught in the Southern ports had been seized by the Confederates. And over two hundred of the officers had left the service to join their fortunes with those of the Confederacy. President Davis had, as we have seen, issued his proclamation authorizing privateering. And such ships as the Confederates could lay their hands upon were fitted out to prey upon the commerce of the United States. On the other side, President Lincoln had declared a general blockade of the Southern ports. The

Naval operations during the summer and autumn of 1861.

newly organized navy had thus several serious problems
before it, any one of which would tax its powers to the
utmost. It met them all, however, most successfully. At

The Confed-
erate priva-
teers. the outset, the Confederate privateers made
many seizures of Northern merchantmen in
the Southern ports, or in the waters near
them. But before the end of the year the Federal navy
had captured most of the vessels fit for privateering
owned by or in the Confederacy, and the Confederates
were not in a condition to create any more. Except for
the ships secured later in Great Britain, the Confederates would have scarcely been able to threaten the
commerce of the United States seriously again.

One very important legal point was brought to issue
by the capture of one of these privateers, the *Savannah*,

The legal
status of the
Confederate
privateersmen. as she was called. President Lincoln had declared, in his proclamation of April 19th, that
any attempt to molest the commerce of the
United States, under claim of authority from the Confederacy, would be treated as piracy. The *Savannah*
was captured on the 3d of June by the United States war-
ship *Perry*, and the crew were taken to New York City
for trial. The question at issue greatly embarrassed
the United States Government. This Government had
declined to sign an agreement at the Congress of Paris
in 1856 with the Powers of Europe for making privateering piracy by international consent. Consequently,
it was forced back to the question whether it would
recognize the Confederates as belligerents or would deal
with them as criminals, as traitors. If the Government
should view them not only as rebels, but as traitors,
criminals, then it must assume the same attitude toward
the persons engaged in rebellion on land as on sea—that
is, all persons taken in arms against the United States
must be made subject to the ordinary criminal law of the

country, and could not be dealt with as prisoners under the laws and usages of war. How the matter would have been determined had no considerations except those of juristic logic have been involved in it, is difficult to say. The capture of Federal prisoners in the battle of Bull Run was what settled the question. Mr. Davis put Colonel Corcoran and a score of other officers in chains, and informed the United States Government that he would deal with them in the same manner as the Washington authorities should deal with the crew of the *Savannah*. The proceedings against the "pirates" were immediately suspended, and the "pirates" themselves were finally exchanged as prisoners of war. The principle involved in this precedent was that during the appeal of the questions between the United States and the Confederacy to the trial of arms, the Confederate combatants must be regarded and treated as belligerents. If they should succeed in this trial, of course this temporary status would be vindicated as permanent. But if they should fail—fail without having secured any terms from the United States—then they would be finally at the mercy of the Government against which they had rebelled for anything more than the ordinary privileges of the accused in criminal procedure.

The United States navy was also successful in establishing the blockade before the end of the year. The attempt to blockade a coast more than three thousand miles long with its numerous bays, inlets and harbors seemed, in the beginning, a herculean task. But it was done with promptness and vigor. There was considerable blockade-running between the Bermudas and the North Carolina coast, and between the Bahamas and the Florida coast, but it never reached proportions to relieve to any considerable degree the wants of the Confederates. Several attempts were made during the last half of the year to break the blockade at particular points, but they were unsuccessful. The first and most promising one occurred in the mouths of the Mississippi River. The New Orleans authorities had commissioned a Captain Hollins, formerly of the United States navy, to change a steamboat into an ironclad ram, which they named the *Manassas*, and with that and some five ships to drive the blockading squadron out of the river. He did drive some of the United States vessels aground, and proclaimed a victory, but these were all safely gotten off, and the blockade was restored, as stringent as before, within twenty-four hours. The other attempts were even less worthy of notice.

It occurred early to the authorities at Washington that the navy might be used for another purpose, one
The Hatteras expedition. more positive and offensive than protecting commerce and maintaining the blockade, viz., for the purpose of lodging troops at certain points in the Confederacy, and establishing coast garrisons, which would serve as bases of operations against the vital interior points of the insurgent country, and as rallying-places for the Union men of these sections. After a good deal of thought and consultation, it was determined to effect a lodgement at Cape Hatteras on the North Carolina coast and at Port Royal about half way between Charleston and Savannah.

The expedition for the occupation of Hatteras was prepared during the month of August, and set out from Newport News on the 26th. It consisted of six war vessels under the command of Commodore Stringham, and several transports containing a land force of about one thousand men commanded by General Butler. The fleet arrived off Hatteras on the following day, and on the morning of the 28th began the attack on the forts, Clark and Hatteras. These forts mounted some fifteen guns and were held by nearly a thousand men, under the command of Commodore Barron, a former United States naval officer. The attack was successful, and, on the 29th, Barron surrendered forts and garrison. Recognizing the strategic importance of the place, the Federal commanders decided to occupy it permanently. They left a small garrison in the forts, which was soon increased, and Hatteras furnished the solid base for the subsequent naval operations along that part of the coast.

It will be remembered that Fort Pickens, which guards the east side of the entrance to Pensacola Bay, had been held by its Federal garrison, while Fort Mc- Fort Pickens. Rae, which is on the west side, had been seized by the Confederates. On the 9th of October, the Confederates threatened Fort Pickens by landing troops from Pensacola on Santa Rosa Island to attack some Federal troops in the rear of the fort, but the movement resulted in no attempt upon the fort. On the 22d of November the garrison of Fort Pickens, aided by the war-ship *Richmond*, undertook to bombard Fort McRae, but effected nothing. The *status quo* was preserved during the remainder of the year.

Further westward, however, the Federal navy took possession of Ship Island on the Mississippi coast, and established here a base for naval operations against Mississippi. Before the end of the Ship Island. year, a permanent garrison of nearly two thousand men, under the command of General John W. Phelps, was settled here.

But the naval movement of greatest brilliancy and success during the year 1861 was the expedition against Port Royal, and the occupation of the coasts The capture of Port Royal. and islands of this most important bay. The expedition was prepared during the month of October. It consisted of about twenty war vessels, under the command of Commodore Samuel F. Du Pont, and an army division of some ten to fifteen thousand men, under the command of General T. W. Sherman, embarked on about thirty transports. This large force started from Fortress Monroe on the 25th of October. Its destination was known only to the President and his Cabinet, and to Du Pont and Sherman. The passage was stormy, and a few of the transports were lost and others disabled. In the night of November 3d, the Commodore's flag-ship arrived off Hilton Head at the entrance to Port Royal. He found two forts, Fort Walker on Hilton Head, and Fort Beauregard on the opposite side of the inlet. They were together defended by about fifty guns and two thousand soldiers. There was also a little fleet within the bay, commanded by Commodore Tatnall, formerly of the United States navy. The soldiers in the forts were under the immediate command of General T. F. Dayton.

Du Pont began the attack in the forenoon of November 7th, and within six hours he had captured the forts, and was landing Sherman's army. Tatnall burned his vessels, and the Confederate soldiers fled in all directions open to them. The war was thus early carried into South Carolina. Before the end of the year the Federal fleet and army had possession of the waters of the South Carolina coast from North Edisto Bay to Warsaw Bay, and of all the principal islands in these waters. They also had possession of Tybee Island at the mouth of the Savannah River. The Stars and Stripes had been again raised in both South Carolina and Georgia, raised never again to be lowered.

The Washington Government also managed, at this time, most successfully, a very serious incident in foreign relations. President Davis had commissioned James M. Mason and John Slidell as diplomatic representatives of the Confederacy to Great

The Trent affair.

Britain and France.   These two men, bearing despatches from the Confederate Government to the Governments of Great Britain and France, and accompanied by their families and secretaries, slipped out of Charleston Harbor in the night of October 12th on the steamer *Theodora,* and landed safely in Cuba.   On the 7th of the following month they left Havana on the British steamer *Trent,* destined for St. Thomas, whence they intended to proceed to England.   Captain Charles Wilkes of the United States war-ship *San Jacinto* happened to be with his vessel in Cuban waters looking for the Confederate privateer *Sumter.*   While in the port of Havana he learned of the presence of Mason and Slidell in the city, and of their destination. Wilkes had read a good deal of international law in British texts and decisions, and he concluded that he had the belligerent right to visit any neutral vessel on the high seas in search of contraband of war, and to seize the persons and papers of diplomatic representatives of governments at war with his Government. There is not much doubt that the British principles, practices and decisions did seem to warrant this conclusion.   Wilkes waylaid the *Trent* in the Bahama Channel the day after her departure from Havana, and, upon the refusal of her commander to heave to, fired a shot across her bow.   She yielded to force and stopped.   She was boarded by Lieutenant Fairfax and a detachment of marines from the *San Jacinto,* who forcibly removed Mason and Slidell and their secretaries from the *Trent* to the *San Jacinto,* and brought them to Fortress Monroe, whence they were taken, by order of the Government, to Boston Harbor and confined in Fort Warren. The despatches carried by these gentlemen were not secured, and their families, spurning the proffered hospitality of Captain Wilkes, proceeded to England.

The news of the event of the 8th of November in the Bahama Channel reached the Government at Washington on the 16th, and the Government at London on the 30th. At first the conduct of Captain Wilkes seemed to be universally approved in the United States. The people applauded it with enthusiasm everywhere. The House of Representatives passed a vote of thanks. Even the Secretary of the Navy, Mr. Welles, declared officially that "the prompt and decisive action of Captain Wilkes on this occasion, merited and received the emphatic approval of the Department."

In Great Britain the event was viewed both by the Government and the people as an insult to their flag, and release of the prisoners with suitable apology or war seemed to be the only alternatives which occurred to anyone as proper demands to be made of the Washington Government. But there were two cool heads in Washington, the President and the Secretary of State, and they had a prudent envoy in London, Mr. Charles Francis Adams. Moreover the British Ambassador to the United States, Lord Lyons, was wise and just and friendly in his feelings toward the Government to which he was accredited.

Mr. Seward had put Mr. Adams in a position to meet any embarrassments, by despatching him, on the day that the news of the affair in the Bahama Channel reached London, the information that Captain Wilkes had acted without authority from Washington, and that the Government was ready to discuss the matter with the British Government.

The British Government made a good deal of bluster before the despatch was communicated to it; and was so embarrassed by its own haste after receiving the communication from Mr. Adams that it delayed making the same known to the public for some days. During this time the arsenals rang with the noise of warlike preparations, and troops were sent on shipboard destined for Canada. The law officers of the crown were appealed to, and they advised the Ministry that the act of Wilkes was illegal, since he did not take the *Trent* into port and subject his capture to the jurisdiction of a regular prize court of the United States. The infraction of international law made by Wilkes consisted, according to their view, in taking the persons of the envoys out of the British vessel without a preceding trial and judgment by a regular prize court of the United States authorizing the same. The opinion of the British jurists was certainly sound and lawyerlike. It made the question of procedure precede, as it should, the argument upon the merits.

Whether they so intended or not, their opinion, and the demand of the British Government based on it, opened to the United States Government the way of escape from danger and embarrassment without loss of dignity. Mr. Seward saw at once his opportunity and advised the President to yield on the point of procedure and release the prisoners, which the President promptly did.

Mr. Seward took advantage of this occasion to assert, that, in demanding the release of Mason and Slidell, the British Government had placed itself upon principles in regard to the right of visitation and search, and in regard to what constitutes contraband of war, always before this denied by Great Britain, while long approved by the United States and most of the states of Continental Europe. Mr. Sumner took the same ground in his famous speech upon the subject made in the Senate on the 9th of January, 1862.

The contention in both cases appears, however, a little strained, to say the least. As we have seen, the British Government rested its whole case on the question of procedure. It declared simply that the forcible removal of the envoys from the *Trent* was illegal because it had not been preceded by a trial in a regular prize court of the United States, and by a judgment from such a court decreeing their removal. Both Mr. Seward and Mr. Sumner were a little over anxious to appear as victors in this diplomatic bout with Great Britain.

The Confederates were greatly disappointed and chagrined at the result. They had been gleeful in their joy at the prospect of the United States having a war with the most powerful state of Europe in addition to the internecine struggle. They now denounced as cowardice the prompt backing down of the Washington Government before " the roar of the British lyon," and scolded Great Britain for not carrying out her threats, although her demands had been accorded. The amicable arrangement of this matter removed all danger of any serious complications between the United States and Great Britain, and solved thus early one of the main problems with which the Washington Government was confronted from the first.

If we cast a comprehensive glance over the situation at the close of the year 1861, we shall indeed find some

Bird's-eye view of the situation at the close of 1861.

justification for President Lincoln's statement in his message of December 3d to Congress, that the cause of the Union was "advancing steadily and certainly southward," but we cannot repress the feeling that this was fully as cheerful a view of the state of things as the facts warranted. The Confederates had, at last, established their line of defence from Yorktown in the east along the southern Potomac to Aquia Creek, thence to Centreville, Leesburg and Winchester, thence along the Alleghanies south-westward to the headwaters of the Great Kanawha, thence to the upper Cumberland Valley, thence westward to

Bowling Green, Russellville and Columbus, and thence to Springfield and the Kansas border. Every slave-holding Commonwealth, except Delaware and Maryland, was thus wholly or partly within their jurisdiction. It was a vast territory, and in it a great power was now fairly organized and equipped for resistance. The authorities at Washington and the people of the North could now no longer deceive themselves with the idea of a speedy termination of the struggle. Neither could they promise themselves any more that success at a single point upon this extended line would be decisive. They saw that a powerful and united effort along the whole line must be made in order to effect anything worth the exertion and the cost. We pass now, therefore, from the consideration of the *petit* war to that of the *grand* war of the rebellion.

CHAPTER XI

MILL SPRINGS, FORT HENRY, DONELSON, SHILOH, PEA RIDGE, AND ISLAND NO. 10

The President's Military Order of January 27th, 1862—Anticipation of the President's Order by the Western Armies—Attempts to Relieve East Tennessee—Zollicoffer's Move to Mill Springs—The Battle of Mill Springs, or, More Correctly, of Logan's Cross Roads—Grant's Manœuvres from Cairo and Paducah—Fort Henry—Fort Donelson—The Battle—The Surrender—The Results of the Victory—Halleck, Buell, and Grant—Failure of the Attempts to Prevent the Concentration of the Confederates at Corinth—Concentration of the Federals at Pittsburg Landing—The Advance of Buell—The Extension of Halleck's Authority—Nelson's Forced March from Columbia to Savannah—Johnston's Preparations for Battle—The Advance of the Confederates to Shiloh—The Federal Position—The Plan of Attack—The Battle—The Death of Johnston—Webster's Battery—The Arrival of Nelson—Suspension of the Struggle—The Two Armies on the 7th—The Renewal of the Battle—The Piercing of the Confederate Centre—The Defeat of the Confederates and their Retreat—The Losses—The Pea Ridge Campaign—Retreat of Price—Curtis's Pursuit—The Position at Pea Ridge—The Flanking Movements of the Confederates—The Battle of Pea Ridge—The Second Day's Battle, and the Defeat of the Confederates—The Losses—The Indian Brigade —The Capture of Island No. 10—The Attack on New Madrid—Preparations against Island No. 10—The Capture of the Island and the Confederate Army—The Beginning of Pope's Popularity—The Advance on Corinth—The Retreat of the Confederates from Corinth—The Fall of Memphis.

By the beginning of 1862, the Northern patience with the work of preparation again manifested signs of exhaustion. The President was made to feel that the temper of the people required another early effort to advance. He had himself become restless under General McClellan's procrastinations. At last he took matters into his own hands, and, on the 27th of January, issued that, from a military point of view, strange order for a forward movement on the part of all the armies of the United States, to be executed on the selfsame day, the 22d of February following. More than once Mr. Lincoln sought to make use of the mystical influence of the impressive events in our national history to inspire the people and the soldiers with patriotic ardor. This military proclamation is intelligible from this point of view, but from no other.

The President's military order of January 27th, 1862.

The two comprehensive objects of the intended movement were the capture of Richmond and the opening of the Mississippi. Undoubtedly it was good military judgment so to manœuvre the armies as to prevent the Confederates in the West from reinforcing those in the East, and *vice versa*, but it is hardly to be supposed that a general advance upon the selfsame day from points a thousand miles apart would best effect these purposes, or would even be a possibility.

The Western armies did not, however, wait for the coming of Washington's birthday to enter upon the campaign. Already, in fact, before the issue of the President's order, they had begun operations.

Anticipation of the President's order by the Western armies.

As we have seen, the Union forces in Middle and East Kentucky had early regarded East Tennessee as their objective point. The strong Union sentiment of the people of East Tennessee was well known in Kentucky and throughout the North. Its occupation by the Union armies would

Attempts to relieve East Tennessee.

rescue a loyal people from the tyranny of the Confederacy, would secure the resources of this section for the Union cause, and would sever one of the main lines of connection between Virginia and the western parts of the Confederacy.   During the autumn of 1861, two attempts were made to advance in the direction of East Tennessee ; one by General Schœpf from the Federal base at Wild Cat Camp in Garrard County, and the other by General William Nelson from Lexington, up the Licking River through Prestonburg and Piketon, and then across the Cumberland Mountains into the valley of Clinch River.   Schœpf's movement was stopped by a rumor that the Confederates were advancing from Bowling Green upon his right flank, and Nelson was checked by the Confederates under Colonel Williams in a little battle between Prestonburg and Piketon, and, although he advanced afterwards to Piketon, he was convinced that the way across the mountains was barred to him by Williams and his forces at Pound Gap.

Nelson withdrew his forces from Piketon, whereupon the Confederates, under the command of Colonel Humphrey Marshall, advanced again into Kentucky. General Buell now sent Colonel James A. Garfield, with the eighteenth brigade of his army, to drive Marshall back. Marshall retreated before Garfield's advance to Prestonburg, and in the morning of the 10th of January, 1862, made a stand at Middle Creek, a little to the west of Prestonburg.   In the engagement which followed both parties claimed the victory.   Both parties, however, withdrew from the position, the Confederates retiring to Pound Gap and the Federals to Paintsville.   The Confederates thus abandoned extreme East Kentucky, and the Federals left East Tennessee, for the moment, in the grasp of the Confederacy.   It was evident now to them that they could not penetrate East Tennessee through the mountains of South-eastern Kentucky, and that they must choose their line of advance further westward.

The Confederates saw this also, and in order both to meet the possibility of an attempt of the Federals to advance towards East Tennessee by the Kingston route further westward, and to put themselves in a better position to invade Middle Kentucky, Zollicoffer abandoned Barboursville and moved his troops westward to Mill Springs and Beach Grove, the former on the south side and the latter on the north side of the Cumberland River, directly opposite to each other. The Confederates now began to fortify these two positions.

Zollicoffer's move to Mill Springs.

General Buell saw at once the necessity for dislodging Zollicoffer from this new base of operations, and in the last days of December, he ordered General Schœpf to take a position at Somerset, a place about eighteen miles to the north-east of Mill Springs, and there await the advance of General George H. Thomas from Columbia, a place thirty-five miles north-west from Mill Springs, who had been ordered to form a junction with Schœpf, and then attack the Confederates on the Cumberland. The Confederate Commander, now General George B. Crittenden, soon learned of the movement, and saw at once that he could save himself only by preventing the junction of Thomas and Schœpf. The two Union armies were to come together at a place called Logan's Cross Roads, the place where the road from Somerset to Mill Springs joined the road from Columbia to Mill Springs, and about ten miles northward from Mill Springs. Crittenden's plan was to occupy this place before either Thomas or Schœpf could arrive, and beat the Union armies singly. It was a correct conception, but Crittenden was too slow in executing it.

The union of Thomas and Schœpf had been accomplished for some hours before the Confederates arrived in front of the Federal outposts.

The Confederates had, however, no choice of alternatives. They must attack. They endeavored to help themselves by a surprise attack. In the early morning of the 19th of January, they hurled themselves impetuously upon the Federal troops. The Federals were at first thrown into confusion, and the Confederates charged forward with shouts of victory. But Thomas drew them by his masterly manœuvres into a position where he turned their left flank, and, in the moment of their confusion while attempting to change front, threw a large fresh regiment upon them in bayonet charge, which routed them completely. The victory of the Federals was decisive, but the darkness intervened before the works at Beach Grove were reached. On the morning of the 20th, the Federals entered the fortifications, only to find that the Confederates had fled across the river to Mill Springs, and were already in full retreat towards Nashville.

The battle of Mill Springs, or, more correctly, of Logan's Cross Roads.

Some five thousand Confederates and eight or ten thousand Federals had taken part in the engagement. The Confederate loss was about five hundred men, among them General Zollicoffer. The Federal loss, on the other hand, was only about half as great. The Federals also made capture of a large amount of arms, ammunition and commissary stores, and of a considerable number of animals and wagons. The Confederates had, undoubtedly, suffered a most serious disaster. It was the beginning of the chapter of disasters which overtook their armies to the west of the Alleghanies during the late winter and spring of 1862.

At the beginning of Thomas's movement against Mill

Springs, Buell requested McClellan to order General Grant, at Cairo, to threaten Columbus, Fort Henry and Fort Donelson, in order to prevent the *Grant's manœuvres from Cairo and Paducah.* Confederates at Bowling Green from sending aid to Crittenden at Mill Springs, and to prevent Bowling Green from being reinforced from the first-named points.

In obedience to an order from McClellan, transmitted through Halleck, Grant sent General J. A. McClernand from Cairo with a force of some six thousand men to menace Columbus, and General C. F. Smith, from Paducah, with a smaller force, to occupy the attention of the Confederates about Fort Henry. Both of these movements were successfully executed between the 10th and 25th of January. No reinforcements were sent from these points to Bowling Green, and the Confederates at Bowling Green, being threatened on their front by General Buell's main army, could do nothing for Crittenden at Mill Springs.

These reconnoissances were destined, however, to lead to far more important results. General Smith found a fort on the west side of the Tennessee River, just across from Fort Henry, which, on account of its elevation above the latter, really commanded it. General Smith reported to General Grant that it was, in his opinion, practicable to seize this point, called Fort Heiman, and from it to reduce Fort Henry.

General Grant had already formed the view that the true lines of operation for the Union forces in the West were up the Tennessee and Cumberland Rivers, *Fort Henry.* thus turning both Columbus and Bowling Green, and forcing the evacuation of Kentucky. After receiving Smith's report, he went to Halleck, at St. Louis, with the plan. Halleck, at first, rebuffed him, but with the help of Flag-Officer Andrew H. Foote, who had gathered a little fleet of iron-clad boats, called gun-boats, at Cairo, he at last prevailed on Halleck to allow him and Foote to undertake the campaign. Halleck's order of January 30th was simply to make preparations to take and hold Fort Henry, and his written instructions only added the direction to occupy the road from Fort Henry to Fort Donelson on the Cumberland, so as to prevent reinforcement from Donelson to Henry, or escape from Henry to Donelson. Grant's army arrived on transports within striking distance of Fort Henry in the evening of February 5th. He ordered McClernand to disembark on the east side of the river and occupy the roads leading from Henry to Donelson, C. F. Smith to disembark on the west bank and assault Fort Heiman, and Officer Foote to bombard the Forts in front. The execution of these movements was to take place at eleven o'clock in the forenoon of the next day, the 6th. The Confederate Commander, General Lloyd Tilghman, had, however, very cleverly divined the plan, and, during the night, he effected the evacuation of Fort Heiman, and the escape of the garrison of Fort Henry by the upper road to Fort Donelson. He remained himself at Fort Henry, with some eighty artillerists, in order to occupy the attention of the Federals until his little army of three thousand men could escape.

The advance of the Federals began as ordered. At a little past noon the battle between the little band in the Fort and Foote's seven gun-boats was opened. It lasted an hour and a quarter, when the Confederates surrendered. When Smith arrived at Fort Heiman, he found it deserted, while McClernand failed to intercept the march of the garrison to Fort Donelson. The loss in killed and wounded was inconsiderable, and the prisoners captured in Fort Henry numbered only about sixty, among them General Tilghman. But one of the great water courses leading into the heart of the Confederacy was now opened, and the first stage of the campaign for the rescue of Kentucky and Tennessee from the power of the Confederacy was successfully accomplished.

In his despatch to General Halleck announcing the capture of Fort Henry, Grant declared that he would take and destroy Fort Donelson on the 8th. In this prediction he was too sanguine. He does not seem to have taken sufficient account of the time it would require to send the gun-boats down the Tennessee and up the Cumberland, nor of the difficulties of the march across from Henry in the torrents of rain which were falling, nor of the strength and extent of the fortifications at Donelson.

On the day following the capture of Henry, however, Grant with his staff and few companies of cavalry rode to within a mile of the outer works around Fort Donelson and made a satisfactory recon- Fort Donelson. noissance of the position. He found the fortifications to consist of a strong Fort on the bank of the river mounting a goodly number of heavy guns to defend the approach by the river, and a line of rifle pits running up the stream, and about a mile away from it, to a slough of the river which lay almost at right angles with the main current. A deep creek, called Hickman Creek, ran around the base of the Fort, on the down-stream side of it, and formed a strong barrier against an attack by a land force moving up the river. Grant also found that there was a range of hills outside of the ridge occupied by the rifle pits, which were higher than any of the points of the fortifications, and that a deep ravine running at right angles with the line of rifle pits cut this line into two parts near the centre. At a glance he saw that he could command the Confederate works by artillery upon these higher points, and could pierce the line of fortifications through the ravine.

By the 12th Grant and Foote were fairly prepared to begin operations. Foote steamed up the Cumberland with the gun-boats, and along with him, on transports, went Colonel Thayer's brigade of infantry ; while Grant, with an army of about fifteen thousand men, set out on the march across the neck of land between Fort Henry and Fort Donelson, about a dozen miles in width. The army was in two divisions, under the command of McClernand and Smith, while Lew Wallace was left behind with some two thousand men to hold Forts Henry and Heiman.

The Confederates had, during the six days since the capture of Fort Henry, been receiving reinforcements. After the disaster at Mill Springs, the Confederate commander at Bowling Green, General A. S. Johnston, had decided to retire behind the Cumberland, in order to avoid being flanked by Thomas on his right. He was evacuating Bowling Green when Grant was starting from Fort Henry to attack Donelson, and he sent Generals Pillow, Buckner, and Floyd with ten to twelve thousand of his best troops to Donelson, having resolved to fight his battle for the possession of Nashville and the south bank of the Cumberland at Donelson.

About noon of the 12th the head of McClernand's column encountered the Confederate pickets. Grant now put his forces into position, the division under

The battle.

McClernand forming the right wing, while Smith's division formed the left wing, resting on the heights nearly opposite the fort. Only one of the ironclads had arrived, the *Carondelet*, commanded by Captain Walke. He immediately fired a few shots at the lower guns of the fort, but made no impression.

On the next day, the 13th, the Federal lines were

drawn closer, and about one o'clock in the afternoon
General McClernand ordered Colonel Morrison's brigade,
supported by Haynie's regiment, to take advantage of
some confusion in the Confederate line caused by the
good artillery fire from the Federal batteries on the
heights behind them, and assault a redan in the middle
of that line which was causing the Federals a good deal
of annoyance.   It was a rash and presumptuous thing on
the part of McClernand, and he forfeited Grant's respect
for his judgment thereby.   Nevertheless, the brave Il-
linoisans almost succeeded, and probably would have
succeeded had not their gallant leader, Colonel Morrison,
been stricken down at the most critical moment.   Morrison was borne bleeding from the field, and Haynie
gave the order to withdraw.   The victory of the Confederates in the battle of the 13th gave them great encouragement, and was in some degree dispiriting to the
Federals.

In the night of the 13th Foote arrived before the Fort
with five gun-boats, and the transports bringing Thayer's big brigade of six full regiments.   General Lew
Wallace arrived also in the early morning of the 14th,
with the troops that had been left at Fort Henry.   With
these large reinforcements, Grant's army now outnumbered that of the Confederates, without the gun-boats,
and the courage of the men was completely restored.

Grant now formed a third division, composed chiefly
of the newly arrived troops, put Lew Wallace in command of it, and caused it to take position in the centre of
his line, between Smith and McClernand.   His plan of
battle for the 14th was to have the army so threaten the
outer works as to hold the Confederate forces in them,
while the gun-boats should attack the batteries on the
river, pass above them, establish communication with
McClernand's right, and then take everything in reverse.

The gun-boats began the attack about three o'clock in the afternoon. They advanced to within about a thou- Attack of the gun-boats. sand feet of the lower batteries, pouring a well-directed fire into the Fort, when the wheel of the flag-ship, the *St. Louis,* was struck and torn away and Foote was severely wounded. At about the same moment another shot from the batteries carried away the tiller-ropes of the *Louisville.* These two boats became immediately unmanageable, and drifted down stream, followed by the others, all more or less battered. The flagging zeal of the Confederates was roused again by the victory of the 14th. Still the Federal reinforcements continued to arrive, and the Federal line kept approaching the river above the fortifications, threatening to bar the way of retreat toward Nashville.

The Confederates were informed of these facts by their scouts, and in the evening of the 14th their commanders met in council to discuss the situation. Despite the triumph of the batteries over the gun-boats, it appeared to them very serious. They at last resolved to assail the Federal right, at dawn the next morning, with a division of their troops commanded by Pillow, turn it, and drive it back upon the centre, and then hurl the Confederate right wing, led by Buckner, upon the exposed flank of the Federals, and thus open the way for the Confederate army to pass out and march by way of Charlotte toward Nashville. Orders were sent in all directions to make the necessary preparations. The weather had become intensely cold, and the shivering Confederates spent most of the dreary night putting themselves in readiness for the deadly conflict, and the dangerous retreat which was, according to the plan, to follow it.

General Grant did not anticipate any such movement on the part of his enemy. He had been summoned by the wounded Foote to a conference on board the *St.*

Louis, which was lying disabled some five miles below the Fort. He set out from his head-quarters, just behind Smith's division, in the early morning of the 15th, to answer Foote's call, all unconscious of the fact that the Confederates were, at the very moment, moving in great force upon the extreme right of his line. He had sent word to his division commanders to hold their positions, but not to bring on an engagement until ordered by him. Returning from his visit to Foote, he was met by one of his staff coming at full gallop, and informed that the Confederates had turned McClernand's right and were driving the entire right wing back upon the centre. He rode rapidly forward to the scene of battle, and his master mind divined at once the plan of the Confederates to escape. He immediately ordered McClernand's broken regiments back into line across the path which the Confederates were trying to open, and rightly supposing that the mass of Buckner's troops had gone out from the trenches in front of the Federal left wing to join in the attempt of the army to cut its way out, and that only a few remained to hold the Federals at bay long enough to secure the retreat, he commanded General Smith to assault and carry these works. Smith's troops carried out this order with great promptness and success, and quickly gained a lodgement in the Confederate rifle pits near the Fort itself. The Confederates now came rushing back to regain their works, but Smith held them at bay, while the Federal right and centre regained their positions of the preceding day. There was no place within the Confederate position which Smith's artillery did not command ; and when the sun went down, darkness drew its protecting wing over a beaten and demoralized army of Confederates, who had now to meet the alternatives of slaughter or surrender.

At midnight their chiefs, Floyd, Pillow, and Buckner,

Grant's divination.

were gathered in council in a little house in the hamlet of Dover, on the bank of the slough of the Cumber-
The surren-
der. land which hemmed the Confederates in on the side looking up the river. Floyd was bent upon making his own escape. He feared it might go hard with him if taken. Pillow was a man who never knew when he was down, and was naturally rather in favor of further resistance. But Buckner, a better soldier and a better man in every way than either of the others, saw the futility of any more fighting, and felt the cruelty to the men of exposing them to any more hardships and suffering. He advocated surrender. Floyd and Pillow at last assented, with the understanding that Buckner should assume command and they should attempt to escape. It was now near the dawn of the 16th. There were two little boats at the Dover landing. Floyd and Pillow boarded these with as many soldiers as could get on, chiefly the Virginians of Floyd's brigade, and steamed for Nashville. Forrest, with his cavalry, swam the slough and rode away along the south bank of the river. At the same time, Buckner ordered the white flag to be raised, and sent a messenger to Grant to open parley. Grant replied that he should require immediate unconditional surrender, and that he should begin the attack at once if this demand were not accepted. Buckner felt obliged to yield, though he did so with very bad grace, and in a rather undignified manner.

It was a magnificent Federal victory. The Confederates lost nearly two thousand men killed and wounded,
The results
of the victory. and from twelve to fifteen thousand taken prisoners, together with the entire equipment of their army. But it was not a cheaply purchased victory to the Federals. They lost between twenty-five hundred and three thousand men killed and wounded. The slaughter and the suffering had been frightful on

both sides. The strategic results of the victory were the evacuation of Middle Tennessee and of the fortress on the Mississippi at Columbus by the Confederates, and their retreat to Corinth and Chattanooga. So soon as General Johnston learned of the disaster at Donelson he marched the remnants of his army, which had retreated from Bowling Green to the north bank of the Cumberland, right on through Nashville to Murfreesborough, at which point he was joined by Crittenden's troops coming from Mill Springs through Carthage and Lebanon, and, after remaining a few days in Murfreesborough, moved his whole force southward to the Memphis and Charleston railroad line, and sent them over this road to Corinth, in Mississippi, in order to form at that point a junction with Beauregard, who had been transferred from Virginia to take command of the defences of the Mississippi Valley. During the same period the Confederates withdrew from Columbus, the " Gibraltar of the West." About one-half of them, commanded by Polk, the Bishop-General, went direct to Corinth, while the other half, led by Beauregard himself, retired to Island No. 10—an island in the Mississippi some forty-five miles below Columbus, at the upper extremity of New Madrid bend—a place where the great river makes a turn so sudden and complete as to run for a few miles in a direction exactly contrary to its general course.

The reaping of the results of the victory to the fullest extent was now, however, hindered by questions of authority and precedence. Halleck was Grant's superior, but he was not Buell's superior. The connection between Halleck and Buell was McClellan. McClellan had, on the 15th of February, ordered Buell to advance on Nashville, and had informed Halleck of this order. Before receiving this information, Halleck had telegraphed McClellan that, in

Halleck, Buell and Grant.

his opinion, a direct move by Buell from Bowling Green on Nashville would be bad strategy, and that the mass of Buell's troops should be sent to him to help him take Fort Donelson, and then operate up the Tennessee River in the rear of the Confederates, forcing them thus to evacuate Tennessee. And upon receiving Halleck's despatch, McClellan replied that Buell must move in force on Nashville as rapidly as circumstances would permit, but that if Grant must have help, three of Buell's brigades and some artillery would be sent to him on the next day. McClellan thus evidently ruled that the operations against Nashville belonged in Buell's department.

Grant sent C. F. Smith's division up the Cumberland to Clarksville, a place about one-third of the way from Donelson to Nashville, and kept them there awaiting orders from Halleck or McClellan to advance toward Nashville, while, in accordance with McClellan's order, Buell sent General William Nelson's division to Fort Donelson to reinforce Grant, and marched with the rest of his army direct upon Nashville. His advance arrived at Edgefield, just across the river from Nashville, on the 23d of February, and Nelson arrived at Donelson on the same day. Having no use for Nelson's troops at the moment, Grant ordered Nelson to proceed with his men on transports, under convoy of a gun-boat, up the river to Nashville, and upon arrival, to put himself in communication with Buell, provided Buell was there or was not far away, but in case Buell was not within two days' march of the place to return to a point below the city and wait for his arrival. When Nelson approached Nashville, he found
Nelson and Buell in Nashville and Edgefield. Buell's forces encamped on the north side of the river with no means of crossing, the Confederates having destroyed the bridges and the river craft. He at once landed his troops, without any orders from Buell or understanding with him, on

the south bank of the river and took possession of the city. Nelson was at the moment nominally under Grant's orders, although Grant had not instructed him to occupy Nashville, as we have seen. Buell seems to have been disturbed, if not terrified, by the situation. He had formed the opinion that the Confederates were gathering in great force some ten miles below Nashville and were on the point of attacking Nelson and repossessing themselves of the city. On the 25th, he sent a message to General C. F. Smith at Clarksville, urging him to bring his division as quickly as possible to Nashville, and informing him of the almost desperate situation of the Federal army at Nashville and Edgefield, as he viewed it. As a matter of fact, the entire Confederate army was at Murfreesborough in a most demoralized and disheartened condition, and did not number all told over seventeen thousand men.

Grant had written to head-quarters in St. Louis several days before, announcing his own intention of going in person to Nashville unless restrained by an order from General Halleck to the contrary Grant in in the returning mail. Receiving no such order, he proceeded to Nashville on the 27th. When he arrived at Clarksville, he found Smith's division embarking to go to Nashville in answer to Buell's request. Smith showed Grant Buell's message of the 25th, remarking that he considered Buell altogether over-anxious. Grant ordered him, however, to join Buell. When Grant saw Buell in Nashville, he told him that the Confederates were getting away as fast as possible, and that there was no danger of an attack upon the Federal forces at Nashville, but Buell asserted that fighting was at that moment going on not a dozen miles away, and that Nashville was in imminent danger. Grant returned to Donelson that evening, leaving the over-cautious Buell in almost as nervous a condition as were the Confederates themselves thirty miles to the south-east.

Grant and Buell together had a force of at least sixty thousand men well armed, equipped, and disciplined, and all flushed with victory. It is true that Grant's army had fought a great battle, and Buell's army had made a long march. But the battle was now ten days past, and moderate marching is much better for the health and spirit of troops than entire rest. Opposed to them was the mere caricature of an army at Murfreesborough, ready to take to its heels at the appearance of a few good regiments. There is no doubt that General Grant was entirely correct in claiming, as he did in his " Memoirs," that if all the Federal troops west of the Alleghanies had then been under the command of a single good general in the field, they could have been marched, directly after the fall of Donelson, to Chattanooga, Corinth, Memphis, and Vicksburg, and have dealt the Confederacy its death-blow in the West. But the over-cautious Buell, acting under the orders of the still more cautious McClellan, and Grant held back by Halleck, who was altogether over-anxious about the danger which he fancied threatened Cairo from Columbus, could not proceed in unison to the completion of the great work which lay just before them. It is true that McClellan was at the time Halleck's superior as well as Buell's, but he was far away, and the time for prompt action was employed by him in controversy with Halleck as to whether Murfreesborough or Columbus should be the next point of attack, while during the very moments when the wires between Washington and St. Louis were occupied with these messages the Confederates were evacuating both of these places, and hastening to concentrate upon Corinth, in Mississippi, for the defence of the Memphis and Chattanooga line.

Communication between Halleck and Grant was inter-
rupted for about a week after the 23d of February, and
the first order which Grant received from   Halleck and
his immediate superior after that time came Grant.
to his hand on March 2d.   It commanded him to march
his forces from Donelson back to Fort Henry, leaving a
small garrison at Donelson. This order was executed
on the 4th.   On the day after his arrival at Fort Henry
he received another order from Halleck, directing him
to send the bulk of his troops, under the command of
C. F. Smith, on an expedition up the Tennessee to Eastport, for the purpose of destroying the Memphis and
Charleston railroad bridges near that point, but to remain himself at Fort Henry.   Grant did not for the moment understand why he should be superseded by Smith
in the command of this expedition.   The reason was revealed to him the next day in a communication from
Halleck, in which Halleck wrote : "Your going to Nashville without authority, and when your presence with
your troops was of the utmost importance, was a matter
of very serious complaint at Washington, so much so
that I was advised to arrest you on your return."   Halleck did not, however, inform Grant that he himself,
and he alone, was the person who made the complaint.
Grant felt deeply injured by Halleck's censure, and asked
to be relieved from any further duty under him.   Halleck had supposed that the interruption of communications between Grant and himself was owing to Grant's
negligence, and that Grant's visit to Nashville was for
the purpose of a grand spree in celebration of his victory.
He now investigated these things, and found there was
no truth in his suspicions.   He wrote to Grant on the
13th, refusing to relieve him of his command, and sent
a communication to Washington two days later exoner-
ating him.

In accordance with Halleck's order, General Smith started from Fort Henry on the 9th of March with about twenty-five thousand men on transports, and steamed up the river to Savannah. He here disembarked the main portion of his troops, but sent General W. T. Sherman with his division farther up the river to Eastport, with instructions to land there, and destroy the Memphis and Charleston Railroad near Iuka, in order to prevent Johnston's army from concentrating with the forces gathering at Corinth and in the vicinity. On account of the high water covering the bottoms, Sherman was not able to reach the railroad. He returned down the river to Pittsburg Landing, a place on the west bank of the river, some ten miles above Savannah, which latter place is situated on the east bank. Here, by order of General Smith, Sherman debarked his men and set up his tents. At the same time Smith sent Hurlbut's division across from Savannah to join Sherman, and Lew Wallace's division across to Crump's Landing, about five miles above Pittsburg Landing. This was the disposition of the troops on the west bank of the Tennessee when Grant arrived at Savannah on the 17th of March, and took command of the movements.

Failure of the attempt to prevent the concentration of the Confederates at Corinth.

By this time the Confederates had gathered in considerable force at Corinth. The Confederate President had ordered General Braxton Bragg to go from Pensacola with a fine division of troops to Beauregard. These had arrived, as well as Polk's men from Columbus, and A. S. Johnston's army was being rapidly transported from Decatur over the Memphis and Charleston Railroad. Grant saw, at once, that the forces on the west bank of the river must be immediately reinforced or withdrawn. He decided for the former alternative, and on the 18th ordered

Concentration of the Federals at Pittsburg Landing.

all the troops at Savannah, except McClernand's division, to go over to Pittsburg Landing.

On account of the illness of their commander, General Smith, these were formed into a division under the command of General W. H. L. Wallace. Another division was formed of the new troops arriving with and after Grant, and placed under the command of General B. M. Prentiss. By the 20th, Grant had an army of about forty thousand men at Savannah, Crump's Landing, and Pittsburg Landing, and the Confederates had about as many in and around Corinth, only twenty-five or thirty miles away.

During all this time Buell had not been able to satisfy his mind whether Johnston was going to join Beauregard at Corinth or would receive reinforcements at Chattanooga from Virginia and return to attack Nashville. He had, therefore, divided his army, sending a large division of some ten thousand men or more, under General O. M. Mitchell to Murfreesborough, and marching slowly with the main body, some forty thousand, toward Savannah, by way of Columbia.

The advance of Buell.

On the 11th of March, President Lincoln issued his War Order, No. 3, according to which McClellan's authority was confined to the Department of the Potomac, while the entire territory west of the longitude of Knoxville, Tennessee, was placed under the superior command of Halleck, and the district between the departments of Halleck and McClellan was assigned to Frémont under the name of the Mountain Department. The connection between the three was now the War Department at Washington, that is, the President and the Secretary of War, Mr. Stanton.

The extension of Halleck's authority.

So soon as Halleck was placed in superior command over Buell, he ordered Buell to move his forces as rapidly as possible to the support of Grant. He repeated the order a few days later with peremptoriness. Still Buell was lingering at Columbia, only fifty miles away from Nashville, as late as the 30th, while Savannah was more than seventy-five miles farther on. Upon that day he received another despatch from Halleck, urging him to go on to Savannah and to dismiss all fear from his mind in regard to Johnston's moving on Nashville from Decatur.

Buell's advance, General William Nelson's division, had now been for twenty days at Columbia. The rea-
Nelson's forced march from Columbia to Savannah.
son for the delay given by Buell was the high water in Duck River, the bridges over which had been burned by the Confederates. The impatient and impetuous Nelson was so irritated by the delay that he rode up and down the bank of the river himself, plunging his horse in here and there until he found a place over which he determined to ford his division, and wait no longer for the completion of the bridges. It was thus that Nelson put his division a number of hours in advance of the main body of Buell's army, and arrived at Savannah in time to reach the scene of the great battle before the end of the first day.

Johnston had arrived in Corinth on the 23d, and on the 29th he assumed the chief command of all the forces
Johnston's preparations for battle.
in and about Corinth, and issued his orders dividing the entire force into three corps and a reserve, and designating Polk, Bragg, Hardee, and Crittenden as their respective commanders. Crittenden was arrested a few days later on charge of misconduct in the Mill Springs campaign, and the command of the reserve was transferred to J. C. Breckenridge. Johnston also made Beauregard his second in general command, and Bragg his chief of staff.

With the exception of Bragg's troops, from Pensacola,

the Confederates were in a bad state of demoralization, and were greatly lacking in supplies and means of transportation. Bragg's judgment was that no offensive operations could be undertaken, but Johnston, smarting under the denunciations which had been hurled at him for yielding Tennessee without giving battle at Murfreesborough, and grieving deeply at the displeasure of his friend, President Davis—although this displeasure had been very mildly, and only impliedly, expressed— determined to attack the Federals gathering at Pittsburg Landing, and to do it before Buell's army could reach the scene of conflict. It may have been good tactics, but there was a large element of desperation in it. Some of the Southern historians are inclined to ascribe the movement to Beauregard. Beauregard was probably in favor of it, while Bragg was opposed to it. But Johnston was commander-in-chief, and his will was decisive.

There is no doubt that, on the 1st of April and thereafter, the Federal commanders regarded an advance of the Confederates from Corinth as so unmilitary as to be without the range of probabilities. The fact that they had taken no precautions to meet an attack is convincing on this point. They had not caused a single intrenchment to be thrown up, and they had placed their raw troops farthest forward on the roads from Pittsburg Landing to Corinth. The divisions of Sherman and Prentiss were in the front, while those of McClernand and Smith were encamped nearer the river, and Lew Wallace's troops were five or six miles to the north. These three divisions were the veterans of the Donelson campaign, and if an attack by the Confederates had been expected, some of these would in all probability have been so placed as to assist in receiving the first shock. In fact, General Grant acknowledges in his "Memoirs" that he had "no idea the enemy would leave strong intrenchments to take the initiative when he knew he would be attacked where he was if he remained."

In the evening of the 2d of April, information reached Johnston at Corinth, that Buell's forces were on the march from Columbia to Savannah. He must strike at once, if at all. He hastened to issue his address to the army, informing the commanders and the men of the plan of attacking the Federals at Pittsburg Landing. His troops now numbered about forty thousand, organized, as we have seen, into three corps and a reserve. On the morning of the 4th the movement began. The cavalry were in the advance. Hardee's corps followed, then Bragg's, then Polk's, and lastly the reserve led by Breckenridge. Johnston expected to march his whole army from Corinth to the Federal outposts in a single day, and to begin his attack on the morning of the 5th. But the roads were so narrow, and in such an execrable condition that he was not able to reach the spot where his columns were to be deployed in line of battle until the afternoon of the 5th. It was then determined to defer the attack until the morning of the 6th.

The Federal forces were encamped upon the wooded plateau bounded on the north by Owl and Snake Creeks, and on the south by Lick Creek, two watercourses of considerable depth at that season, running in a general parallel direction, some three miles apart, toward the Tennessee River. This plateau was intersected by three roads, one running from Pittsburg Landing to Corinth, one from Hamburg Landing to Corinth, and one from Hamburg Landing to Purdy, a county town in Tennessee north of Corinth. There was also a road leading from Pittsburg Landing to Crump's Landing, which bowed westward and crossed Snake

Creek about a mile from its mouth in the Tennessee. This road connected Lew Wallace's division with the rest of the army.

The advanced line of the army on the morning of the 6th of April was composed of the divisions of Sherman and Prentiss, all raw troops. Sherman's first brigade was on the extreme right of the line and touched Owl Creek at the bridge over which the road to Purdy passed. His fourth brigade came next to the first, and the third next to the fourth. These two brigades connected at Shiloh church, on the road from Pittsburg Landing to Corinth, some two and a half miles from the Landing. Sherman's second brigade was placed on the extreme left, and touched Lick Creek at the point where the road from Hamburg Landing to Purdy crossed it. Between Sherman's second and third brigades, Prentiss's division was located, but it did not quite fill up the gap between them. About half a mile to the rear of Sherman's third brigade was McClernand's division, and about the same distance in the rear of Prentiss was Hurlbut's division. Finally W. H. L. Wallace's division was in reserve in the rear of both McClernand and Hurlbut.

The Federals had a good position. Their flanks were protected by the waters and marshes of the creeks, and the topography of the plateau furnished good points of defence. The Confederates were forced to attack directly in front, and to depend upon human power, valor, and endurance for success.

Johnston's plan was to turn the Federal left, by persistently advancing his own right, and thus drive the Federals into the marshes of Snake Creek, The plan of between the bridge over Snake Creek and the attack. Tennessee River. Once huddled into this miry corner, and thrown into confusion, there could be but one re-

sult. The Confederate generals explained this plan to
their subordinates, and went into the battle with the
colonel of every regiment fully cognizant of it.

Before it was fairly light in the morning of the 6th,
they came storming forward in three lines of battle,
Hardee's corps in the advance, followed by
Bragg's and then by Polk's, with Breckenridge's in reserve. The Federals were not prepared to
meet the sudden and impetuous attack. They were
fairly surprised. The soldiers of Sherman and Prentiss
were, of course, the first to feel the shock. For raw
troops they did as well as could have been expected.
Their commanders behaved like heroes. Sherman developed, at one stroke, that genius for strategy and command which made him, in the opinion of many, the
greatest soldier produced by the war. He seemed to be
omnipresent. His towering form and ringing words imparted strength and courage wherever he passed, and
his quick perception and sound judgment enabled him
to place his battalions just where they could do most
efficient work. Horse after horse was shot under him,
and twice he was struck. But begrimed and bleeding
and suffering, his uniform riddled with balls, his hat
even pierced, he never lost for one moment his courage,
coolness, or judgment. If any one man saved the Federal army from irreparable disaster in the forenoon of
the 6th, it was certainly Sherman.

But no amount of personal bravery and military tact on
the part of one man, or a thousand men, could stem the
tide of the furious onset. The Confederates poured into
the intervals on the right and left of Prentiss's division,
turning the positions of both Prentiss and Sherman by
the left, at the same time, and almost surrounding Prentiss. The Federals yielded their ground, however, slowly.
McClernand, Hurlbut, and W. H. L. Wallace brought

up their divisions in support, and the battle raged with
great fury along the entire line. By this time Grant had
arrived on the field. He came up from Savannah, and
in passing Crump's Landing ordered Lew Wallace to put
his division in readiness to march, and await further
orders. On arriving at Pittsburg Landing, and finding
the real battle in progress there, he sent a messenger to
Wallace with an order for him to march his division to
Sherman's right. Grant then went on to the field, and
rode from regiment to regiment trying to preserve some
concert of action among the troops of his considerably
shattered and demoralized army. Again and again he
and his generals rallied the men, but the Confederates
still pressed victoriously forward. McClernand's division
formed no less than six lines of battle in retiring, and at
last, with the remnants of Sherman's troops, took position in front of the bridge across Snake Creek, resolved
to defend it at all hazards, since it was here that Lew Wallace, who had not yet come up, was expected to appear,
and since it was over this bridge and road alone that the
army could save itself from capture in case of ultimate
defeat.

On receiving Grant's order to march to Sherman's
right, Wallace struck out for a point on Owl Creek
above its junction with Snake Creek, and about three
miles from the Tennessee River, supposing that Sherman's right was about in that position, and not knowing
that Sherman had fallen back. About noon Grant sent
one of his aids to look for Wallace, and two hours later
he sent two more of them. About four o'clock in the
afternoon they found Wallace, and the aid first sent
out, leading the division back from its perilous wander-
ings to the bridge across Snake Creek, to which point he
ought to have marched directly from Crump's Landing.
Had he done so he could have been on the battle-field by

noon, as Grant intended. But as it was, he arrived too late to be of any service on the first day of the great conflict.

Meanwhile the Confederates had made a desperate attempt to turn the Federal left entirely and drive the shattered army into the marshes of Snake Creek. Johnston himself led the charge. The movement seemed to be on the point of success, when Johnston fell mortally wounded, and expired amid the shouts of victory. The Confederates passed onward. W. H. L. Wallace's division was scattered, the commander himself being killed. Prentiss was surrounded, and part of his division with himself captured. Still Sherman and McClernand held the bridge over Snake Creek, and were resolved to sacrifice the last man in its defence. Thousands of the Federals had fled from the field and were huddled under the bank of the river. Bragg now determined to carry the last position on the Federal left, and drive the remnants of the divisions of Hurlbut, Wallace, and Prentiss into the river. The almost exhausted Confederates rallied at the sound of his voice, and made themselves ready for the final charge.

The death of Johnston.

But at this critical moment, when victory seemed the certain reward of one more grand effort, bitter disappointment was being prepared for them. The siege guns, which had been landed a few days before, were lying on the heights just above the Landing. It was up and over these heights from the other side that Bragg's line must come. Colonel J. D. Webster, of Grant's staff, perceived, at this moment, the extreme danger to the Federal army, and the advantage which might be gained from a proper employment of this heavy artillery lying uselessly around. He hastily collected a few gunners and threw this heavy ordnance into battery, and, with a slight infantry support, likewise hastily

Webster's battery.

gathered from broken regiments, prepared to receive
Bragg's line, now pressing up out of the ravine in front
of the position.   A well-directed fire from the artillery
sent the Confederates reeling backward, but the brave
and resolute General rallied them again, and they turned
and rushed up the slope before the Federal gunners
could reload their pieces.   The weak infantry support
deserted, terror-stricken, the artillerists, and the capture
of the guns, and with them a large part of the army,
seemed the work of only five minutes more of resolute
advance.

But before the half of that little period had expired
the intrepid Nelson, always in the advance of Buell's
army, came driving up from the Landing at   The arrival
the head of the first brigade of his division,   of Nelson.
and received Bragg's line within three hundred feet of
the battery.   Instantly deploying right and left with
the precision of trained soldiers, they poured such a vol-
ley at short range into the Confederate ranks as shattered them into fragments and drove them headlong
down into the ravine.   The shells from the gun-boats
had also contributed in effecting the defence, but were
of more service during the retreat of the Confederates
than during their advance.   The repulse of Bragg by
Webster's hastily constructed battery, supported at the
critical moment by Nelson's infantry, and the maintenance of the position on the extreme right in front of
Snake Creek bridge by Sherman and McClernand had
saved the army from disaster.

Night was rapidly approaching, and Beauregard, now
in chief command of the Confederates, called his exhausted soldiers back to the camps occu-   Suspension
pied by the Federals the night before, in   of the strug-
order to give them rest and refreshment and   gle.
reorganize them for the renewal of the contest on the

morrow. He did not know that General Buell was himself already at Pittsburg Landing, and that three divisions of his army were nearing the battle-field. Least of all did he know that it was a brigade of Buell's army which finally effected the repulse of Bragg.

During the night the remainder of Nelson's division crossed over from the opposite bank of the Tennessee, and the divisions of Crittenden and McCook arrived at that point. In the early morning hours of the 7th these two divisions also effected the crossing, and before the Confederates were ready to renew the conflict twenty thousand men of Buell's army, fresh and eager for battle, had formed themselves in front of the position successfully held at the close of the previous day. Nelson was on the extreme left, next came Crittenden, and then McCook. On the right of McCook came the divisions of Grant's army, now reduced to three—first McClernand's, then Sherman's, and on the extreme right the troops commanded by Lew Wallace. The whole Union army was thus, on the 7th, drawn up for battle in two wings, the right wing commanded by Grant, and the left by Buell. It numbered scarcely less than fifty thousand, about one-half of whom were fresh troops.

On the other hand, the Confederates had brought their last man into action on the 6th. They had lost by the casualties of the battle at least ten thousand men, and, advancing as they did by the lines of entire corps, the regiments, brigades, and divisions of the different corps had become inextricably mingled. Moreover, the spoils of the Federal camps had added greatly to their demoralization. Their officers spent the whole of the night in the vain attempt to reorganize their commands; and the shells from the gun-boats kept the soldiers from obtaining the rest necessary for further exertion. In a word, the Confederate army resumed its positions, on the morning of the 7th, decimated, fatigued, and considerably disorganized.

The Federal commanders felt assured of victory. The Confederate chiefs, unaware of the presence of Buell's troops, also counted upon certain success. The Federals had in store for the Confederates, on the 7th, as great a surprise as the Confederates had dealt out to them on the morning of the 6th.

Before daylight the Army of the Ohio was in motion. To the brave and restless Nelson was confided the duty of opening the battle. He soon found the *The renewal* Confederates in strong force directly in front *of the battle.* of him, for they still adhered to their plan of battle of the day before of turning the Federal left. The Confederate commanders now quickly discovered that they had a division of fresh troops to overcome before they could accomplish this purpose. They drew reinforcements from their own centre and left in order to strengthen their right in the work required of that part of their army. They thus gave Nelson a severe battle for several hours, driving him back at different points.

By this time, however, the Federal commanders had discovered that the Confederate centre, resting on, or near, the main road to Corinth, in the deep *The piercing* forest about a quarter of a mile east of Shiloh *of the Confed-* Church, had been weakened to support their *erate centre.* right in front of Nelson. McCook was therefore ordered to break the Confederate line at this point. Beauregard commanded here in person, and the first attempt was repulsed. Then Rousseau's entire brigade, consisting of three battalions of regulars and three regiments of volunteers, was hurled upon it. General Sherman says, in his report, that he saw, from his position farther toward the Federal right, this superb brigade advancing, and deploying, and entering "this dreaded woods," and feeling entirely confident of its success, ordered his own division to keep abreast of it in the movement.

It was now a little after two o'clock, and the Confederates knew that the crisis of the battle was at hand.

The defeat of the Confederates and their retreat. Led by Beauregard in person, they struggled manfully and obstinately, but in vain. The whole Federal line was now advancing surely, steadily, and in perfect order. Calling Breckenridge to him, Beauregard acknowledged defeat, and imposed upon the brave Kentuckian the duty of covering the retreat, charging him not to allow the retreat to be turned into a rout.

Most faithfully did Breckenridge execute his trust. The Confederates gave way at all points, but slowly and in comparative order. The Federals, exhausted by their tremendous efforts, advanced only about one mile farther, and then rested for the remainder of the day, in possession of the battle-field, and but little more. On the following day Sherman tried a little pursuit, and had one of his regiments badly cut up by a cavalry charge. After this the Confederates returned to Corinth unmolested.

The Federals had won the battle, but at a terrible cost. The killed, according to their official report, numbered 1,754, the wounded 8,408, and the captured and missing 2,885. The Confederates acknowledged a loss almost as great, except in captured and missing. It would be substantially correct to say that the Confederates returned to Corinth about twenty-five thousand strong. In less than a week from their return they were reinforced by Van Dorn and Price, coming from Arkansas after their defeat at Pea Ridge, which will now be related, and could again muster an army of

forty thousand men. It is not surprising then that the
authorities at Washington regarded the Federal victory as
rather barren, and demanded of Halleck to be informed
whether " the neglect or misconduct of General Grant
or any other officer contributed to the sad casualties" of
the battle of the 6th.

West of the Mississippi, in Missouri and Arkansas, the
Federals had been equally successful in the spring campaign of 1862. On the 26th of January, the   The Pea
Federal army, commanded by General S. R.   Ridge cam-
Curtis and about twelve thousand strong,   paign.
began to move from Rolla against Price, who was intrenched at Springfield with about ten thousand men.

To the surprise of Curtis, Price evacuated his fortifications at the approach of the Federals, retired into
Arkansas, and took refuge in the defiles of   Retreat of
the Boston Mountains, some fifty miles south   Price.
of the Missouri line. Here he was joined by reinforcements under McCulloch, McIntosh and Pike, and on the
3d of March General Earl Van Dorn took command of
the entire force, and prepared to return and face Curtis.
Van Dorn estimated his strength at sixteen thousand
men. The Federal General reported him as having
almost double that number.

Curtis had pursued Price as far as Fayetteville, a town
in Arkansas some thirty miles south of the Missouri
line. His army had been reduced to less   Curtis's pur-
than eleven thousand men during the march   suit.
from Rolla. When he learned of the increased force
under Van Dorn, and of its return movement, he was
convinced that he must not await an attack at Fayetteville, but must retire into the Ozark hills, a few miles to
the north-west, where he could find a defensive position
which would offset, in some degree, the superior force of
the Confederates.

These hills are cut from east to west by three deep ravines, nearly equidistant from one another. The most

The posi-
tion at Pea
Ridge. southerly one is called Cross Hollows, the middle one Sugar Creek Valley, and the northerly one Cross Timber Hollows. These valleys are traversed almost at right angles by the post road from Fayetteville to Springfield. The point where it intersects Cross Hollows is called the village of Cross Hollows, that where it intersects Sugar Creek Valley is called Mottsville, and that where it intersects Cross Timber Hollows is called Elkhorn Tavern. There is also a road leading from Bentonville to Springfield along the western slope of these hills, and at a point in this road opposite Sugar Creek Valley a road branches off to the east, runs up Sugar Creek Valley to a place called Leetown, which is located about a mile and a half west of Mottsville, and then crosses the ridge between Sugar Creek Valley and Cross Timber Hollows, and finally runs eastward up Cross Timber Hollows to Elkhorn Tavern.

General Curtis selected for his position the ridge between Sugar Creek Valley and Cross Timber Hollows, so as to cover both the post road from Fayetteville to Springfield and the road from Bentonville to Elkhorn Tavern *via* Leetown. In the afternoon of the 6th of March Curtis's entire army took this position, after his rear guard under Sigel had succeeded in cutting its way through the swarms of Confederates around Bentonville. The little army was organized into four divisions, commanded by Generals Sigel and Asboth and Colonels Jeff. C. Davis and Carr. The line of battle faced southward, of course. The divisions of Sigel and Asboth formed the right, reaching out a little to the west of Leetown; the division commanded by Colonel Davis formed the centre; and the division led by Carr, reaching out a little to the east of Mottsville, formed the left.

It does not seem to have occurred to General Curtis that the Confederates might pass up the road from Bentonville to Springfield beyond the point where the road branches off to Leetown, and come up through Cross Timber Hollows, where there was no road at all, into his rear. But that was exactly what they did do. They executed this movement during the night of the 6th, and on the morning of the 7th Curtis found them pushing up this ravine to Elkhorn Tavern and threatening to cut his connection with Springfield. He immediately ordered his whole line to change face from front to rear, making now Carr's division his right, and the divisions of Asboth and Sigel his left, with Davis, of course, still in the centre. It was in this perilous position that he fought the battle of the 7th of March.

The flanking movements of the Confederates.

His plan was not to wait for the Confederates to attack, but to strike the centre of the Confederate line, while the line was being formed, pierce it, drive one part of it eastward, and the other westward, and then when each part had its flank exposed, throw his right upon one part, and his left upon the other. With this purpose in view, he formed an assaulting column from Davis's division, and placed it under the command of the valiant Colonel Peter Osterhaus. He then ordered Osterhaus to advance to the attack, and went himself to his right in order to hold it firm while Osterhaus should break the Confederate centre. Osterhaus pressed forward impetuously and, at first, successfully, but the Confederates soon moved strong reinforcements from their right and repulsed him. Curtis now ordered Davis to support Osterhaus with the remainder of his division. The Confederates felt, at this moment, certain of victory. They had pressed the Federal right slowly back, and had now full possession of

The battle of Pea Ridge.

Elkhorn Tavern and the road to Springfield. When Osterhaus yielded, they rushed forward with great impetuosity. But Davis's fresh troops brought them to a halt. The Confederates were led at this point by McCulloch and McIntosh, who performed feats of most extreme daring in order to encourage their men. The battle was waged here most hotly, and it seemed as if the Confederates were on the point of success, when both McCulloch and McIntosh were struck down. There was no one among their survivors who could rally and lead forward the soldiers accustomed only to their voices and their chieftaincy. The Federal centre was now relieved of the pressure upon it, but the right was continually losing ground. Van Dorn himself was directing the movement of the Confederates against the Federal right, and he had brought many of the troops from his own right to his left, to accomplish his purpose. Curtis now learned that there were practically no Confederates in front of his left, and he ordered Asboth to lead his division to the support of Carr on the right, and Sigel to go to the support of Davis. Both of these movements were successfully accomplished, and the Federal right was thereby enabled to hold its ground. It had however been forced back about a mile from the position held by it at the beginning of the day.

Night now intervened, and the Federal commander found himself in a very precarious situation. The Confederates were between him and Springfield, and the alternatives for the morrow were victory or surrender. In the darkness he formed his new line of battle, the third since the beginning of the conflict. He now knew that the Confederates were massing opposite Carr's division. He, therefore, placed Asboth on Carr's right, and ordered Davis and Sigel to move up nearer to Carr's left, while Osterhaus remained about Leetown to prevent the Confederates from flanking the new Federal left. Carr's division was now almost the centre of the new Federal line. The Federal General knew well the ground over which he must fight, since it had been his own position of the day before.

The attack on the morning of the 8th was begun by Davis. The Confederates returned his fire with terrible effect from their new lines and batteries. The Federal right centre was again sorely pressed, and was retiring slowly, when Curtis suddenly threw forward his extreme right, *The second day's battle, and the defeat of the Confederates.* planting his cannon on eminences which commanded the left flank of the Confederates. At the same time Sigel appeared on their right flank, advancing with irresistible force. The Confederates were caught in a *cul de sac*, and were raked by the crossfires of the Federals from both the right and the left. They broke and fled in all directions. The main body of them went northward on the road from the Elkhorn Tavern toward Springfield until they passed out of the gorge in the hills, and then made for Huntsville in a south-easterly direction. Sigel followed them for a short distance, but they melted away before him in the defiles, and the Federal soldiers were too much overcome with fatigue and hunger to pursue them further at the moment.

Curtis had saved his army from surrender, and Missouri from another invasion, but at a terrible cost. He reported a loss of nearly fifteen hundred, and estimated the Confederate loss at a higher, *The losses.* though not definite, figure. Van Dorn reported his loss at eight hundred, and estimated the Federal loss at two thousand. It is rather difficult to understand how he could have known much about the Federal loss. He also reported that he went into the battle with only fourteen thousand men, while he estimated the Federal

force at about twenty thousand. Van Dorn's communication was addressed from Jacksonsport, some two
hundred miles south-eastward from the battle-field, and
was dated the 27th of March. It was addressed to General Braxton Bragg at Corinth. It was evident that he
was moving to join the Confederate army gathering at
Corinth. Price with the Missourians followed him a
little later, and Curtis pursued Price across the entire
"State" of Arkansas, reaching finally the town of Helena on the Mississippi River.

There are some facts about this battle of Pea Ridge
that are very painful for the historian to record, and for
The Indian brigade. the civilized world to learn. They relate to
the employment of Indians by the Confeder-
ates, and the exercise of their savage methods of war-
fare in this battle. General Curtis reported that they
tomahawked and scalped his men, and made bitter complaint of the utter demoralization which such practices
were bound to produce.

It is from some points of view to be regretted that the
questions involved in the great conflict were not fought
out by Americans of the white race on both sides. But
after the employment of Indians by the Confederates, it
certainly did not become them to object to the employment of negroes by the Federals. Negroes were more
or less barbarians, but they were not savages, and their
conduct, on the whole, was that of a civilized soldiery.
It was especially exasperating to the Northern people
that the man who organized and commanded this Indian
brigade was a Bostonian by birth, and a Harvardian by
education, Albert Pike, and it was some relief to the conscience of the Confederates that such was the case. The
Indian soldiers were not, however, of much service to
the Confederates. The roar of heavy artillery frightened them so much that they could not be held in any

regular order, and after the battle the brigade was not again effectively reorganized.

At the very moment when Grant and Buell were winning the costly victory around Shiloh Church, events were taking place a hundred and fifty miles to the north-west on the line of the Mississippi of a far more satisfactory character to the Federal arms. *The capture of Island No. 10.*

After the victory at Donelson and the evacuation of Columbus, Halleck had ordered General John Pope to proceed to Cairo, and organize an expedition against the Confederate forces at New Madrid and Island No. 10, to which places, as we have seen, about one-half of the Confederates from Columbus had retired. On the 21st of February, Pope went from Cairo up the Mississippi to Commerce on the Missouri bank, having decided that it was best to assemble his land force for the attack on New Madrid there, and march them from that point. By the end of the month he had collected an army of twenty thousand men, and had set his column in motion for the march through the dismal Mingo swamp which lies between Commerce and New Madrid, fifty miles apart. In five days it was accomplished, and on the 3d of March the entire force deployed in front of New Madrid. Pope found the place fortified and defended by twenty-one heavy guns and five regiments of infantry. He also found six gun-boats, carrying from thirty to forty guns, lying along the shore, and as the water of the river was almost on a level with the bank, these guns commanded the flat terrain back from the river to a considerable distance. The Confederate force in the fortifications was directed by General J. P. McCown and the fleet of gun-boats by Flag-Officer George Hollins. Pope decided immediately to delay the attack until he could bring down some siege artillery from Cairo.

While waiting for these guns he occupied Point Pleasant, a point twelve miles down-stream from New Madrid, cutting off thus water communication with New Madrid and Island No. 10 from below. The Confederate gun-boats made several attempts to silence the Federal battery at Point Pleasant, and drive the Federals away. The Federals, however, not only stood their ground, but advanced their artillery nearer to the river and made it impossible for transports to pass.

While the attention of the Confederates was occupied with this movement in their rear, the siege guns sent

The attack from Cairo arrived before New Madrid. They
on New Ma- were placed in position during the night of
drid.
 the 12th of March, and fire was opened from them on the fortifications and the gun-boats on the morning of the 13th. The cannonade continued during the entire day. Several of the gun-boats were disabled and the earthworks were badly damaged. Night came on before Pope was ready to assault the intrenchments with infantry, and with it a terrible storm of rain and electricity. When morning dawned, it was found that the Confederates had abandoned New Madrid, leaving all their heavy artillery, thousands of small arms, a vast magazine of ammunition, and a large quantity of stores of every description. The men had been transported across the river, and ordered to make their way to Island No. 10, and the gun-boats had withdrawn to a point below Point Pleasant. Pope's entire loss in this brilliant movement did not exceed sixty men. He estimated the loss of the Confederates as much larger, but no exact report of the same was ever made by anybody.

Pope began at once his operations for the reduction of Island No. 10. He dragged the heavy guns captured from the Confederates down the river to a point opposite the extremity of dry ground on the Tennessee bank,

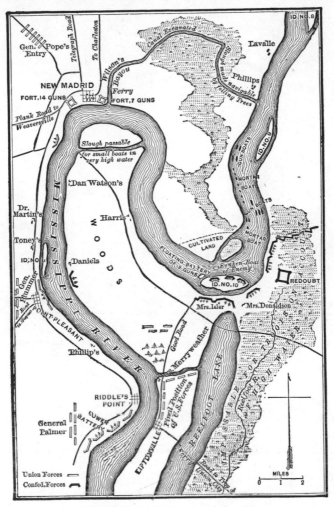

New Madrid and Island Number Ten.

and planted them here in battery, in order to prevent
any communication from below with Island No. 10 by
means of a road which led from this point Preparations against
Island No. 10.
on the Tennessee shore up to a point on the
same shore opposite the island.   On the
east side of this road lay the dismal Reelfoot Lake and
swamps, which cut off all land retreat from Island No.
10, except over the road, the lower extremity of which
Pope now closed by means of his artillery on the opposite bank.   The Confederates saw the trap which Pope
was preparing, and their five gun-boats attacked the battery with great determination, but were driven off, with
the loss of one of the boats, and with much damage to
two others.

Upon the advice of his most capable engineer, General
Schuyler Hamilton, Pope now ordered his engineer regiment, commanded by Colonel J. W. Bissell, to cut a
canal across the neck of the first peninsula made by the
bend of the river at New Madrid, in order to enable him
to bring troops from Cairo on transports, and pass them
through the canal and down the river to the place on
the Tennessee shore mentioned above, without danger
from the guns on Island No. 10.   This great work was
accomplished in less than twenty days, and on the 4th
day of April Pope had water communication between
Cairo, *via* the New Madrid canal, and his position below
Island No. 10 which commanded both the land and water
approaches to that island from the south.   During this
time, however, the Confederates had lined the Tennessee shore between New Madrid and this position
with heavy guns in order to prevent the transports
from passing down from the lower end of the New Madrid canal.   Pope found it necessary, therefore, to have
some gun-boats to precede his transports, and silence
these guns.   He could not bring them through the

canal. It was not deep enough. They must run past the batteries at Island No. 10. Foote, whose fleet was waiting just above the island, hesitated at first to hazard the experiment. But when it became clear to him that the capture of the island required the risk, he ordered Captain Walke to make the attempt with the *Carondelet*. At ten o'clock in the night of the 4th, and in the midst of a heavy thunderstorm, Walke started on the perilous mission. Despite the Cimmerian darkness, his boat was discovered and fired upon from every battery, but was not struck by a single ball. In the night of the 6th, the *Pittsburg* ran the gauntlet also untouched. During the forenoon of the 7th, these two gun-boats cleared the way from New Madrid down the river to, and below, Point Pleasant against the most strenuous efforts of the Confederates to prevent it. About midday Walke signalled to Pope that the Confederate batteries were silenced. The transports containing the troops now came down and crossed over to the Tennessee side and occupied the road, which was the only outlet of escape from the island by land. Before midnight of the 7th, almost the entire Federal army was in this position.

The Confederate Commander, now General Mackall, had left a small force in the works on the island, and The capture of the island and of the Confederate army. under cover of the darkness had attempted to escape with the main body of his troops by crossing over to the Tennessee shore and marching down this road. Foote soon discovered the movement and proceeded at once against the works. The little force there surrendered without resistance. Mackall, of course, found his way blocked by a superior force. He surrendered also with but little resistance. The Federals had won a complete victory, without the loss of a single man. Pope reported the capture of about seven thousand men, one hundred and fifty-eight cannon, seven thousand stands of small arms, and an immense quantity of ammunition and stores.

There is no question that this bloodless triumph was planned and executed with remarkable ability. It stood out in bold contrast with the bloody barren victory which was at the same time being won at Pittsburg Landing. It is not at all astonishing that the Administration at Washington and the people in the North were greatly impressed with the difference between the two, and were moved thereby to estimate Pope's ability and merits higher than those of Grant, Sherman, or Buell, at that juncture. It must not, however, be forgotten that except for the repulse of the Confederates at Pittsburg Landing all that had been won by the victories at Mill Springs and Fort Donelson would have been lost again, and perhaps also all that had been won at Pea Ridge and Island No. 10. Had the Confederates been successful at Shiloh, they would probably have been able to reoccupy Tennessee and Arkansas, and Southern Kentucky and Missouri. As it was, the re-establishment of the Federal supremacy over these four important Commonwealths was made secure and substantially permanent by this great, though costly and apparently indecisive, victory.

The beginning of Pope's popularity.

Halleck now gathered the armies of Grant, Buell and Pope, with large reinforcements, together at Pittsburg Landing for the capture of Corinth, and took command of the entire force in person. He had all told, the latter part of April, about one hundred thousand men. He put Thomas in command of the Army of the Tennessee, and made Grant second to himself in command of the whole force. On the 1st day of May, he began his advance on Corinth. The

The advance on Corinth.

Army of the Tennessee, led by Thomas, formed his right wing, the Army of the Ohio, led by Buell, his centre, and the Army of the Mississippi, led by Pope, his left wing. Beauregard had been reinforced by the troops of Van Dorn and Price from Arkansas, and by part of Lovell's force from New Orleans. He could muster about sixty thousand men. He had fortified the place quite strongly, and Halleck was thoroughly convinced that the great battle of the war was to be fought before Corinth. He, therefore, proceeded with the greatest caution, advancing his whole line at once and intrenching as he went. Of course the advance in this manner was very slow, on the average about a mile a day. It was the 27th of May before he got up near enough to Corinth to execute his plan of cutting the Mobile and Ohio Railroad south of Corinth. In the night of the 27th he started Colonel Elliot with a thousand picked cavalrymen to do this work.

On the 29th, the whole army was so near Corinth that Halleck thought the battle might take place on the 30th. He supposed that the Confederates were massing on his left to attack Pope. But Beauregard probably never had any idea at all of fighting a battle at Corinth. His plan was to draw the Federals farther south, away from their base on the Tennessee River, thus compelling them to weaken their active forces to guard their long lines of communication, and then fight them with much greater advantage. At any rate he had determined upon this course before the middle of May, and during the entire last week of the month he was shipping his stores southward as fast as possible over the railroad. Both Grant and Logan knew, on the 28th, that this was going on, but Halleck could not be made to believe it.

About four o'clock in the morning of the 30th an

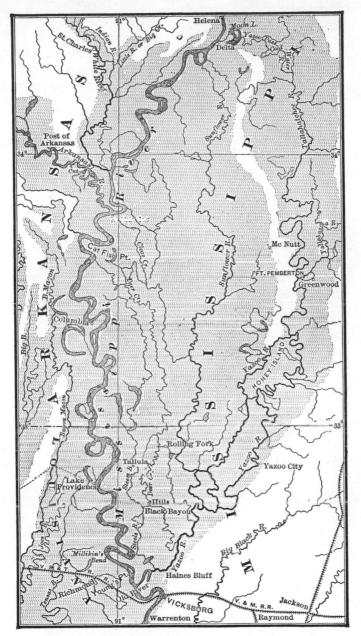

Mississippi Valley—Helena to Vicksburg.

escaped Confederate soldier came into General Nelson's camp, and informed Nelson that the Confederates were retreating from Corinth. Nelson immediate- ly ordered his division to advance, and ad- vised Buell of his movement. By seven o'clock both his division and McCook's were inside of the Confederate works. The Confederate army was disappearing over the ridges to the south. Colonel Elliot struck the railroad some eighteen miles below Corinth in the morning of the 30th only to find that all the trains carrying the stores and war material, except a single one, had passed. Halleck had been deceived and eluded by the more astute Beauregard. The Federals were too much worn out by their work with the spade to make any effective pursuit. Halleck sent a few companies of cavalry to harass the retreating column, but they stopped at the crossings of the Tuscumbia only a few miles away. Beauregard halted at Baldwin, some thirty-two miles below Corinth. Halleck now sent Pope's army, strengthened by one of Buell's divisions, to find him. Beauregard retired from Baldwin on the 7th of June before Pope's advance. Pope very nearly forced him to battle on the 8th, but Halleck restrained the impetuosity of his subordinate, and Beauregard escaped the danger which for a moment again threatened him. On the 9th, the Confederate troops were again united at Tupelo, a place on the Mobile and Ohio Railroad some fifty-two miles south of Corinth. Halleck felt that his line was becoming too much extended and called Pope back to the neighborhood of Corinth.

The retreat of the Confederates from Corinth.

The fall of Corinth led naturally to the fall of Memphis, not, however, without some fighting. When Pope started from above Fort Pillow to go to Halleck at Pittsburg Landing, he left Foote's fleet and two regiments of infantry to hold the river

The fall of Memphis.

above the Fort.   In the morning of the 10th of May th
Confederate fleet which held the river below the Fort
consisting of eight vessels, under command of Captaii
Montgomery, steamed up the river and attacked th
Federal boats.   After an engagement of two hours, ii
which two vessels on each side were much injured, th
Confederates were compelled to retire.

The garrison at Fort Pillow evacuated the place abou
the 4th of June, in consequence of Beauregard's retrea
from Corinth.   The Federal forces entered the Fort on
the 5th and the way to Memphis now appeared to be
open to them.   Montgomery, however, was determined
to make them fight for its possession.   The Federal
fleet anchored in the night of the 5th only a mile or two
above the city.   In the morning of the 6th Montgomery
moved forward to contest their farther advance.   The
Federal fleet consisted of five gun-boats and four rams.
On account of Foote's illness, the gun-boats were under
the command of Captain Davis, and the rams under the
command of their inventor, Colonel Ellet.   The battle
lasted about two hours, and ended in the destruction
of seven out of the eight vessels of the Confederates.
Ellet's rams did the work for the most part.   The
city was occupied by the Federal forces a little later in
the day, and soon became the head-quarters of General
Grant.   The Mississippi was now open to Vicksburg.

The campaign of the spring of 1862 in the departments west of the Alleghanies had thus been highly
successful to the Federals, and had brought to the front
the men who were destined to play the chief rôles in
the future conduct of the war, Halleck, Grant, and
Sherman.